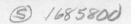

THE NEW
LEXINGTON
PRESS

GLOBAL CLIMATE CHANGE

GLOBAL CLIMATE CHANGE

*A Senior-Level Debate
at the Intersection of Economics,
Strategy, Technology, Science, Politics,
and International Negotiation*

Andrew J. Hoffman, Editor

The New Lexington Press
San Francisco

Substantial discounts on bulk quantities of The New Lexington Press books are available to corporations, professional associations, and other organizations. For details and discount information, contact the special sales department at (415) 433–1740; Fax (800) 605–2665.

For sales outside the United States, please contact your local Simon & Schuster International office.

The New Lexington Press Web address: http://www.newlex.com

 Manufactured in the United States of America on Lyons Falls Turin Book. This paper is acid-free and 100 percent totally chlorine-free.

Library of Congress Cataloging-in-Publication Data

Global climate change : a senior-level debate at the intersection of economics, strategy, technology, science, politics, and international negotiation / Andrew J. Hoffman, editor. — 1st ed.
        p. cm. — (The New Lexington Press management and organizational sciences series)
    Includes index.
    ISBN 0–7879–4103–4 (alk. paper)
    1. Climatic changes—Environmental aspects—Congresses. 2. Global environmental change—Congresses. 3. Environmental policy—Congresses. I. Hoffman, Andrew J., date. II. Series.
QC981.8.C5G646 1998
363.738'746—dc21   97–33911

FIRST EDITION

PB Printing   10 9 8 7 6 5 4 3 2 1

CONTENTS

PART THREE
Closing Thoughts

For my mother and father,
whose world we have inherited.

For my sister and brothers,
who are making it their own.

And for my nieces and nephews,
who will live with the choices we now make.

PREFACE

ON MAY 23, 1997, the Kellogg Graduate School of Management hosted four hours of private dialogue on climate change policy among nearly fifty senior representatives from industry, environmental groups, the Clinton administration, and academia. This meeting was followed by a one-and-a-half-hour open discussion, during which the public was invited to ask questions. This was not the typical kind of conference found at a business school. Academics do not often organize closed-door meetings to facilitate collaborative problem solving and information exchange. As any organizational behavior professor will tell you, the reward systems of academia determine what kind of activities they undertake. And at most business schools, practitioners' conferences (and books) are not where aspiring academics should wisely devote their energy. The key to academic success is the publication of academic journal articles. This kind of conference will not register in the tenure review process and siphons precious time away from more profitable pursuits.

But I believe that this kind of conference is exactly what business schools *should* be organizing. It offers a chance for academics to inject their perspectives and skills into efforts to resolve the kinds of problems businesses face today and to keep their ideas relevant and vital in a rapidly changing world. There are three other reasons why I believe business schools should organize such conferences.

First, business schools have the *capability* to make such conferences happen. A business school provides a setting where corporate executives can come to exchange ideas among themselves in a uniquely neutral territory. Business leaders, many of whom have MBAs, feel a certain level of comfort within the familiar confines of a business school and are perhaps more likely in that setting to engage in true intellectual exchange rather than to resort to political and economic posturing.

Second, business schools have a *responsibility* to support this kind of activity. Many social issues today are too complex for solutions to be found through one organizational entity, such as government. Environmental problems, for example, involve an increasingly complex interplay of social, political, scientific, technological, and economic considerations. Finding solutions will require an equally complex interplay and exchange among activists, politicians, scientists, engineers, business managers, and academics. What better place to bring all these stakeholders together than the neutral ground of a college or university? And when issues (like climate change) have such serious implications for corporate strategy, in terms of both development and implementation, who has more of a responsibility to facilitate this exchange than business schools? As multinational corporations have greater and greater impacts on global systems, exercising what Paul Kennedy describes as "more global reach than global responsibility,"[1] their input and perspectives must be brought to bear on global issues.

Third, this kind of activity is perfectly consistent with the *purpose* of a business school. Just as chemistry professors study the behavior of chemicals and civil engineering professors study the behavior of physical structures, business school professors should study the behavior of corporations and their managing executives. Further, just as other professors engage in cutting-edge research on emerging technologies (such as cloning, intelligent operating systems, or cold fusion), so too should business school professors. Emerging issues of importance to corporate executives should also be of importance to business school professors. Topical business issues, such as the environment, health care, international relations, labor trends, and the global economy, are precisely where business school professors ought to be devoting their attention.

In fact, Stephen Barley, the editor of one of the top academic journals in my field, organizational behavior, challenged organizational behavior professors to embark on this task in his opening speech at the 1996 Stanford Conference on Organization Research.[2] He argued that most academic contributions to contemporary social issues presently come from lawyers and economists, not professors of organizational behavior (or professors of corporate strategy or general management, for that matter). It is time for business schools to inject their talents and capabilities into searches for solutions to contemporary social problems.

So in the end I am excited to have been a part of this dialogue. It was a privilege to moderate a meeting on so important a topic among such senior-level executives. While the academic rewards system may overlook the endeavor, it is consistent with my perception of the business school professor's capabilities, responsibilities, and purpose. The goal of this dialogue was not to generate material for an academic journal; rather, it was an attempt to facilitate change in the very world those journals describe. If the openness and honesty of the dialogue presented in this book is any indication, change is on its way.

ACKNOWLEDGMENTS

In acknowledging the role of the Kellogg Business School in making a conference like this possible, I must thank the many people who graciously gave of their time. First there is Claire Buisseret. She was my right arm—collecting names, sending faxes, arranging the logistics, and helping to copyedit the dialogue transcript. I could not have done this without her. I also wish to thank Max Bazerman and Don Jacobs for making the many resources of the Kellogg Environmental Research Center, the J. L. Kellogg Graduate School of Management, and the James L. Allen Center available for this event. Jim O'Connor, Roger Beach, Roger Stone, and Matt Arnold were extremely generous in helping to develop an agenda and solicit the attendance of the many participants. Eight energetic business students—Lou Abela, Mike Breault, Dani Cunningham, Isabelle Gecils, Maite Limlingan, Michael Payne, Rachel Ringel, and Kurt Weinsheimer—helped make the day go smoothly, allowing me to concentrate on facilitating the discussions. Rich Honack and Kelley MacDonald handled public relations and the media. And finally, I should thank two sets of individuals simultaneously. I thank Tim Wirth and Dirk Forrister, who by agreeing to attend precipitated the participation of the thirty-plus business and environmental leaders who came. I also thank those leaders, who by agreeing to attend sparked the interest of Tim Wirth and Dirk Forrister and made them feel that this was a meeting worth attending. Needless to say, a lot of effort and a little bit of good timing made all the pieces fall into place. Thanks to all who made it possible.

Boston   ANDREW J. HOFFMAN
September 1997

NOTES

1. P. Kennedy, *Preparing for the Twenty-First Century* (New York: Random House, 1993): 47.
2. "Renewing Organizational Theory," Stanford Conference on Organization Research, Asilomar, Pacific Grove, California, April 21–23, 1996; see also R. Stern and S. Barley, "Organizations and Social Systems: Organization Theory's Neglected Mandate," *Administrative Science Quarterly*, 1996, 41: 146–162.

THE EDITOR

Andrew J. Hoffman is assistant professor of organizational behavior at Boston University. From 1995 until 1997 he was on the organization behavior faculty at the J. L. Kellogg Graduate School of Management at Northwestern University. His main research activities focus on the managerial and technical aspects of corporate environmentalism. In particular, he applies organizational behavior models to understanding how and why corporations adopt environmental practices and procedures. In 1997 he authored *From Heresy to Dogma: An Institutional History of Corporate Environmentalism,* published by The New Lexington Press. He has also published articles in leading academic, professional, and popular journals. Before earning his Ph.D. he was a compliance engineer for the Environmental Protection Agency, a consultant for Metcalf & Eddy, Inc., an analyst for the Amoco Oil Corporation, and a custom home builder. He earned his doctoral degree (1995) from the Sloan School of Management and the Department of Civil and Environmental Engineering at MIT and his bachelor's degree from the Department of Chemical Engineering at the University of Massachusetts at Amherst (1983).

THE CONTRIBUTORS AND PARTICIPANTS

Richard Abdoo is chairman of the board, president, and CEO of Wisconsin Energy Company and all of its subsidiaries. Abdoo joined Wisconsin Electric Power Company in September 1975 as director of corporate planning. He was elected vice president in May 1981, senior vice president in May 1984, and executive vice president in 1989. He is a member of the American Economic Association and is a registered professional engineer in the states of Michigan, Ohio, Wisconsin, and the Commonwealth of Pennsylvania. Abdoo graduated from the University of Dayton (1965) with a bachelor's degree in electrical engineering and received a master's degree in economics from the University of Detroit (1969).

Matthew Arnold is director and founder of the Management Institute for Environment and Business (MEB), a program of the World Resources Institute that engages the private sector in environmental stewardship. Arnold is a key contributor to all aspects of MEB's strategy, program development, and operations, and served on its board of directors from 1990 to 1996, when MEB merged with the World Resources Institute. He coauthored *The Power of Environmental Partnerships* and coedited *Stakeholder Negotiations: Exercises in Sustainable Development.* Arnold holds A.B. and M.B.A. degrees from Harvard University and an M.A. degree from the Johns Hopkins School of Advanced International Studies.

J. Robert Banks is vice president of health, environment, and safety (HES) and of public policy at Sun Company, Inc. Previously he served as vice president of HES and in other HES leadership positions over a fifteen-year period. He began his career with Sun in 1966 at the Marcus Hook Refinery and has held a number of positions in the engineering, operations, and planning areas. He also participated in the start-up of the Great Canadian Oil Sand Plant in Fort McMurray, Alberta, and served as the business manager of Sun's FIMRS Project—a major business venture to build or acquire facilities for processing heavy, high-sulfur crude oil. Banks serves on the U.S. Environmental Protection Agency's Community-Based Environmental Protection Committee, is a member of the Corporate Environmental Health and Safety Management Roundtable, and chairs the Advisory Committee for the Risk Management and Decision Processes Center at the Wharton School of the University of Pennsylvania. A graduate of Penn State University (1953) with a B.S. in chemical engineering, Banks also attended the Harvard Advanced Management Program in 1986.

Max H. Bazerman is J. Jay Gerber Professor of Dispute Resolution and Organizations at Northwestern University. Professor Bazerman taught at the Sloan School of Management at MIT, Boston University, and the University of Texas before joining the J. L. Kellogg Graduate School of Management in 1985. He was named the J. L. Kellogg Distinguished Professor of Dispute Resolution and Organizations in 1989 and in 1991 became the J. Jay Gerber Distinguished Professor. Bazerman's research focuses on decision making, negotiation, fairness, social comparison processes, and the natural environment. He was profiled by *The Organization Frontier* in 1993 as the leading management expert on the topics of negotiation and decision making. Bazerman earned his B.S.E. from the University of Pennsylvania (1976) and his M.S. (1978) and Ph.D. (1979) in organizational behavior from Carnegie-Mellon University.

Andrew W. Bermingham is managing director of Montreux Energy Corporation in the United States and is responsible for the organization of the Aspen Energy and Environment Roundtable. Montreux Energy organizes two strategic forums on the future of global energy investment. Held each spring in Switzerland, the Montreux Energy Roundtable was established as a private forum for strategic discussion of key energy investment issues. It convenes public and private sector leaders from the oil and gas industry, utilities, the financial community, government ministries, and international organizations. In response to the risk and liability of global environmental challenges, the Aspen Energy and Environment Roundtable was created in 1994 as a private annual forum held each fall to discuss investment opportunities in clean and sustainable energy solutions. Bermingham joined Montreux Energy at its outset in 1990. Prior to that he worked with the International Energy Agency in Paris from 1988 to 1989. Mr. Bermingham holds a bachelor's degree in economics from Middlebury College (1985) and an M.S. in mineral economics from the Colorado School of Mines (1992).

John Bobek is vice president of strategy and globalization at Johnson Controls, Inc. He provides strategic business planning, direction, and tactical support that will help globalize the business offerings and initiatives of the Controls Group of Johnson Controls, Inc. Prior to coming to Johnson in 1991 Bobek was vice president of service products for Asea Brown Boveri's process automation business, providing maintenance, repair, and performance services for process control systems used in a wide variety of continuous processes, such as pulp and paper and chemicals, worldwide. Prior to that Bobek headed a service business for Combustion Engineering, which provided maintenance, repair, and performance services to electric utilities for coal-, oil-, and gas-fired electric power generating stations. He earned a master's degree in business administration from the Amos Tuck Business School at Dartmouth College and a bachelor's degree in economics from Tufts University.

John Browne is group chief executive of the British Petroleum Company, p.l.c. Mr. Browne joined BP in 1966 as a university apprentice. In 1984 he became group treasurer and chief executive of BP Finance International, and in April 1986 he took up the position of executive vice president and chief financial officer of the Standard Oil Company in Cleveland, Ohio. In 1987, following the BP-Standard merger, in addition to his existing position, Mr. Browne was appointed chief executive officer of Standard Oil Production Company. In 1989 he became managing director and chief executive officer of BP Exploration, based in London, and in September 1991 he was appointed to the board of the British Petroleum Company, p.l.c., as a managing director. Mr. Browne became group chief executive of the company on July 1, 1995. He holds a degree in physics from Cambridge University and an M.S. in business from Stanford University.

Magalen O. Bryant is chairperson of the board of the National Fish and Wildlife Foundation. Mrs. Bryant founded Tara Wildlife Management and Service, Inc., for the purpose of providing continuation and enhancement of wildlife habitat. Bryant also helped found the Delta Environmental Land Trust Association (D.E.L.T.A.), a nonprofit organization dedicated to the conservation and reforestation of the remaining five million acres of the irreplaceable lower Mississippi River delta ecosystem. Bryant has received both the Chevron Conservation Award and the Governor's Award for Conservation in Mississippi. She was also awarded The Tower of Dulles Award from the Committee for Dulles and the first Colonial Award given by George Washington University.

Claire E. Buisseret teaches French in Wilmette, Illinois. Until August 1997, she was department assistant for the Kellogg Environmental Research Center and the Center for the Study of Ethical Issues in Business, both at the J. L. Kellogg Graduate School of Management at Northwestern University. Buisseret holds a B.A. in English and French from Loyola University of Chicago and an M.S. in education from Northwestern University.

Robert C. Carr is senior vice president of planning and economics at Amoco Corporation. He is responsible for the identification and analysis of companywide strategic issues (external and internal) and the development of corporate responses to them. Carr has been vice president and treasurer for Amoco Corporation, vice president of planning and administration for Amoco Production Company, and vice president and controller of Amoco Corporation since joining Amoco in 1990. Prior to this Carr spent twenty-four years with Mobil Corporation and its subsidiaries, leaving in 1988 as chief financial officer of Montgomery Ward, Inc. Carr earned a bachelor's degree in political science from Harvard University (1962) and a master's degree in international affairs from the Johns Hopkins School of Advanced International Studies (1964).

Louis O. DelGeorge is vice president of Commonwealth Edison Company (ComEd). Mr. DelGeorge joined ComEd in 1974 after spending five years at the Bettis Atomic Power Laboratory as a nuclear reactor component designer. DelGeorge was responsible for the licensing of ComEd's LaSalle County, Byron, and Braidwood facilities. He has held various positions of increasing responsibility in nuclear engineering, nuclear licensing, and nuclear plant support services. DelGeorge directs the life cycle management and environmental activities for Unicom Corporation, ComEd's holding company. In this capacity he is responsible for all environmental services, including site remediation, affecting the company's nuclear and fossil generation and its transmission and distribution system. In addition DelGeorge has responsibility for policy development on nuclear waste management issues. DelGeorge has a B.S. degree in engineering mechanics and a Juris Doctor degree.

John C. Dell is senior vice president at Duff & Phelps Credit Rating Company (DCR). Mr. Dell manages the DCR group responsible for electric and gas utility ratings and fixed income research. Dell is a member of the Credit Rating Committee. Prior to joining DCR in 1992 he was a managing director with Continental Bank in Chicago, where he was responsible for banking relationships with electric utilities, gas pipelines, LDCs, and telecommunications companies. He is a member of the Utility and Telecommunications Securities Club of Chicago. Dell earned a B.A. from Rollins College in Winter Park, Florida, and an M.B.A. from the University of Wisconsin.

Clement Erbmann is managing director at First Analysis Corporation (FASC). Mr. Erbmann joined First Analysis in 1989. He is responsible for FASC's international business. Previously he was a vice president at Donaldson, Lufkin, & Jenrette, where his work included dealing with corporate stock repurchase programs, strategic block accumulation, and restricted stock sales. In addition, he started and built a wealthy individuals' brokerage office as a vice president of Goldman Sachs, and he managed funds for wealthy individuals while a vice president at Morgan Stanley. He received an M.B.A. from Northwestern University and a bachelor's degree in business from the University of Cape Town (South Africa).

Dirk Forrister is chairman of the White House Climate Change Task Force. Mr. Forrister has been chairman of the task force since it was established by the Council on Environmental Quality and the National Economic Council in February 1997. The task force is charged with informing the public about global climate change to build support for the Clinton administration's priorities in the international negotiations to be completed in Kyoto, Japan, in December 1997. Prior to coming to the task force, Forrister served as assistant secretary of energy for congressional, public, and intergovernmental affairs. Previously he worked as a special assistant for policy to Secretary of Energy Hazel O'Leary, advising her on a variety of energy and environmental issues, primarily global climate change. Before serving in the Clinton administration, Forrister was a legislative assistant and counsel to Congressman Jim Cooper of Tennessee on energy, environment, and telecommunications issues. Forrister has a Juris Doctor degree from Rutgers University School of Law (1985) and a B.A. from David Lipscomb University, in Nashville, Tennessee (1980).

William H. Hicks is publisher of The New Lexington Press. The New Lexington Press is a scholarly imprint of Jossey-Bass Inc., Publishers, in San Francisco, California. Mr. Hicks has been in publishing for thirty-three years, covering college textbooks, professional books, and now scholarly publications. In 1985 he joined Jossey-Bass as the senior editor for the Jossey-Bass Management Series. Last year he became the publisher for The New Lexington Press.

Richard P. Honack is assistant dean and director of marketing and communications at the J. L. Kellogg Graduate School of Management. Mr. Honack joined Kellogg in April 1995. Prior to that Honack worked for more than twenty years in the newspaper industry, holding positions in marketing, general management, strategic planning, and editorial. He held a variety of positions with the *Chicago Tribune* from 1984 to 1995 and the *Chicago Sun-Times* from 1977 to 1984. He is a regular discussion leader at the American Press Institute and has been a guest speaker at numerous conventions, seminars, and college classes on the subjects of management, marketing, sales, and planning. He has consulted with newspapers around the world on marketing strategies and creative thinking. He is also a faculty adviser for Kellogg's Global Initiatives in Management program. Honack is a past director and executive committee member of the International Newspaper Marketing Association. Honack holds an M.M. degree from Kellogg and a B.S. degree in journalism education from Indiana University, in Bloomington, Indiana.

Donald P. Jacobs is Gaylord Freeman Distinguished Professor of Banking and dean at the J. L. Kellogg Graduate School of Management. Dean Jacobs has been a member of the Kellogg School faculty since 1957 and dean since 1975. Jacobs's research interests include banking, capital markets, monetary policy, corporate finance, and international finance. His work has been published in many scholarly journals, and he is an author of *Financial Institutions* and editor of *Regulating Business: The Search for an Optimum.* He teaches corporate governance and bank management at the master's level at the Kellogg School and also teaches corporate governance and financial topics for the school's executive education programs at the James L. Allen Center. Jacobs earned his B.A. in economics from Roosevelt University (1949) and his M.A. (1951) and Ph.D. (1956) in economics from Columbia University.

David Kee is director of the Air and Radiation Division of the U.S. Environmental Protection Agency, Region V. In addition to his current responsibilities for the region's air quality and radiation programs, Mr. Kee is a member of the United States–Canada Air Quality Committee and serves on the U.S. Great Lakes Policy Committee. Mr. Kee has been in the service of the government since 1963, beginning as an economist with the U.S. Public Health Service, moving to the Illinois Pollution Control

Board in 1970, and joining the U.S. Environmental Protection Agency in 1971. Kee has a B.S. in economics from the University of Illinois.

Richard L. Klimisch is vice president of the Engineering Affairs Division of the American Automobile Manufacturers Association (AAMA). Dr. Klimisch has been vice president since June 1993. In this position he oversees joint research and policy development on pollution, safety, noise, IVHS, OSHA, fuels, and lubricants. From 1983 to 1993 Klimisch was executive director of the General Motors environmental activities staff. This staff oversaw worldwide GM activities related to vehicle safety, fuel, economy, and all aspects of pollution. Klimisch was the spokesman for GM on recycling, fuel economy, and alternative fuels. He was one of the founders of the Vehicle Recycling Partnership (VRP) and served as chairman of this consortium prior to his movement to AAMA. He has authored over thirty scientific papers, two books, and two patents in the fields of chemical kinetics, catalysis, emission control, atmospheric chemistry, and alternative fuels. Klimisch received his Ph.D. (1964) in chemistry from Purdue University and his B.S. (1960) in chemistry from Loras College, in Dubuque, Iowa.

Allen M. Koleff is vice president of environmental, energy, and process technology at Stone Container Corporation. Mr. Koleff began his career in 1962 at A. E. Stanley Manufacturing Company, where he was a process engineer, manager of facilities planning, and international manager of manufacturing and technical service. He joined Stone in 1975 as vice president and general manager of a Stone affiliate and took over responsibility for corporatewide environmental management in 1977. Koleff holds a B.S. degree in chemical engineering from Illinois Institute of Technology.

Jonathan Lash is president of the World Resources Institute (WRI). From 1978 to 1985 Lash served as senior attorney at the Natural Resources Defense Council. From 1985 to 1987 he served as Vermont's commissioner of environmental conservation, and from 1987 to 1991 he headed the Vermont Agency of Natural Resources. For two years before coming to WRI, Mr. Lash directed the environmental law and policy program of the Vermont Law School. In 1993 Mr. Lash was named cochair of the President's Council on Sustainable Development and the National Commission on Superfund. Mr. Lash is the first U.S. member of the Earth Council and is cochair of the OECD's newly formed Advisory Group on the Environment.

Eugene L. Lecomte is president emeritus of the Insurance Institute for Property Loss Reduction. Mr. Lecomte joined the institute in 1979 and served as its president and CEO until 1996. Prior to that Lecomte served as president of both the Massachusetts Automobile Rating and Accident Prevention Bureau and the Workers' Compensation Rating and Inspection Bureau of Massachusetts. Lecomte is an honors graduate of Northeastern University.

Amory B. Lovins is vice president of the Rocky Mountain Institute. Mr. Lovins cofounded the institute—a fifteen-year-old, forty-three-person independent, nonprofit resource policy center—and directs its research and finance. A consultant physicist educated at Harvard and Oxford, he has received an Oxford M.A. (by virtue of being a don), six honorary doctorates, a MacArthur Fellowship, and the Nissan, Mitchell, "Alternative Nobel," and Onassis Prizes. He has also published twenty-five books and several hundred papers and consulted for scores of industries and governments worldwide. He works chiefly on transforming the car, real estate, and electricity industries toward advanced resource productivity. His technical writings on climate change began in 1968 and include the 1981 book *Least Cost Energy: Solving the CO$_2$ Problem.* The *Wall Street Journal*'s centennial issue named him among the twenty-eight people in the world most likely to change the course of business in the 1990s.

Dan Martin is director of the MacArthur Foundation's World Environment and Resources Program, which supports conservation, public education, policy studies, and sustainable development projects relating to key environmental issues. He has also served as director of the foundation's General Program, which concentrates on special funding initiatives and issues regarding the media, and as director of the Population Program, which addresses the complex issues of population, reproductive rights, and reproductive health. Prior to his work at the foundation he was president of the Jessie Smith Noyes Foundation (from 1984 until 1986), a private foundation specializing in grantmaking in the areas of environment, population, and education. A graduate of Knox College, Martin earned his doctorate in political philosophy and international politics from Princeton University (1968).

Robert K. Massie is executive director of the Coalition for Environmentally Responsible Economies. Mr. Massie has been working on issues of corporate governance, activism, and responsibility for nearly two decades. He began working for the U.S. Senate Subcommittee on Investigations and later for Ralph Nader's Congress Watch. From 1989 to 1996 Mr. Massie taught at Harvard Divinity School, where he ran the Project on Business, Values and the Economy. In 1994 he ran as the statewide Democratic nominee for lieutenant governor of Massachusetts. An ordained Episcopal minister, Mr. Massie received his master's degree from Yale Divinity School and his doctorate in business policy from Harvard Business School (1989), where his research focused on the methods used by large institutional investors to make decisions about social issues.

Bret Maxwell is managing director at the First Analysis Corporation and board member at the Enron Renewable Energy Corporation. Mr. Maxwell joined First Analysis in 1982 with expertise in the solid waste management field. His prior experience includes consulting for Arthur Anderson & Company on manufacturing control systems and engineering work for General Electric Company on automated inspection systems, robots, and sensing devices. He received a bachelor's degree in industrial engineering and an M.B.A., both from Northwestern University.

W. Henson Moore is president and CEO of the American Forest and Paper Association. Prior to joining the American Forest and Paper Association, Moore was a partner in the Washington office of Bracewell & Patterson, a Houston law firm, where he worked on natural resource and environmental issues. Moore served as Deputy secretary of the U.S. Department of Energy from 1989 to 1992 and in 1992 became deputy chief of staff to President George Bush. From 1975 to 1987 Moore represented the Sixth Congressional District of Louisiana. He served on several committees, including Energy and Commerce, Agriculture, Budget, and Ways and Means. Moore holds B.A. and M.A. degrees in government and a law degree from Louisiana State University.

Patrick J. Mulchay is executive vice president and COO at Northern Indiana Public Service Company (NIPSCO). He has been with NIPSCO since 1962, starting with various positions in division operations and training. From 1991 to 1994 he was vice president and general manager of gas operations for NIPSCO. He has an A.A.S. in electrical engineering technology and a B.S. in management from Purdue. He also has an M.B.A. from the University of Notre Dame.

Oliver Nicklin is president and founder of First Analysis Corporation. He is an acknowledged expert in the broad environmental waste services field. Prior to founding First Analysis he served for twelve years with William Blair & Company, an investment banking, brokerage, and research firm in Chicago. His other experience includes strategic planning and European project evaluations for the Amoco and Exxon Corporations. A major emphasis throughout his career has been finding, evaluating, and nurturing emerging growth situations. He received a bachelor's degree in chemical engineering from the University of Texas and an M.B.A. from Harvard University.

Fielding L. Norton III is director of research and development at Employers Reinsurance Corporation. The scope of his team's activities includes developing data analysis and modeling techniques for optimizing the company's global portfolio of reinsurance risk; conducting, sponsoring, and evaluating the results of basic and applied research to support the development of novel risk-transfer solutions; and providing technical input to the assessment of business opportunities and public policy issues. Norton's scientific research is focused on investigating problems of global climate change. Prior to joining ERC, Norton served as program manager for the Risk Prediction Initiative in Bermuda, as teaching and research fellow at Harvard University, and in numerous roles as an educator of children and adults. Norton earned a B.S. in education from the University of Kansas and an M.S. in applied physics and a Ph.D. in earth and planetary sciences from Harvard University.

James J. O'Connor is chairman and CEO of Unicom and of Commonwealth Edison Company. Mr. O'Connor became a ComEd director in 1978 and assumed his position as chairman in 1980. O'Connor is a director of Corning Incorporated, First Chicago NBD Corporation, the First National Bank of Chicago, the Tribune Company, and United Airlines. In the electric power industry he is a director and vice chairman of the Nuclear Energy Institute, chairman of the Advanced Reactor Corporation, director and past chairman of the Edison Electric Institute, and past chairman of the board of the Institute of Nuclear Power Operations. O'Connor received his B.S. degree in economics from Holy Cross College and holds an M.B.A. from Harvard (1960). He received his J.D. degree from Georgetown Law School (1963).

James R. Olson is senior vice president of external affairs at Toyota Motor Sales, USA, Inc. Mr. Olson is responsible for all public relations activities in the United States, including Toyota and Lexus product news, media relations, and publications. Olson also oversees Toyota's community relations, government relations, and video communications activities. Olson joined Toyota in 1985 as corporate public affairs manager after a sixteen-year career with Ford Motor Company. He has a bachelor's degree in English literature from Stanford University and a master's degree in broadcast journalism from Northwestern University.

Julio M. Ottino is Walter P. Murphy Professor and chair of the Chemical Engineering Department at Northwestern University. Professor Ottino's research centers on fluid mechanics, chaos, and granular flows. In 1986 he was the Chevron Visiting Professor at the California Institute of Technology, and in 1990 he was a senior research fellow at the Center for Turbulence Research at Stanford University. He currently serves as associate editor of *Physics of Fluids* and the *American Institute of Chemical Engineers Journal*. Ottino received his Ph.D. from the University of Minnesota.

Dennis R. Parker is vice president for safety, health, and environmental affairs at Conoco, Inc. Mr. Parker's experience with Conoco began in 1967 and includes assignments in engineering and operations. In 1981 he served as executive assistant to the chairman and CEO. In 1982 he became president of Conoco Far East, an affiliate in Tokyo, Japan. Three years later he moved to Houston as general manager of Conoco's worldwide petroleum coke business. He was named general manager of international crude oil trading in 1987. The following year he became manager of the company's refinery in Ponca City, Oklahoma. In 1991 he took on the additional title of vice president of coordination management, linking the company's varied Ponca City operations with Houston headquarters. Parker holds a B.S. degree in chemical engineering from the University of Missouri-Rolla and an M.B.A. from Oklahoma City University. He completed Harvard University's Advanced Management Program in 1987.

Stephen C. Peck is vice president of the Electric Power Research Institute's Environment Group. Dr. Peck is responsible for R&D on global climate change, air quality, electric and magnetic fields, and land and water quality. Before joining EPRI in 1976 he was on the faculty at the University of California at Berkeley. Peck received a B.A. degree in mechanical sciences from Cambridge University and an M.Sc. degree from the London School of Economics. He received his M.B.A. and Ph.D. degrees from the University of Chicago.

Steven W. Percy is chairman, CEO, and CFO of BP America, Inc. From 1992 to 1996 he was president of BP Oil in the United States and executive vice president of BP America. He serves as director of BP America and is a member of the BP America advisory board. Percy returned to BP America from his assignment as group treasurer of the British Petroleum Company, p.l.c., and chief executive of BP Finance International. He is a member of the American Petroleum Institute, the Ohio Business Roundtable, and serves on the University of Michigan Business School's corporate advisory board. His educational background includes a B.S. in mechanical engineering from Rensselaer Polytechnic Institute, an M.B.A. from the University of Michigan, and a J.D. from the Cleveland Marshall College of Law.

Marvin Pomerantz is chairman and CEO of the Mid-America Group and chairman and CEO of the Gaylord Container Corporation. Mr. Pomerantz founded Great Plains Bag Corporation in January 1961 and served as its president and general manager for over fourteen years. In 1971 he was named vice president of Continental Can Company, Inc., and in January 1975 he was named vice president and general manager of the Forest Products Brown Systems Operation. In August 1980 he was named president of the Diversified Group of International Harvester, and from September 1981 until his resignation in July 1982 served that company as its executive vice president. In 1981 he was the recipient of the Oscar C. Schmidt Iowa Business Leadership Award, presented by the University of Iowa College of Business Administration. In 1995 he was inducted into the Iowa Business Hall of Fame. Pomerantz graduated from the University of Iowa (1952) with a B.S. degree in commerce.

Paul R. Portney is president of Resources for the Future (RFF). From 1989 to 1995 Dr. Portney was RFF's vice president, and he has also served as the director of RFF's Center for Risk Management and of its Quality of the Environment Division. From January 1979 until September 1980 he served as chief economist at the Council on Environmental Quality in the Executive Office of the President. He is the author or coauthor of a number of journal articles and books, most recently *Footing the Bill for Superfund Cleanups: Who Pays and How?* He lectures frequently on developments in U.S. and international environmental policy. Portney received his B.A. in economics and mathematics from Alma College and his Ph.D. in economics from Northwestern University.

Howard Ris is executive director of the Union of Concerned Scientists (UCS). He oversees all of the organization's research, public education, and legislative programs on global environmental and security issues. He served as the director of UCS's Nuclear Arms Control Program from

1981 until 1984. Prior to joining UCS in 1981, Ris directed the New England River Basins Commission's hydroelectric power program. From 1976 to 1978 he was a senior policy analyst in the Massachusetts Executive Office of Environmental Affairs. He has also been a consultant to several state and federal agencies on a wide variety of environmental planning issues. Ris served on the Energy and Transportation Task Force of President Clinton's Council on Sustainable Development. Ris holds a B.A. degree in mathematics from Duke University and a master's degree from the State University of New York College of Environmental Science at Syracuse University.

Bruce E. Rittmann is John Evans Professor and coordinator of environmental health engineering at Northwestern University. Professor Rittmann's research combines concepts and techniques from engineering with those from microbiology, biochemistry, and microbial ecology. Rittmann is most recognized for his research on biofilm kinetics, the biodegradation of organic micropollutants, and the application of molecular and modeling tools to understand and control complex microbial systems used in environmental biotechnology. Rittmann recently was awarded the first A.R.I. Clarke Prize for Outstanding Achievements in Water Science and Technology from the National Water Research Institute, and he previously won the Walter Huber Research Prize from the ASCE, the University Scholar Award from the University of Illinois, and the Presidential Young Investigator Award from the National Science Foundation.

Arthur E. Smith, Jr., is principal executive and counsel for environmental affairs at Northern Indiana Public Service Company (NIPSCO). Smith heads an in-house staff of over twenty-five specialists in all environmental media. In addition to compliance, due diligence, and permitting services, the department provides environmental policy and legal counsel to top management. Smith is the former chief civil litigation specialist with the U.S. Environmental Protection Agency and assistant U.S. Attorney, N.D., of Illinois. He received his B.A. in biology and his M.A. and M.S. in environmental sciences from Columbia University and his J.D. from Seattle University School of Law.

Michael D. Spence is executive vice president at Texas Utilities Services, Inc.; Texas Utilities Properties, Inc.; and Chaco Energy Company. Spence is a member of the Texas Society of Professional Engineers and the Institute of Electrical and Electronic Engineers. Spence received his B.S. degree in Electrical Engineering from Texas A&M University (1963).

Roger W. Stone is chairman, president, and CEO of Stone Container Corporation, a Chicago-based Fortune 500 international pulp and paper company. Mr. Stone is a director of the American Forest and Paper Association, director of the Canadian Pulp and Paper Association, chairman of Kraftliner Manufacturers Institute, a vice chairman of the National Council for Air and Stream Improvement, Inc., a director of Morton International, McDonald's Corporation, and Option Care, Inc. He is an associate of Northwestern University, on the advisory board of the J. L. Kellogg Graduate School of Management, and a Trustee of the Committee for Economic Development. Stone is a graduate of the University of Pennsylvania's Wharton School of Finance (1967).

Terence H. Thorn is senior vice president of environmental and international government affairs at Enron Corporation, one of the world's largest integrated natural gas and electricity companies. Thorn is responsible for environmental policy and compliance and works closely with all Enron companies worldwide. Prior to this position he was president and CEO of Transwestern Pipeline Company, an Enron subsidiary. He has worked on five Clinton administration international trade missions and is chairman of the International Committee of the Business Council of Sustainable Development. He has a B.A. and an M.A. in history and international relations from the University of Maryland.

Chandler Van Voorhis is CEO of GreenWave, a radio and Internet talk show that focuses on business and environment relations. He also serves as personal adviser to Magalen O. Bryant. Until 1996, Van Voorhis was president of the Alliance for Environmental Education. He is a graduate of Woodberry Forest School and Centre College.

Kimberly A. Wade-Benzoni is visiting assistant professor of organization behavior at the J. L. Kellogg Graduate School of Management at Northwestern University. Her current research interests in conflict management and decision making include intergenerational resource allocations, egocentric interpretations of fairness, self-enhancement biases, dysfunctional aspects of standards, and relationships. She has coauthored several book chapters, articles and research papers. She received a bachelor's degree in electrical engineering from Cornell University and master's and doctoral degrees in organization behavior from Northwestern University.

George A. Walker is vice president of health, environment, and safety at Unocal Corporation, the world's largest publicly traded independent exploration and production company. In 1996 he served as chair of the management committee for the Western States Petroleum Association. He is a former member of the American Petroleum Institute's Health, Environment, and Safety General Committee. Previously Mr. Walker held positions as general manager of health, environment, and safety programs for Unocal's Petroleum Products and Chemicals Division and manager of Unocal's refinery in Wilmington, California. He was the WSPA representative to the South Coast Air Quality Management District RECLAIM Advisory Committee.

Timothy E. Wirth is undersecretary of state for global affairs at the U.S. Department of State. Dr. Wirth has responsibility for overseeing environment, population, human rights, refugee, narcotics, and related programs. Wirth was elected to the United States Senate from Colorado in 1986 and served until 1993; he chose not to run for reelection. In the Senate he specialized in issues related to natural resources, the environment, and financial institutions. Prior to his election to the Senate Wirth represented the Second Congressional District of Colorado for twelve years. As a congressman he was chairman of the Subcommittee on Telecommunications, Consumer Protection and Finance and was voted one of the twenty-five most effective members of Congress. In 1992 he served as national cochair of the Clinton-Gore presidential campaign. From 1969 to 1970 Wirth served as deputy assistant secretary of education at the Department of Health, Education and Welfare (HEW). He was awarded a White House fellowship in 1967 and served as special assistant to the secretary of HEW, John Gardner. Prior to his election to Congress Wirth worked in private business in Colorado. Wirth earned his bachelor's degree (1961) and master's degree (1964) at Harvard University and his doctorate (1973) at Stanford.

Hoyt H. Wood, Jr., is senior vice president at Employers Reinsurance Corporation. In 1973 Mr. Wood joined Employers Reinsurance Corporation as a casualty underwriter in the home office. In 1979 he transferred to the corporation's Kansas City branch, where he continued to focus on treaty business. In 1981 he returned to the home office, and in 1983 was named manager of the Home Office Casualty Treaty Department. In 1991 he assumed responsibility for all domestic underwriting activities and was elected senior vice president. Wood is a graduate of the University of Missouri, Kansas City.

I

INTRODUCTION

BACKGROUND ISSUES AND OVERVIEW

Andrew J. Hoffman

IN 1970 the Council on Environmental Quality issued the first warning that industrial activity might be changing the weather. Climatologists began hypothesizing that human activity was triggering atmospheric changes, but they couldn't decide whether these changes were cooling or warming the surface of the earth. Scientists identified two primary mechanisms by which people might be changing the world's climate: (1) by increasing the carbon dioxide (CO_2) content of the atmosphere through the burning of fossil fuels, we were raising the earth's temperature by creating the "greenhouse effect"; and (2) by clouding the atmosphere with dust and soot, we were cooling the earth's temperature by blocking out sunlight. By 1983 the argument for global warming had prevailed, and the Environmental Protection Agency issued a report warning that it might already be too late to avoid the rising atmospheric temperatures expected from increasing levels of carbon dioxide and other "greenhouse gases."

The issue reached the level of global concern in June 1988 when the World Conference on the Changing Atmosphere (the first of its kind) convened in Toronto. Sponsored by the United Nations and Canada, the conference established the ongoing Intergovernmental Panel on Climate Change (IPCC) and recommended an initial global reduction of carbon

Andrew J. Hoffman is assistant professor in the Organizational Behavior Department of the Boston University School of Management.

dioxide emissions by 20 percent of 1988 levels by 2005.[1] Although these recommendations were not binding, they brought the concept of the greenhouse effect to the forefront of public debate.

In the ensuing years, few environmental issues have evoked a comparable level of passionate debate among industry leaders, environmentalists, and government officials as the greenhouse effect (later dubbed "global warming" and, ultimately, "climate change"). This debate has created an unprecedented political exchange concerning the validity of scientific data. Scientists have sparred over competing scientific interpretations of climate models. In this scientific battle, industry has been far from a silent observer. Often closely involved with the funding and dissemination of scientific research, industry groups have coalesced around polarized positions on the issue. Although it is hard to argue against the existence of increasing levels of greenhouse gases in the atmosphere (chiefly carbon dioxide, methane, and nitrous oxide), there have been plenty of arguments about what impact those increases will have on the global climate.

Industry's most vocal lobbying group,[2] the Global Climate Coalition (GCC)—an organization representing electric utilities and automobile, mining, oil, and coal companies, established in 1989 to coordinate business participation in the scientific and policy debates on global climate change—has consistently argued that "it is too early to determine what causes global warming."[3] The group presses for political restraint while delivering skeptical critiques of scientific research that suggests action may be needed. Similarly, the Western Fuels Association—a cooperative of consumer-owned electric utilities operating coal-fired power plants in the Rocky Mountain, Great Plains, and Southwestern states and Louisiana—has produced and disseminated free copies of a 1996 video entitled *The Greening of Planet Earth,* which argues that "rather than fearing increased atmospheric CO_2 emissions, we should welcome such emissions since . . . a CO_2-enriched atmosphere will bring a better world, a more productive world."[4] In an attempt to interject itself directly into the public debate, the group also produces and distributes free to journalists[5] the biweekly newsletter *World Climate Report,* which continually challenges the scientific data on climate change.

Recently, however, as the scientific evidence for global warming has mounted, the focus of the debate has begun to shift away from science and toward economics. Yet, although the focus is different, the polarization continues. The GCC states that lower emission targets could bind the United States "to economic and regulatory obligations that could have serious impacts on American industry and its job holders for the next forty years."[6] The Western Fuels Association's *World Climate Report* states that controls on greenhouse gas emissions "would boost the cost of production, lead to increased imports, slash employment and domestic output, and in some cases eliminate all U.S. production."[7] In an uncharacteristically independent move, the Mobil Corporation placed an advertisement in the *New York Times*[8] (see Exhibit 1.1) arguing that controls on CO_2 emissions will mean that "jobs will disappear and lifestyles will be pinched as our industrial infrastructure shrinks" and predicting that gasoline prices will increase "50 cents to $1.50 per gallon." These conclusions were based on a report produced by Charles River Associates and funded by the American Petroleum Institute.

Ultimately little is to be gained from this kind of confrontational, sensationalistic posturing. First, it makes industry into the perfect villain for the media. In his recent book *The Heat Is On,* Ross Gelbspan charges that the oil and coal industries are engaged in a "deliberate campaign . . . to confuse the public about global warming and the disruptive weather patterns that mark its initial stages" and that "in tandem with the Organization of Petroleum Exporting Countries (OPEC)," they are attempting "to frustrate diplomatic attempts to address the crisis meaningfully."[9]

Pessimistic appeals also damage industry's credibility in the overall environmental arena. From claims that "the personal auto will be put out of financial reach of many Americans by politically inspired auto [emission] standards"[10] in the early 1970s (it wasn't) to predictions that the 1990 Clean Air Act amendments would cost electric utilities between $4 and $5 billion a year (actual costs were orders of magnitude less),[11] industry has repeatedly predicted that economic disaster would result from environmental protection measures. As Bob Herbert points out in a 1997 *New York Times* editorial, "The problem with the industry groups is that they lack credibility. They *always* claim that taking steps to improve air quality will lead to economic catastrophe."[12]

Ultimately, when industry continues to contradict the trajectory of social thought, it becomes excluded from the political debate that continues to progress. The momentum for climate change controls has begun and will continue, with or without industry participation. Over the past two years, while the GCC and the Western Fuels Association have continued to deny the scientific evidence for climate change, the following developments have occurred:

- In 1995 the IPCC concluded that "the balance of evidence suggests a discernible human influence on the global climate" and that it "is expected to continue to change over the next century."[13] The report reviewed a wide range of potential consequences, from a rise in sea level to increased storm severity and adverse impacts on human health. Although there are dissenting views, the report is supported by over two thousand scientists from over one hundred countries.

GLOBAL CLIMATE CHANGE

Exhibit 1.1. Mobil Corporation Ad.

Stop, look and listen before we leap

International efforts to deal with climate change are lurching from speculation toward actions that could wreak havoc on nations even as the underlying science and economics continue to signal caution.

While governments have agreed that there may be reasons for concern over the buildup of greenhouse-gas emissions, primarily carbon dioxide (CO_2), there is no consensus on what constitutes "dangerous levels" of emissions nor is there agreement on when, where and how best to reduce their impact. Yet, an action plan with binding commitments on developed nations could take shape by year's end.

We are concerned that policy makers are not considering the implications of controlling CO_2 emissions. Studies have examined some of the emission-control plans tabled to date and concluded that they will impose painful burdens on developed economies, particularly if timetables are short and targets unrealistic. For Americans, such solutions mean jobs will disappear and lifestyles will be pinched as industrial infrastructure shrinks.

A study just issued by Charles River Associates (CRA) provides additional weight to the impact of emission controls in an age of global markets. The report shows how ill-timed or ill-considered abatement measures could stunt world economic growth, unsettle global trading patterns and set the stage for a new era of trade protectionism.

CRA analyzed two abatement scenarios—one a more modest stabilization proposal, the other a more aggressive reduction plan. Both policies appear to fall within the boundaries of acceptability by the U.S. government. The authors utilized a carbon-rationing plan to achieve required reductions in CO_2 emissions. In practice, rationing will increase energy prices for both industry and the consumer.

The cost of limiting emissions could range from $200 to $580 per ton of carbon, depending on the timing and severity of the plan selected. To put this in perspective, this equates to an additional cost to consumers of 50 cents to $1.50 per gallon of gasoline in today's dollars.

The expected blow to U.S. prosperity would be considerable, according to CRA: an annual drop in gross domestic product ranging from $105 billion in the year 2010 to $460 billion in 2030, both in today's dollars. At the lower range, this works out to a loss in annual household income of roughly $1,000.

One key finding of CRA's study is that the economic burden of emissions controls is borne not only by the industrialized countries, but also by developing societies, who under current proposals need do nothing. The developed world feels the pain as it is forced to switch fuels and revamp its industrial infrastructure. The developing world, which now exports 60 to 75 percent of its products to industrialized countries, will see those markets shrivel as economic growth stalls and demand for protectionist measures grows. Developing countries that import energy will benefit from lower fossil-fuel prices, but in most cases that gain won't offset the loss of trading markets. And energy exporters—be they developed or developing—will be particularly hard hit as energy markets shrink.

The CRA study injects a healthy dose of realism into the climate-change debate. In the coming months, we'll continue to look at what other experts are saying. Meanwhile, we urge international policy makers not to make 1997 a year of hasty decisions. The entire world's prosperity depends on a course of wise, sustainable action.

Mobil The energy
to make a difference™

Source: ©1997 Mobil Corporation. Reprinted with the permission of Mobil Corporation.

- In 1996 the Clinton administration announced that during the United Nations conferences planned for 1997 in Kyoto, Japan, it will seek a binding international agreement to reduce greenhouse gas emissions among industrialized nations.[14]

- In February 1997 two thousand economists (including eight Nobel laureates) endorsed a report concluding that "global climate change carries with it significant environmental, economic, social and geopolitical risks" and that "preventive steps are justified. . . . Economic studies have found that there are many potential policies to reduce greenhouse-gas emissions for which the total benefits outweigh the total costs. For the United States in particular, sound economic analysis shows that there are policy options that would slow climate change without harming American living standards, and these measures may in fact improve U.S. productivity in the longer run."[15]

- In December 1997 a group of U.S. negotiators led by Undersecretary of State for Global Affairs Timothy Wirth will go to Kyoto, Japan, to complete a negotiated treaty on the control of greenhouse gases that has been two years in the making.

Given the momentum toward imposing some level of controls on greenhouse gas emissions and the clear inevitability that negotiations with significant implications for U.S. industry would take place in December 1997, the Kellogg Environmental Research Center saw a need for rational and open discussions on climate change issues. Continued polarization is not in the long-term interests of industry. Therefore Kellogg hosted a small, senior-level exchange of views on policy responses to climate change, inviting representatives of the Clinton administration, CEOs of major companies at risk from contemplated climate change policies, and heads of national environmental organizations. The meeting took place at the James L. Allen Center of the J. L. Kellogg Graduate School of Management on Friday, May 23, 1997.

This meeting provided a unique opportunity for all sides to gain a better understanding of the diverse perspectives shaping climate policy as we approach the critical negotiating period before Kyoto. We invited over twenty-five senior executives from the electric utility, oil, automobile, forestry, and financial sectors as well as seven senior representatives from the environmental community to meet with Timothy Wirth, undersecretary of state for global affairs, and Dirk Forrister, chairman of the White House Climate Change Task Force. (The attendee list is reproduced in Exhibit 1.2.)

Exhibit 1.2. Attendee List for Senior-Level
Dialogue on Climate Change.

A SENIOR-LEVEL DIALOGUE
ON CLIMATE CHANGE POLICY

J. L. Kellogg Graduate School of Management, Friday, May 23, 1997

ATTENDEE LIST

ADMINISTRATION REPRESENTATIVES

Dirk Forrister, Chairman, Climate Change Task Force, White House

David Kee, Air and Radiation Division Director, U.S. Environmental Protection Agency, Region V

Timothy E. Wirth, Undersecretary of State for Global Affairs, U.S. State Department

INDUSTRY REPRESENTATIVES
Energy

Richard A. Abdoo, Chairman, President, and CEO, Wisconsin Energy Company

Andrew Bermingham, Managing Director, Montreux Energy Corporation

John Bobek, Vice President, Strategy and Globalization, Johnson Controls, Inc.

Louis DelGeorge, Vice President, Commonwealth Edison Company

Patrick J. Mulchay, Executive Vice President and COO, Northern Indiana Public Service Company

James O'Connor, Chairman and CEO, Commonwealth Edison Company

Stephen C. Peck, Vice President, Environment Group, Electric Power Research Institute

Arthur E. Smith, Jr., Principal Executive and Counsel, Northern Indiana Public Service Company

Michael D. Spence, Executive Vice President, Texas Utilities Company

Petroleum

J. Robert Banks, Vice President, HES, Communications and Public Policy, Sun Company, Inc.

Robert Carr, Senior Vice President, Planning and Economics, Amoco Corporation

Dennis R. Parker, Vice President, Safety, Health and Environmental Affairs, Conoco, Inc.

Steven W. Percy, Chairman, CEO, and CFO, BP America, Inc.

George A. Walker, Vice President, Health, Environment, and Safety, Unocal Corporation

Paper and Forestry

Allen Koleff, Division Vice President, Environmental Process and Energy Technology, Stone Container Corporation

Marvin A. Pomerantz, Chairman and CEO, Gaylord Container Corporation

Roger W. Stone, Chairman and CEO, Stone Container Corporation

Exhibit 1.2. *(continued).*

Financial

John C. Dell, Senior Vice President, Duff and Phelps Credit Rating Company

Clement Erbmann, Managing Director, First Analysis Corporation

Bret Maxwell, Managing Director, First Analysis Corporation, and Board Member, Enron Renewable Energy Corporation

F. Oliver Nicklin, President, First Analysis Corporation

Fielding L. Norton, III, Director of Research and Development, Employers Reinsurance Corporation

Hoyt H. Wood, Jr., Senior Vice President, Employers Reinsurance Corporation

Automobile

Richard Klimisch, Vice President, Engineering Affairs, American Automobile Manufacturers Association

J.R. Olson, Sr. Vice President, External Affairs, Toyota Motor Corporation, USA

ENVIRONMENTAL REPRESENTATIVES

Matthew Arnold, President, Management Institute for Environment and Business, WRI

Magalen O. Bryant, Chairperson of the Board, National Fish and Wildlife Foundation

Amory Lovins, Vice President and CFO, Rocky Mountain Institute

Dan Martin, Director, World Environment and Resources Program, The MacArthur Foundation

Robert Massie, Executive Director, Coalition for Environmentally Responsible Economies

Paul Portney, President, Resources for the Future

Howard Ris, Executive Director, Union of Concerned Scientists

ACADEMIC REPRESENTATIVES

Max Bazerman, J. J. Gerber Distinguished Professor of Dispute Resolution, Kellogg Graduate School of Management

Bill Hicks, Publisher, The New Lexington Press

Andrew Hoffman, Visiting Assistant Professor of Organization Behavior, Kellogg Graduate School of Management

Richard Honack, Assistant Dean and Director of Marketing and Communications, Kellogg Graduate School of Management

Donald Jacobs, Dean, Kellogg Graduate School of Management

Bruce Rittmann, John Evans Professor of Environmental Engineering, Northwestern University

Julio Ottino, Chair, Chemical Engineering, Northwestern University

We explicitly focused on the economic and strategic implications of climate change policy and avoided a debate over the merits or credibility of scientific data and models. As recent history has shown, debates over the science can too easily digress into an unproductive contest between one body of scientific data and another. Instead the parties were asked to share their economic concerns and offer proposals to help clarify how climate change policy could be implemented with the least economic risk and greatest environmental benefit.

Rather than create a debate atmosphere, we tried to facilitate a dialogue, focusing on what the attendees could do to respond to the climate change issue, not on how they would be affected or how they would react to what others might do to them. As is evident from the conference agenda (Exhibit 1.3), we purposefully chose to have few organized statements, to minimize perfunctory remarks and maximize discussion of the issues. Open discussion focused on the major issues to be addressed in an international climate change treaty, such as timetables, goals, joint implementation, compliance flexibility, the status of the developing world, the so-called no-regrets policy, and opportunities for common ground where government, industry, and environmentalists could work together to ensure that meaningful emission reduction goals would be set and achieved.

Through this dialogue we hoped to develop insights into the best timing and focus of a rational U.S. policy, to identify likely impediments to effective implementation, and to consider ways attendees could work alone and together to maximize environmental benefits while minimizing economic risks. We wanted to counter the fictional notion of "the" oil industry or "the" electric industry speaking as one monolithic entity. Rather than simply allowing the Western Fuels Association or the GCC to paint a picture of industry with one broad brush, this forum offered industry representatives a chance to speak for themselves and to explain their legitimate economic and strategic concerns to constituents from the government and the environmental community. In this way we hoped to engage industry more positively in the climate change dialogue.

That is why we have published this book. It includes transcripts of the dialogue that transpired on May 23, 1997, as well as a collection of more carefully crafted thoughts of the attendees and company representatives. Although possibilities are limited for bringing about marked change in the span of a single day, the ideas exchanged at the conference, and the additional ideas presented here, add an important new component to the ongoing debate on climate change.

Exhibit 1.3. The Dialogue Agenda.

A SENIOR-LEVEL DIALOGUE
ON CLIMATE CHANGE POLICY

J. L. Kellogg Graduate School of Management, Friday, May 23, 1997

AGENDA

1:00 P.M.　**Registration and Refreshments**

1:15 P.M.　*Private Session I: Welcome, Introductions, and Agenda*

　　　　　Donald Jacobs, Dean, Kellogg School

　　　　　Andrew Hoffman, Assistant Professor, Kellogg School

1:25 P.M.　*The U.S. Position on Climate Change Negotiations*

　　　　　Timothy Wirth, Undersecretary of State for Global Affairs

1:40 P.M.　*Implications of Climate Change Policy*

Can climate policies be constructed in a way that will achieve environmental goals while minimizing economic costs? Topics should include the economic and environmental implications of a climate change treaty, such as industry interests and objectives, proposed timetables and targets, technological possibilities, competitiveness and economic issues, global trading patterns, and enforcement mechanisms.

Moderator:　*Andrew Hoffman,* Assistant Professor, Kellogg School

Remarks:　　*Steven W. Percy,* Chairman, CEO and CFO, BP America, Inc.

　　　　　　Roger W. Stone, Chairman and CEO, Stone Container Corp.

　　　　　　Amory Lovins, Vice President and CFO, Rocky Mountain Institute

3:00 P.M.　**Coffee Break**

3:15 P.M.　*Private Session II: Seeking Common Ground*

Can industry members work together and with other stakeholders to ensure that meaningful goals are set and met? Topics should include the general responsibilities of industry, government and environmentalists in controlling climate change, and areas of common ground in achieving them.

Moderator:　*Andrew Hoffman,* Assistant Professor, Kellogg School

Remarks:　　*James O'Connor,* Chairman and CEO, Commonwealth Edison Co.

　　　　　　Paul Portney, President, Resources for the Future

4:30 P.M.　*Closing Thoughts on Private Sessions*

　　　　　Dirk Forrister, Chairman, White House Climate Change Task Force

4:45 P.M.　**Coffee Break**

Exhibit 1.3. *(continued).*

5:15 P.M.	***Public Session: Strategy for Sound Climate Change Policy***

Brief presentations from panelists, followed by question-and-answer period for all dialogue attendees (who will be seated in front row of the auditorium). Topics should focus on the issue of climate change as it pertains to each industry and observations on the differences and commonalities among stakeholders as revealed in the private session.

Welcome: *Donald Jacobs,* Dean, Kellogg School

Moderator: *Andrew Hoffman,* Assistant Professor, Kellogg School

Panelists: *Dirk Forrister,* Chairman, White House Climate Change Task Force

Amory Lovins, Vice President and CFO, Rocky Mountain Institute

Steven W. Percy, Chairman, CEO and CFO, BP America, Inc.

Stephen C. Peck, Vice President, Electric Power Research Institute

Richard L. Klimisch, Vice President, American Automobile Manufacturers Association

Paul Portney, President, Resources for the Future

6:45 P.M.	**Cocktails**
7:00 P.M.	**Dinner**

BACKGROUND ISSUES

To fully appreciate the arguments and the dialogues presented in the following pages, a specific kind of literacy is necessary. Global climate change is an extremely complex issue, lying at the intersection of science, technology, economics, politics, and international diplomacy. To help the reader better understand the concepts discussed in this book, the next few pages cover some important background issues separately.[16] This chapter then concludes with an overview of the ideas generated in the dialogue.

Scientific Issues

Climate change and ozone depletion are often misunderstood as being synonymous. Although they are related, the two problems are actually quite different. To understand each of them, one must start with the sun. The part of the sun's light that humans can see is composed of a spectrum of colors, as can be seen in a rainbow. In addition to this visible

Figure 1.1. The Ozone Layer.

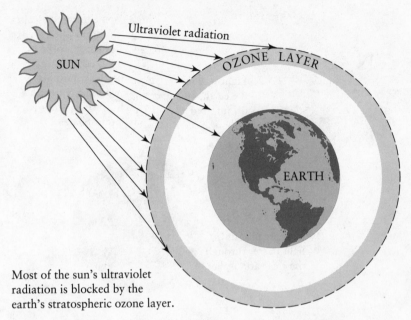

Most of the sun's ultraviolet
radiation is blocked by the
earth's stratospheric ozone layer.

Source: W. Kempton, J. Boster, and J. Hartley, *Environmental Values in American Culture* (Cambridge, MA: MIT Press, 1995): 30. Reproduced with permission, © 1995 Massachusetts Institute of Technology.

light, the sun gives off other forms of light, or radiation, not visible to our eyes. To either side of the spectrum of visible light are ultraviolet (UV) light and infrared light, also called radiant heat. Whereas the problem of ozone depletion concerns the effects of UV light, the problem of the greenhouse effect, or global warming, involves the effects of visible and infrared light. The two pertinent facts about these forms of radiation are that (1) UV light, if unfiltered, is very damaging to biological tissue, and (2) when visible light strikes an object, it warms it up, and the warm object then radiates infrared light, or heat. The earth's atmosphere acts both as a filter (blocking much of the sun's UV light, as depicted in Figure 1.1) and as an insulator (retaining radiant heat, as shown in Figure 1.2). Thus we can summarize the essence of the two (distinct) problems of ozone depletion and climate change as follows: ozone depletion lets more ultraviolet light through the atmosphere; the greenhouse effect warms the planet because the atmosphere passes visible light through to the earth's surface, but greenhouse gases block some of the resulting radiant heat from getting away.

Figure 1.2. The Greenhouse Effect.

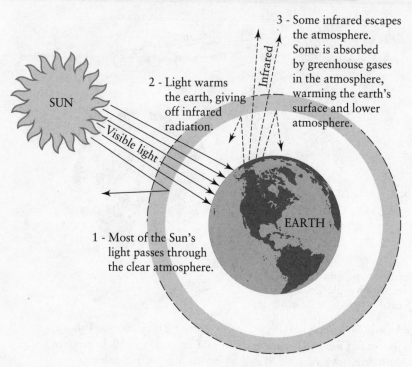

Source: W. Kempton, J. Boster, and J. Hartley, *Environmental Values in American Culture* (Cambridge, MA: MIT Press, 1995): 31. Reproduced with permission, © 1995 Massachusetts Institute of Technology.

OZONE DEPLETION. Ozone (O_3), a gas molecule made up of three oxygen atoms, is formed naturally in the stratosphere—the earth's upper atmosphere. This stratospheric ozone, along with clouds and dust particles, shields humans and all other living things from the sun's UV radiation. Higher levels of UV light would increase human skin cancers worldwide and damage other species. UV light also causes eye cataracts and reduces human immune response, increasing the rate and severity of diseases. The ozone layer is being thinned by human-made chemicals called chlorofluorocarbons, or CFCs (used for refrigerators, air conditioners, foam insulation, and many other things), and, to a lesser extent, halons (used primarily in fire extinguishers). These human-made chemicals released on earth gradually rise to the stratosphere, where they react with ozone molecules and convert them into other substances. Ozone loss has been most pronounced over Antarctica, because the chemical reactions occur more quickly in cold air, but ozone loss and corresponding increases in UV radiation have now also been measured in the populated mid latitudes.[17] Unfortunately, CFCs take ten years to reach the stratosphere and then remain there from fifty to one hundred years. In 1996 researchers at the National Oceanic and Atmospheric Administration's laboratory in Boulder, Colorado, detected a reduction in ozone-destroying chemicals at ground level.[18] Since it takes two to three years for the air masses now at ground level to migrate to the stratosphere, scientists predict that ozone destruction in the stratosphere will peak sometime between 1997 and 1999. Sometime after that the ozone layer should begin to recover. This turnaround can be traced back to 1987, when twenty-three nations agreed in Montreal to phase out the manufacture and use of ozone-destroying chemicals.

GLOBAL WARMING. The earth's atmosphere creates a natural greenhouse effect that, like a greenhouse building for plants, traps the sun's heat and keeps it warmer inside.[19] Visible light passes through the atmosphere, striking the earth's surface and heating it. This surface heat radiates back up as infrared light. Naturally occurring greenhouse gases absorb part of this infrared radiation in the lower atmosphere, thus keeping the earth warmer. Without that natural greenhouse effect, the earth's average surface temperature would be a chilly 0°F (−18°C) rather than its present global average of 59°F (15°C).

The primary natural greenhouse gases are water vapor (in clouds), carbon dioxide (CO_2), methane (CH_4), nitrous oxide (N_2O), and tropospheric (near-the-surface) ozone (O_3). Human activities are increasing atmospheric concentrations of all of these greenhouse gases, except water vapor. Humans have also introduced new greenhouse gases—chlorofluorocarbons (CFCs), hydrofluorocarbons (HFCs), and perfluorinated carbons (PFCs)—that do not occur naturally and cause ozone depletion as well as greenhouse warming. The sum total of these increased and new greenhouse gases is expected to alter the earth's climate globally. Even though these gases occur only in trace quantities (for example, a mere 0.03 percent of the atmosphere is carbon dioxide), their increase can be unambiguously measured. However, scientists disagree concerning the extent to which any climatic effects of these increases can be directly attributed to human activities.

Whereas the greenhouse effect is a natural phenomenon, anthropogenic (human-caused) increases in the greenhouse effect are referred to by the term *global warming* or *global climate change*. The major anthropogenic greenhouse gases are shown in Table 1.1. They are ranked in the table by their net effect on atmospheric heat retention (that is, according to how much they change the balance between heat loss and retention illustrated in Figure 1.2). This ranking takes into consideration both the potency of each gas and how much of it humans released during the 1980s.[20] Carbon dioxide alone accounts for 55 percent of the anthropogenic increases in the greenhouse effect. Since a worldwide CFC ban is already being phased in as a result of the 1987 Montreal protocol and methane and nitrous oxide together account for only 21 percent of the total anthropogenic effect, it is clear that carbon dioxide is the most important greenhouse gas at present. It is also more important than the other compounds because its life span in the atmosphere is much longer: over 1,000 years, compared with 10 to 150 years for the others.[21]

Carbon dioxide is generated and stored as part of a natural cycle in the earth's ecosystem. Biological processes on land contribute 110 trillion tons of carbon (as CO_2) to the atmosphere each year. This is balanced by uptake of CO_2 through photosynthesis. The oceans are also speculated to emit and absorb CO_2, but scientific models have been uncertain as to the extent of this phenomenon. Anthropogenic activities contribute an additional 5.7 trillion tons to the atmosphere through the burning of fossil fuels (coal, oil, and gas), plus another 600 million to 2.5 trillion tons through land-use changes (mostly the loss of tropical forests.) Atmospheric CO_2 levels began to increase in the nineteenth century with the industrial revolution and increasing deforestation and are expected to reach double preindustrial levels by the year 2065.

Table 1.1. Major Anthropogenic Greenhouse Gases.

Greenhouse gas	Effect	Life span (years)	Activities causing emissions
Carbon dioxide (CO_2)	55 percent	1,000	primarily fossil fuel burning; secondarily deforestation
Chlorofluorocarbons (CFCs)	24 percent	100	refrigerators; foam insulation and packing; previously aerosol cans (now banned)
Methane (CH_4)	15 percent	10	rice paddies; ruminant animals; coal mining; natural gas leaks; landfills; biomass burning
Nitrous oxide (N_2O)	6 percent	150	nitrogenous fertilizers; burning fossil fuels; biomass burning

Source: W. Kempton, J. Boster, and J. Hartley, *Environmental Values in American Culture* (Cambridge, MA: MIT Press, 1995): 33. Reproduced with permission.

Although the main effect of increasing greenhouse gases would seem to be simply to raise the earth's temperature, the reality is more complex. Since the earth's temperature drives evaporation and the movements of the atmosphere and the oceans, the dynamic effects of increased greenhouse gases on global climate are more diverse than a simple temperature increase. Using sophisticated computer programs, climatologists have tried to predict the effects of increased CO_2 and other greenhouse gases. Commonly predicted effects include drier weather in midcontinental areas (including the U.S. Midwest), sea level rise, more violent storms, and northward migration of vector-borne tropical diseases and climate-sensitive species.[22] If enough greenhouse gases were to accumulate in the atmosphere, many species would not be able to migrate quickly enough and would become extinct. In addition to the uncertainty inherent in simulations of complex ecological processes, a second problem is the level of CO_2 used in the simulations. Climatologists have been basing their models on a benchmark of a doubling of CO_2 over fifty to one hundred years. However, more recent calculations have shown that when atmospheric CO_2 peaks (projected to occur in two to three hundred years), levels will be closer to six or eight times the baseline level.[23] Furthermore, small temperature changes have surprisingly large effects on climate. For example, past ice ages were caused by average temperature reductions of approximately 9°F (5°C). And finally, the specific effects of increased greenhouse gases are predicted using complicated computer models, which vary in their results even when given the same inputs.[24] Although most climatologists consider the above-listed effects plausible, they cannot be predicted with certainty.

Technological Issues

How might global warming be arrested? Technological prescriptions include adaptation, prevention, and an additional approach called geoengineering. These can be combined, but to simplify the following discussion, they will be considered as mutually exclusive policies.

The *adaptation* strategy is this: rather than trying to prevent global warming, we should switch crops, move farmers north, and build dikes to hold back the rising sea. Serious economic analyses have argued that such an adaptation strategy would be less expensive than reducing greenhouse gas emissions. These analyses have been criticized, however, because they assume that economic activity is independent of nature, they typically assign no monetary value to environmental damage, they discount future costs to their present value, and they do not consider damages nations might inflict on other countries in taking these measures.

The *geoengineering* approach to climate change, like adaptation, would not change greenhouse gas emissions. Rather, this approach would mount engineering projects on a planetary scale to nullify an increased greenhouse effect. Proposals have included spreading dust in the upper atmosphere to reduce incidental sunlight and seeding the ocean with iron to increase the growth of phytoplankton, which takes in CO_2. A National Academy of Sciences (NAS) panel found some geoengineering options feasible, using existing technology and at a "reasonable cost."[25] However, the NAS panel cautioned that the earth's systems are nonlinear, involve complicated feedback loops, and are likely to be unstable and exhibit unintended side effects from such activities.

The *prevention* approach is to reduce the emission of greenhouse gases. Since there is currently no technology to remove the CO_2 from exhaust gases, most prevention schemes limit the activities that emit greenhouse gases. Reductions in CO_2 emissions could be accomplished by increasing the efficiency of fossil fuel–burning machines and power plants and using alternative energy sources such as wind or solar power or cleaner-burning fossil fuels. For example, burning natural gas yields a nearly 35 percent reduction in carbon dioxide emissions over oil and a nearly 60 percent reduction over synthetic fuels. Emissions do not need to be completely eliminated. One estimate is that stabilizing the global climate would require reductions of 15 percent in methane emissions and 60 to 80 percent in emissions of CO_2 and the other major greenhouse gases.[26] Fossil fuels are crucial to transportation, industry, and home energy. Reductions of 60 to 80 percent may seem impossible to many people if we are to maintain our standard of living.

Economic Issues

The United States is the world's largest emitter of greenhouse gases, producing 19 percent of the total.[27] Of total U.S. greenhouse gas emissions in 1995, carbon dioxide made up 84.8 percent, methane 10.6 percent, nitrous oxide 2.4 percent, HFCs and PFCs 1.7 percent, and sulfur hexaflouride 0.5 percent.[28] Controls on these greenhouse gas emissions would translate fundamentally into controls on energy generation. And any controls on energy generation will have a direct and increasing impact on virtually every industrial sector in the United States. Of particular sensitivity are the electric utility and transportation sectors, which produce 35 and 31 percent of U.S. carbon dioxide emissions, respectively.[29]

These facts lead many analyses based on aggregate economic data to argue that major changes to the energy system would be unacceptably expensive.[30] Estimates of the drain on the U.S. gross national product (GNP) reach as high as 3.5 percent if aggressive emission reduction targets are set. Others have argued, however, that modest controls on greenhouse gas emissions would not damage the economy.[31] This school of thought holds that the world has significant opportunities to control emissions by making its energy systems and automobiles more efficient. Since energy efficiency is desirable anyway for economic reasons, these economists argue, achieving it in the interest of heading off global warming amounts to a policy of "no regrets." This more efficient use of energy could actually increase GNP by 1 or 2 percent.[32] The fact is, however, that just like the scientific models, there is great uncertainty in the economic models used to predict the effects of emissions control measures. These uncertainties arise from the structural assumptions supplied to the model. For example: Is the economy already using energy efficiently? Will carbon tax revenues be used to offset other corporate taxes? Are the benefits of averting the damage caused by climate change included? Variance in the structural assumptions fed into the model can predict, conversely, a net loss or a net gain in GNP from greenhouse gas emissions controls.

A different picture emerges from analyses examining specific technological substitutions. For example, Johansson and colleagues recently analyzed, technology by technology, the effects of switching to cost-effective renewable energy sources and increasing energy efficiency. They estimated that world CO_2 emissions could be reduced by about 40 percent per capita by 2050.[33] Although such per capita improvement would certainly be impressive, after factoring in expected world population growth, global CO_2 emissions would be reduced by only 26 percent by 2050 (developing-country emissions would increase slightly, while the industrialized world would reduce emissions by two-thirds).[34] The 26 percent figure is well short of the 60 to 80 percent reduction needed for climate stabilization. This analysis conservatively assumed that renewables would not be used if they cost more than fossil fuels and that no credit would be given for environmentally friendly economic development. It also neglected the energy-independence benefits of high renewables use. In contrast to the aggregate economic analyses, this analysis predicted a large supply of cost-effective non-CO_2-producing technology.

A study by the U.S. Office of Technology Assessment (OTA) itemized some policies that could reduce CO_2 emissions: taxes on energy or carbon-emitting fuels, tax credits or low-interest loans to encourage use of renewable energy sources and energy efficiency, legislation to require new products (cars, appliances, buildings) to achieve higher energy efficiency, federal support for research and development of new technologies, and public information and education.[35] The OTA pointed out that many of these CO_2 reduction policies would have additional benefits as well, such as reducing local air pollution and increasing the nation's energy security. And despite the scientific uncertainties, many economists consider it prudent to begin soon to slowly restrain greenhouse gas emissions as a form of insurance against the possible economic costs. Insurance industry forecasters say that a 15 percent increase in hurricane wind speeds, precipitated by climate change, would double insured losses.[36] The primary mechanism by which this cutback should be instigated, they agree, is through the use of economic incentives in the form of carbon taxes or tradable emissions permits.[37]

Geopolitical Issues

In 1988 representatives from around the world convened in Toronto at the World Conference on the Changing Atmosphere. Two outcomes of this meeting were the establishment of the IPCC to conduct ongoing scientific research on climate change and a recommendation for an initial global reduction of CO_2 emissions by 20 percent of 1988 levels by 2005.[38] Although this recommendation was not binding, it served to place the issue of climate change on the international political agenda.

In 1990 the IPCC produced its first assessment, which formed the basis for negotiations among nations over the Framework Convention on Climate Change (FCCC). This treaty took nearly fifteen months of intensive negotiations to develop and was introduced for the signatures of 172 heads of state at the United Nations Conference on Environment and Development held in Rio de Janeiro in 1992. By the end of 1993 the treaty was in force, having been ratified by 142 countries. The treaty established a set of voluntary measures, calling for all parties to stabilize their greenhouse gas emissions at 1990 levels by the year 2000, to protect greenhouse gas sinks (such as forests), and to help finance and provide technology to developing countries to help them meet general commitments. It also required detailed national reports outlining programs to respond to climate change, emissions inventories, and projections of future emissions. Finally, the convention established the ongoing Conference of the Parties to the FCCC, which would be the primary legal forum for negotiating future international actions to address climate change.

Three years later the first session of the Conference of the Parties to the FCCC (COP-1) met in Berlin to consider the adequacy of the nonbinding commitments made in Rio and to assess the need for post-2000 controls. In this meeting (held in March 1995) participating governments decided that few "Annex 1" countries (their term for developed countries, including Organization for Economic Cooperation and Development (OECD) member countries and countries with economies in transition to market economies) demonstrated an ability to meet the voluntary goals of the FCCC. The participants felt that current planned actions to mitigate climate change were insufficient and that more aggressive legal instruments were necessary. At the same time, it was agreed that the scientific rationale for action had proved more and more compelling. A new decision document (known as the Berlin Mandate) was signed to establish a process that would outline policies and procedures and set emission control and removal (by sinks) objectives for the years 2005, 2010, and 2020.

Negotiation Issues

At COP-2, held in December 1996 in Geneva, the U.S. government for the first time articulated support for firm, legally binding goals for reducing greenhouse gas emissions. The U.S. delegates did not propose any specific timetables or targets, however, and they stated that the most aggressive proposal, recommended by the Alliance of Small Island States (AOSIS), was unrealistic and insupportable. The AOSIS proposal required Annex 1 countries to reduce their carbon emissions to 1990 levels by 2000 and then to 80 percent of 1996 levels by 2005, to be maintained at that level thereafter. Instead the U.S. government proposed a shift away from such short-term goals (pre-2005) and a focus on medium-term goals that would become binding between 2005 and 2015. Overall the Geneva talks were aimed at putting on the table proposals that would set the foundation for reaching an international agreement on climate change controls at the COP-3 meeting, to be held in December 1997 in Kyoto, Japan.

U.S. "NON-PAPER" ON CLIMATE CHANGE

The U.S. position at COP-2 was summarized in a "non-paper" produced by the State Department.[39] In it the United States called for verifiable, binding, medium-term targets for developed countries that would be realistic and achievable, designed with maximum flexibility, and implemented through national programs. The U.S. position also underscored the need for all nations, including developing nations, to take actions to limit greenhouse gas emissions. Finally, the United States called for continued work on longer-term (fifty to one hundred years) global goals. This approach forms the foundation for the U.S. negotiating position at the Kyoto COP-3 meeting planned for December 1997. (For further depth, see the June 1997 Draft Protocol Framework, printed in the Appendix.)

In the U.S. view, there is sufficient scientific evidence to suggest that climate change could be detrimental to human health and could threaten ecosystems, food supplies, and water resources in many regions of the world, and all parties should proceed with the understanding that the science provides a compelling basis for action to address climate change. Notwithstanding this position, the U.S. government also believes that efforts to further develop and refine our understanding of the science of climate change must continue, even as steps are taken to ameliorate its impact. Such understanding, coupled with advances in the development and application of new technology, will ultimately enable a more efficient and successful long-term approach to addressing this pressing problem.

The United States believes that the next steps in fighting climate change must be as cost-effective as possible. Analyses completed to date suggest that more flexible approaches offer significant cost-saving opportunities, and these must be brought into the FCCC's basic framework. Flexibility includes allowing each nation to determine the most appropriate policies and measures to meet agreed targets and allowing emissions trading and joint implementation between parties to minimize the cost of reductions.

The United States arrived at this basic framework for a number of reasons. It is clear that the 1992 Rio convention's framework of a nonbinding "aim" is not working, even though at the national level numerous voluntary partnerships with industry are working well. Most developed countries, including the United States, will not achieve the goal of returning emissions to 1990 levels by 2000. A binding commitment would create a stronger incentive for nations to decide on a realistic target, make the effort required to meet that target, ensure a level playing field, and foster the development and deployment of advanced technologies.

The United States seeks to focus on appropriate medium-term steps while continuing efforts to develop longer-term goals. This is based on a belief that short-term targets (such as before 2010) are unrealistic and cannot be accepted. Short-term targets would be unnecessarily burdensome to national and global economic growth and development. Embracing them could mean that few, if any, countries would ratify the agreement.

Finally, the United States recognizes the need for climate change to be addressed on a global basis. As a result it believes that it is imperative that the agreement reached in Kyoto include specific provisions that advance the implementation of commitments by developing nations to reduce their greenhouse gas emissions. While recognizing that developed countries must show leadership in addressing this problem, the United States believes it is very clear that all nations must be part of the solution.

The consensus reached at COP-2 provides climate negotiators with a blueprint for action; however, in Kyoto it will be time to develop and agree on concrete proposals. What follows is an outline of the U.S. view on a number of issues and suggestions for several other options that merit closer scrutiny. Further views on specific numbers should be included in targets and timetables in the future as the results of continuing analyses and assessments emerge.

Linkages

A number of key variables under consideration are interdependent, and this interdependence must be recognized in negotiating the next steps. The United States believes that it is critical to include developing countries at this stage, because finding a solution to the climate change problem will require a concerted, global effort. Further, the U.S. government believes that its goal of obtaining a binding agreement, medium-term targets, and national flexibility in implementation depends on involving the developing world. These four concepts are all linked, and so all four must be included in the legal instrument.

Defining the Form of the Target

The United States remains convinced that emissions targets should be set in a manner that allows for adjustment on the basis of new and evolving science. The following outlines some of the United States' current thinking on the form and structure of the target.

MULTIYEAR TARGETS. The United States believes that the target set in the next step should cover a multiyear period. This would accomplish several objectives. First, a multiyear target would compensate for year-to-year variability in weather and economic cycles. U.S. analyses of the effects of such variability provide a striking example of the importance of this issue: unusually hot or cold years can change total U.S. emissions by as much as 2 percent—or about 40 percent of the emissions reductions sought from the energy sector by the year 2000. Because swings in weather, energy prices, or economic cycles cannot be predicted with confidence, a single-year target would require each country to build in an extra margin of greenhouse gas reductions to ensure compliance, significantly and unnecessarily raising costs.

Second, a multiyear target would give each country important flexibility to determine the pace at which its emissions budget should be expended over the period (evenly, front-loaded, or back-loaded). This flexibility may be particularly important in helping the parties reduce their compliance costs in view of differing national circumstances. To provide this flexibility, targets could be set with budgets covering a multiyear period, for example, 2010 to 2020. Enforceability is a key issue in defining a multiyear period.

EMISSIONS "BANKING" AND "BORROWING." The United States strongly urges consideration of emissions "banking" between multiyear average target periods. Such a process would allow countries whose emissions are below the target level in one period to offset higher-than-target emissions in later periods. Banking of emissions could reward efforts to make reductions in earlier periods. Similarly, the United States would consider allowing countries to "borrow" emissions against their targets for later periods in order to emit more in a current period. Borrowing will require that a credible accounting and repayment mechanism be put in place, and it could also entail additional restrictions (for example, to limit the proportion of emissions reductions postponed).

DIFFERENTIATION AMONG ANNEX I COUNTRIES. A number of Annex 1 countries have suggested proposals for differentiation of commitments of the members of this group. Although the United States acknowledges that clear distinctions can be (and are) drawn between different countries and groups of countries, it does not believe that developing a complex, formulaic approach that differentiates at the level of individual nations is a viable alternative at this stage in the negotiations. To date no formula has been proposed for a differentiated approach that equitably addresses all nations' concerns.

An effort to define an acceptable differentiation scheme would likely derail the negotiations, either by being too divisive and time-consuming or by disadvantaging a group of countries that might then choose not to sign or ratify. Either outcome could negate the value of the differentiation effort. Instead the United States endorses the adoption of a common approach with respect to targets that retains each country's flexibility with respect to the choice of domestic policies and measures to implement the target. The United States also supports international trading instruments to minimize and equalize countries' marginal costs of making reductions. Such an approach would enable the completion of the agreement by December 1997.

COMPREHENSIVE APPROACH. The United States continues to support the inclusion of all greenhouse gases and of both sources and sinks in a comprehensive, verifiable approach to addressing the climate change problem. Gases other than carbon dioxide account for about 30 percent of the radiative forcing from all emissions since the industrial revolution. Furthermore, different gases represent different strategic opportunities from the perspective of mitigating effects on the climate. For example, reductions in methane emissions could yield a lower rate of warming over the next several decades than comparable reductions in carbon dioxide. To forgo reducing such a significant source of radiative forcing would not only be counterproductive, it would also both reduce flexibility and decrease the cost-effectiveness of the overall effort.

Assuming a comprehensive approach, several issues still require additional consideration. These include the different level of certainty with regard to measurement of non-CO_2 emissions in various sectors, problems with verification, and the relative importance, or weighting, to be assigned to different gases. Significant technical difficulties also exist concerning how to measure reductions from sinks. The United States insists that any approach must be fully quantifiable and verifiable and include appropriate accounting procedures prior to its inclusion in the legal instrument. This approach must be able to incorporate changing methodologies for the measurement of the sources and sinks of all gases. The United States is currently working to address these concerns and believes that a solution that is technically and politically satisfactory is achievable before Kyoto.

EMISSIONS TRADING. The United States believes that the Kyoto agreement should include provisions for emissions trading among countries that have assumed binding, quantified emissions targets. This includes countries that agree to such targets in the Kyoto agreement, and additional countries that do so subsequently. Through emissions trading, such countries would have the opportunity to meet their emissions targets at the lowest possible costs. This is a matter of ensuring environmental gains in the most cost-effective way.

Trading makes sense when the costs of controlling greenhouse gas emissions differ among countries. In this case it is more cost-effective for those with high emission control costs to buy a portion of the emissions budgeted to a country whose costs are lower rather than to attempt further reductions itself. Trading would be strictly voluntary and would occur only if both countries agreed. Under such an approach the environment is protected, the country with higher costs saves money, the country with lower costs is rewarded, and the overall cost of meeting the targets is reduced. The United States has had domestic success using emissions trading to substantially reduce the costs of complying with clean air standards for acid rain. Experience with international emissions trading has also been gained under the Montreal Protocol on Substances that Deplete the Ozone Layer through its industrial rationalization provisions. Based on such successes, the United States believes that an effective and enforceable regime for emissions trading among countries with a binding target should be developed and should be included in the Kyoto agreement. A number of issues regarding how such an international regime might be structured still need to be addressed.

Emissions trading, as noted, would take place only between countries that have assumed a binding emissions target. The target will give each such country an allowable amount of greenhouse gases it can emit during a time period—in other words, an "emissions budget" for the relevant period, expressed in metric tons of carbon or the equivalent. In its most basic form the emissions trading scheme would allow one country to transfer (sell or trade) some of its allowable emissions to another country. The first country would then be responsible for meeting its emissions target, minus the amount transferred. The second country would be responsible for meeting its emissions target, plus the amount transferred.

The United States anticipates that many countries will wish to develop emissions trading further, to allow private firms or other entities within their borders to engage in emissions trades with counterparts in other nations. In addition to government-to-government trades and firm-to-firm trades, the United States also envisions mixed transactions in which firms in one country trade directly with the government of another country.

Certain fundamental institutional features are necessary for countries that engage in international emissions trading to ensure that trading is verifiable, efficient, and environmentally beneficial. These include compatible mechanisms for accurately measuring, tracking, and reporting domestic emissions. Countries also must have the means to track amounts of emissions transferred to or from other countries, to reduce or augment their national emissions target accordingly, and to ensure the integrity of trades undertaken by their nationals. The United States believes that guidance for these areas should be developed by and agreed to at COP-3 in Kyoto.

JOINT IMPLEMENTATION. The FCCC parties have been engaged in discussions of joint implementation (JI) for several years. During this time support has grown for JI between countries subject to emissions targets and those that are not. Through JI, a country with a target could gain credit toward satisfying it by taking actions that reduce emissions in a country without a target. Such an approach has the potential to reduce the first country's cost of meeting its target, while increasing investment in and diffusion of technology to the second country.

The United States believes that the Kyoto agreement should include the establishment of a JI regime providing for emissions credits. Such a regime would encourage the rapid development and implementation of cooperative, mutually voluntary projects between partners, encourage private sector investment and innovation in development and dissemination of technologies, and provide an incentive through financial and technical assistance to further the development of non–Annex 1 country programs to limit increases in greenhouse gas emissions.

To realize the potential of JI, the process of developing criteria, currently under way in the Subsidiary Body for Scientific and Technological Advice, must continue. Such criteria will be essential to ensure that JI becomes a credible and significant contributor to solving the climate change problem. The U.S. Initiative on Joint Implementation (USIJI) has been one of the most successful and aggressive programs in the development and application of criteria. The United States intends to remain active in the further development of criteria, working both in the domestic context of the USIJI and internationally. The United States believes that criteria development can be completed prior to the year 2000, in time to include JI credits in national greenhouse gas reduction compliance programs. For such a program, the United States stresses the importance of three criteria in particular: acceptance by the governments of the participating countries, reporting of data and methodological information with regard to the project, and the need to ensure "additionality" (for example, a reduction in net greenhouse gas emissions as a result of the project).

ACTIVITIES IMPLEMENTED JOINTLY. Activities implemented jointly (AIJ) is a pilot program to evaluate the viability of project-based reductions in the absence of targets and without credit. While AIJ will provide valuable insights for JI, the United States sees no role for a continued pilot effort beyond the year 2000.

CONTINUING TO ADVANCE THE IMPLEMENTATION OF COMMITMENTS FOR ALL PARTIES. It is widely recognized that the threat of climate change is a global problem that can only be overcome through global action. Although industrialized countries account for the majority of the world's past and current greenhouse gas emissions, greenhouse gas emissions are growing most rapidly in the developing countries; emissions there are projected to exceed those of the developed countries by about 2020. The FCCC and the parties to it, based on their decisions to date, recognize both realities.

The Berlin Mandate began a process to enable the parties to the FCCC to take appropriate action for the period beyond 2000. It provides for developed countries to elaborate on policies and measures and to set quantified emission limitation and reduction objectives for greenhouse gas emissions. For developing countries, the Berlin Mandate process will not introduce any new commitments but calls upon them to reaffirm existing commitments in Article 4.1 and to continue to advance the implementation of those commitments. The Geneva Declaration from COP-2 provides that the outcome of the current negotiating effort should fully encompass the remit of the Berlin Mandate. Two key points emerged from these documents: the next steps under the FCCC must include all parties, and actions ultimately taken by developed and developing countries should be appropriately balanced, recognizing the common but differentiated responsibilities and respective capabilities noted in the FCCC and upheld both in the Berlin Mandate and the Geneva Declaration.

To date all parties have been making progress toward implementing their commitments under the FCCC, including those related to the submission of first national communications under Article 12. Through the U.S. Country Studies Program, many developing countries are already far along in preparing national inventories of greenhouse gas emissions and in developing national action plans. A number of developing countries have also initiated projects under the Pilot Phase for Activities Implemented Jointly.

Beyond these current efforts to implement existing FCCC commitments, a wide range of possibilities exist through which the world can "continue to advance the implementation of existing commitments," as contemplated by the Berlin Mandate. Much work remains to be done to gauge the level of effort developed countries will undertake pursuant to the Berlin Mandate. Still, it is not too early to advance thinking about the range of possibilities for continuing to advance the implementation of existing commitments, recognizing the need for all parties to take action.

NATIONAL COMMUNICATIONS, POLICIES, AND MEASURES. Although the parties have adopted guidelines for the preparation of initial communications from developing countries, they have yet to consider options for reviewing those communications. Such a review process could include systematic efforts to assist developing countries in identifying and implementing no-regrets and cost-effective options for mitigating greenhouse gas emissions. The review could seek to identify key sectors and technological options within them. It could also consider the possibilities for promoting voluntary agreements with industry aimed at identifying and encouraging the implementation of no-regrets measures. Partnership agreements have proven highly effective in the United States at enlisting private sector support for mitigating greenhouse gas emissions and in helping to capture efficient emissions reductions opportunities that are otherwise obstructed by market barriers. In addition, negotiators could explore various means by which parties could obtain both the know-how and the technology needed to implement the options identified.

NEXT STEPS. Beyond these kinds of efforts, the United States recommends developing guidelines to revise the FCCC annexes, which establish which parties assume which commitments under the FCCC, and for considering how better to reflect the common but differentiated responsibilities and capabilities of different parties. In the U.S. view, as countries develop to and beyond a certain point, they must graduate to assume responsibilities commensurate with their development. The present groupings do not reflect dynamic changes in the world that have occurred since 1992, changes that will only accelerate in the future.

Another option would be to consider agreeing in the context of the Berlin Mandate to further negotiations to establish a specified date in the future by which all parties would be expected to have quantitative commitments with respect to their greenhouse gas emissions. Two variables might also be considered. First, the date need not be the same for all parties—a schedule could be possible for phasing in quantitative commitments. Second, the nature of the quantitative commitments need not be the same for all parties—different levels of commitment based on various factors, including levels of development, could be established. It would be important to consider carefully mandates for these negotiations, including when they could begin, when they would conclude, and what results should be anticipated.

As noted, the range of possibilities is very wide. It represents a kind of continuum beginning with modest efforts but potentially extending to those that would bring the world's leaders significantly closer to a truly global response and to the FCCC's ultimate objective. It is as yet too soon to determine precisely where along this continuum the Kyoto treaty should strive to reach as part of the Berlin Mandate process. Inevitably this will depend in large measure on the level of action that developed countries are prepared to undertake, and it is not yet clear what that level will be. Still, in the U.S. view it is not too early to think boldly about the possibilities and about how best to position ourselves for the future, recognizing that the steps taken in Kyoto will represent only a second milestone along a much longer path toward the FCCC's ultimate objective.

COMPLIANCE. The United States has called for a binding target both to promote a realistic negotiation and to promote compliance with the result. The question is what other elements should be included in the compliance regime, recognizing that, on the one hand, effective compliance is important for both environmental and economic competitiveness reasons, and on the other hand, too stringent a compliance regime could result in vague commitments or scare off countries from joining the agreement. Several categories of elements could promote compliance; they are discussed below.

The first element is *the structure of commitments.* In terms of the target, as a matter of drafting it needs to be articulated as clearly and quantitatively as possible; as a matter of substance it should be as objectively measurable as possible. In terms of commitments to advance implementation of Article 4.1, these should, ideally, also be as specific as possible. The desire of developing countries for flexibility could be met by providing flexibility in the choice of implementation options rather than by vague, heavily qualified commitments (such as those in the current convention).

The second element is *how to ascertain compliance.* Ascertaining compliance will involve a combination of requirements on parties to monitor and report on their emissions and an international mechanism to verify such monitoring and reporting. The FCCC's current obligations regarding national inventories, national communications, and an international in-depth review process provide an excellent basis. The new agreement may require strengthened national or international mechanisms. (For example, parties bound by the target could be required to have in place a domestic emissions monitoring system, at a minimum for

CO_2 and for specified sources.) There will also be a need to promote uniformity of measurement.

The third element is *supporting implementation.* Particularly in terms of developing-country performance, the availability of sources of technical assistance (such as systematic support for efforts to develop national action plans) and expanded programs aimed at developing, diffusing, and deploying climate-friendly technologies could be effective in promoting compliance.

The fourth element is *dispute settlement.* The current convention allows any party to challenge another party's compliance with its obligations before a neutral third party, with a recommendatory result. (Parties can opt for a binding result, but it is not required.) Whether this system would suffice for the new agreement or whether it would need to be enhanced needs to be considered, taking into account, among other things, the extent to which the target is clear and objectively measurable (which is not currently known). Ways to enhance the system include, for example, requiring the issuance of binding judgments or specifying particular consequences flowing from a binding judgment of noncompliance.

Additionally or alternatively, the dispute settlement system could be supplemented by a multilateral consultative process, akin to that being developed under the current convention. Unlike dispute settlement, such a process is considered nonadversarial in that implementation issues can be raised without asserting an actual treaty violation; the parties themselves, rather than third parties, consider the issues, and it is multilateral rather than state-against-state.

The fifth and final element is *dealing with nonparties.* Development of a compliance regime regarding a global issue also requires consideration of how to deal with nonparties (the so-called free-rider problem), so that the environmental objective of the agreement is not undermined. Ways to seek to minimize the nonparty problem include the provision of positive incentives for countries to join the regime (for example, assistance, differentiated obligations, other participatory privileges), an entry-into-force clause that requires ratification by countries that account for a particular percentage of global emissions of greenhouse gases, and the use of measures against nonparties.

OVERVIEW OF THE CLIMATE CHANGE DIALOGUE

With this complex blend of scientific, technological, economic, geopolitical, and negotiation issues as a backdrop, we convened this senior-level dialogue on climate change. What became apparent very quickly was that consensus was not a likely outcome. The diversity of both the issues involved and the interests represented in the room ensured a lively but unresolvable debate. Richard Klimisch, vice president of the American Automobile Manufacturers Association, has aptly labeled climate change "the mother of all environmental issues." Yet despite this lack of consensus, several common themes emerged from the dialogue in the form of questions the group considered relevant to their interests. The remaining pages of this chapter present seven of these dominant themes; these should help in understanding the chapters and dialogue that follow.

1. *Does the science on climate change support the necessity for action?* Presenting the strongest statement on the certainty of climate change, Timothy Wirth opened the dialogue by asserting that "the debate about the existence of climate change is over. . . . The threat is significant enough that it's time to take out an insurance policy. We don't know exactly where, how much, how fast; but it is time to move." Representatives from environmental organizations echoed the firmness of Mr. Wirth's sentiments. Presenting a counterargument, however, Roger Stone stated that he did not believe that the science debate is over and that he was "concerned that we are blindly accepting a policy that would result in permanent and destructive changes to our economy." In Chapters Ten and Eleven, Eugene Lecomte and W. Henson Moore write with similar skepticism and argue for similar restraint. However, in terms of the vocalized opinions in the dialogue, most corporate executives endorsed action in a more cautious tone. Although a great deal of uncertainty remains concerning the timing and consequences of climate change, most feel that some type of measured response is warranted.

Dan Martin also suggested that, aside from the scientific evidence, there may be a strategic reason why industry should support a climate change treaty. He argued that as companies face competition from companies in state-run economies, a climate change treaty will present an opportunity to level the playing field. All countries would be forced to abide by one common set of environmental laws through the institution of globally enforceable standards. Therefore he believes that a climate change treaty would be in the best interests of industry.

2. *Are there going to be costs associated with climate change controls?* The costs of climate change controls is a hotly contested question. Amory Lovins opened his second talk by arguing that "we do not need to worry about how the climate science turns out or whether this is a real problem or not." Instead, as he stated in his earlier talk, "protecting the climate will be highly profitable rather than costly if we do the

cheapest things first, and ... pursuing [the] profit motive will put industry in its rightful place as the largest part of the solution." This is not a universally held opinion; indeed, it stirs considerable debate. Lovins's argument centers on the idea that, "figuratively," there are "$10,000 bills lying all over the floor" of factories "of every imaginable variety" and that we can take action without damaging the economy. He believes that most of the analyses of the impact of climate change policies are economic- and not engineering-based. Based on real-world experience, he feels that the obstacles to effectively capturing these opportunities are not economic or technological but cultural and institutional. Max Bazerman, Claire Buisseret, and Kimberly Wade-Benzoni expand on this idea in their chapter on judgment error as it relates to climate change. They point out that "even the brightest humans fall victim to a variety of systematic and predictable cognitive errors. We believe that teaching our citizens, leaders, and negotiators to be aware of these errors is central to the negotiation of a global climate change solution."

Although several executives concede that there are opportunities in energy conservation, many remain cool to the idea. Most are convinced that climate change policy will impose costs on industry and that hidden opportunities are not as abundant as suggested. In one spirited exchange, Paul Portney challenges Amory Lovins on these unseen opportunities: "I'm willing to make a concession to Amory. It is that markets are not as perfect as at least some people in the economics profession sometimes suggest that they are. If I could just get you to concede that businessmen and women are not as stupid as you persistently suggest that they are. The notion that we have to put a gun to businessmens' and women's heads to get them to take advantage of all this free money is silly."

Nevertheless, market opportunities are an area that dominates the discussion of economic impact. In particular it is widely accepted that power generation in the developing world will increase dramatically in the coming decades. James O'Connor predicts that increase to be on the order of 34 to 46 percent between 1993 and 2008. Regardless of the climate change issue, this will be a market opportunity for companies that produce power generation equipment and services. Dirk Forrister adds that the inclusion of joint implementation in the final negotiated climate agreement should only increase the incentives for power generation companies to seek projects overseas.

Conversely, domestic construction of power-generating capacity is expected to become all but nonexistent. Instead utility executives see demand management and performance contracting as areas of vital growth, particularly as the electric utility industry faces deregulation in state legislatures across the country. While pointing out that "environmental issues are not at the top of the agenda" for the utility industry, James O'Connor predicts that deregulation will bring lower rates and will force utilities to increase profits in these other ways.

Other companies (such as British Petroleum and Enron) are investing significant resources in the development of renewable energy sources such as wind and photovoltaics. Richard Abdoo suggests that nuclear power will become an acceptable solution to the climate change problem, as it is a non-carbon-producing power source. Others counter with strong disagreement.

3. *If there are costs, what might their magnitude be?* Regardless of the potential opportunities in newly emerging markets, the potential costs of controlling carbon dioxide emissions are a prevalent concern. The most commonly stated estimate of the costs, through taxes or some other market mechanism, is $100 per ton (although Dirk Forrister is uncomfortable with this number). Other estimates also exist. The Mobil advertisement in Exhibit 1.1 predicts a cost range of between $200 and $580 per ton. The precise number is a critical factor in analyses of the economic impacts of climate change policy. Based on the $100-per-ton figure, Paul Portney says that economic models predict a cost to gross domestic product (GDP) of 1 percent, or about $70 billion per year. This would amount to about half of the $150 billion per year we presently spend on all of the environmental regulatory programs now in place in the United States. Jonathan Lash, however, argues that if economic models use more optimistic assumptions GDP does not fall but rises as much as 2.4 percent, or about $170 billion, per year. Given the size of these amounts of money and the variance between them, many argue that continued research will be necessary to fashion the least costly climate change programs.

In considering the wide variance in cost estimates, many recall the exaggerated economic predictions surrounding the sulfur dioxide controls of the Clean Air Act amendments. Increased competition and railroad deregulation are credited with bringing compliance costs down from their originally high estimates. Virtually all of the executives in the room, environmental and industrial, endorsed the use of market incentives as a mechanism for bringing about economically viable climate change programs. Mandatory, command-and-control programs were universally rejected.

In any market-based incentive scheme, Allen Koleff, Roger Stone, and W. Henson Moore want the forestry industry to be recognized for its unique contribution to climate change mitigation through the carbon sequestration inherent in its products. Mr. Moore points out in his chapter that U.S. forests have a current standing inventory of sixty billion metric tons of sequestered carbon, an amount equal to roughly forty years of total U.S. emissions (at 1.5 billion metric tons per year). Also, these forests and the products developed by the forest products industry (paper, furniture, lumber, and so on) store another 265 million tons of carbon per year. Given this capability, he calls on the administration to include some type of system to encourage and reward these activities.

4. *What kind of flexibility should be in the final program?* The most talked about issues in the dialogue were the concepts of "where" and "when" flexibility. These are seen as critical to the development of an economically sound program to reduce carbon emissions. "Where" flexibility refers primarily to joint implementation. JI allows companies to invest in carbon reductions in foreign countries and receive credit for those reductions at home. The logic is similar to the SO_2 tradable permit program in the Clean Air Act amendments—if it costs $100 per ton to eliminate carbon in the United States and $5 per ton to eliminate carbon in China, then JI will allow U.S. companies to make the Chinese investment and receive domestic credit. Industry and the administration support this concept. However, Howard Ris and Paul Portney point out one reservation, arguing that developing countries may get the short end of the stick in such a scheme. As the developed world makes all of the inexpensive changes in the developing world (picks the low-hanging fruit), developing countries will be left with the more expensive changes when (or if) they are brought into the program.

"When" flexibility allows companies a period of time to satisfy climate change requirements. In this arrangement companies would not be forced to prematurely retire capital stock, and technology developers would have more time to develop and perfect substitutes. Companies would be able to make the transition to cleaner technologies at a pace that is economically and technologically appropriate. One dissenting opinion to "when" flexibility is presented in Chapter Nine by Terence Thorn of the Enron Corporation, who feels that flexibility in timing will only foster bad habits and will allow companies to put off until tomorrow what they should be doing today.

5. *Should the developing world be included in the treaty?* Presently the administration is not pushing for early entry of developing countries (non–Annex 1 countries). The arguments are that we are the number-one emitter of carbon and therefore we should cut back first, and on an aggregate basis we have put more carbon into the atmosphere over the past fifty years than anyone else (we have "fouled the nest") and therefore we should take concerted action and assume leadership in responding to the

problem of climate change. Executives are uncomfortable with this position. They feel that although this may make sense on an emotional level, it makes little sense on an economic or environmental level. John Dell points out that countries in the developing world (particularly China, Brazil, and India) are expanding their power generation base so rapidly that by the early part of the next century they will become the dominant carbon emitters. As such they must be included in the solution. If they are not, any efforts by the developed world will be eclipsed and become futile. Dell also argues that leaving the developing world out of the solution would place industry in the United States, Western Europe, and the rest of the developed world at a distinct economic disadvantage. In such a situation, Allen Koleff warns, industry will be forced to move overseas, to countries where the standards do not exist.

Contrary to the notion that environmental standards are uniformly lax in the developing world, John Bobek suggests that the developing world may, in fact, be more aware of efficiency concerns than the developed world. He argues that their restricted energy availability drives them to be more likely to invest in energy-efficient technologies than the developed world. Amory Lovins adds that for the developing world every dollar spent on energy generation is one dollar taken away from other development needs or from the manufacture of the products that use that energy. Energy efficiency is a rational way for them to improve their standard of living. Over time, energy efficiency can become a source of competition for industries in those countries.

6. *How important is research and development to this issue?* The subject of research and development is introduced into the dialogue by Paul Portney and thereafter continues as a consistent theme. Portney argues that great uncertainty surrounds both the science of climate change and the economic impact of any climate change controls. In order to make reasonable efforts at finding appropriate responses, research and development must be part of the equation. He chided the executives in the room for being "conspicuously absent in testifying before Congress for larger research and development budgets for the Department of Energy, the Environmental Protection Agency, and NASA." He challenged them that "to make business's position in the climate policy debate even more credible, you ought to be up there shoulder to shoulder with people from the administration and the environmental community, lobbying for more expenditures on research and development" while also beginning "to commit your own resources, perhaps in industry consortia, into research and development efforts." Dirk Forrister stressed that research and development is a major part of the U.S. position on climate change. And

the British Petroleum position presented by both Steven Percy and John Browne contains a strong research and development component in the area of renewable energy.

7. *How important is education and behavioral change?* The topic of education emerges toward the end of the private dialogue and dominates the public question period. Amory Lovins suggests that the reason we are not taking advantage of the economic opportunities in energy efficiency available to us is due to flawed engineering education—engineers are taught to optimize the components of a process and not the whole system. By doing the latter, he argues, a host of opportunities will become visible. Others point to the behavior of individual citizens as a central cause of climate change. David Kee points out that urban sprawl is one major contributor and that the driving mentality of the average American must be altered to offset climate change. In responding to public questions, Paul Portney concedes that technology cannot continually bail us out of environmental problems. Behavioral change will sooner or later be necessary to find a permanent solution.

However, the role of business in promoting that behavior change is generally considered to be secondary. Richard Klimisch points out that efforts to sell alternative fuel vehicles have failed. Consumers do not want them, and therefore they will not be aggressively developed. If producers do not provide consumers with the products that they want, he argues, someone else will. Andrew Bermingham suggests that we cannot control what we do not know. Therefore, to offset urban sprawl, perhaps we should have a carbon meter next to the odometer in our car. Just as we have the recommended daily allowance of vitamins on our box of corn flakes, he suggests, why not have the carbon content labeled as well?

Richard Abdoo repeatedly challenges the U.S. government to lead behavioral change by example. How can the government expect industry to change how it behaves, he argues, if the government does not practice energy efficiency in its buildings and in its automobile fleets? He feels very strongly that the government must set an example for others to follow and must then provide the proper signals and incentives to reward that behavior.

Finally, Max Bazerman and Amory Lovins both stress that the obstacles to achieving profitable solutions to the climate change problem are not technological or economic. Rather they are cultural and procedural, what economists call "market failures." Both suggest that some kind of alteration in the way we frame and conceive of the problem is necessary to alter how we develop solutions. Education is the way to bring that about.

A ROAD MAP

This book is divided into three parts. Part One presents a series of prepared remarks by individual industry and environmental leaders. These chapters are intended to present the climate change issue from their respective vantage points. They offer insights on issues specific to the writers' organizations as well as ideas that are of general interest to all organizations. Part Two presents an edited text of the dialogue that took place on May 23, 1997. These three chapters reveal some of the same ideas presented in Part One, but they allow the reader an opportunity to see how others reacted to and challenged them. It is an exciting and illuminating dialogue. The book closes in Part Three with concluding thoughts on the benefits of this particular dialogue and the worth of such a dialogue in the larger scheme of things.

NOTES

1. V. Scheffer, *The Shaping of Environmentalism in America* (Seattle: University of Washington Press, 1991): 182.
2. In virtually every article written for the *New York Times* on the topic of climate change since 1995, the Global Climate Coalition is cited as the chief spokesperson for industry. In an article in the *Wall Street Journal* the group is explicitly referred to as "industry's main lobbying group." See J. Fialka, "Global-Warming Treaty Faces Host of Political Clouds," *Wall Street Journal,* May 27, 1997: A20.
3. "Climate Session Opens with Words of Warning," *New York Times,* July 9, 1996: 4.
4. Western Fuels Association, *The Greening of Planet Earth: The Effects of Carbon Dioxide on the Biosphere* (Arlington, VA: Western Fuels Association, 1996), video.
5. More specifically, it sends the newsletter to the eight-hundred-person mailing list of the Society of Environmental Journalists.
6. F. Palmer, "Fossil Fuels or the Rio Treaty—Competing Visions for the Future," speech at COALTRANS 96, Madrid, Spain, October 21, 1996.
7. T. Moore, "Global Warming: Uncertain Science, Certain Disaster," *World Climate Report,* 1997, 2(18): 2.
8. The ad appeared on March 6, 1997, on page A19. It is reprinted in full here as Exhibit 1.1.
9. R. Gelbspan, *The Heat Is On* (Reading, MA: Addison-Wesley, 1997): book jacket, 8.
10. "Bad Auto-Emission Controls Being Forced on Motorists," *Oil & Gas Journal,* September 11, 1972: 45.
11. J. Bailey, "Utilities Over-Comply with Clean Air Act, Are Stockpiling Pollution Allowances," *Wall Street Journal,* November 15, 1995.

12. B. Herbert, "Bad Air Day" (editorial), *New York Times*, February 10, 1997: A18.

13. International Panel on Climate Change, *Climate Change 1995: IPCC Second Assessment Synthesis of Scientific-Technical Information Relevant to Interpreting Article 2 of the UN Framework Convention on Climate Change 1995* (Cambridge, England: Cambridge University Press, 1996).

14. J. Cushman, "In Shift, U.S. Will Seek Binding World Pact to Combat Global Warming," *New York Times*, July 17, 1996: A6.

15. Redefining Progress, *Economists' Statement on Climate Change* (San Francisco: Redefining Progress, 1997).

16. Much of this discussion is drawn with permission from W. Kempton, J. Boster, and J. Hartley, *Environmental Values in American Culture* (Cambridge, MA: MIT Press, 1995): 28–38.

17. T. Appenzeller, "Ozone Loss Hits Us Where We Live," *Science*, 1991, *254*(1): 645; J. Kerr and C. McElroy, "Evidence for Large Upward Trends of Ultra-Violet-B Radiation Linked to Ozone Depletion," *Science*, 1993, *262*(5136): 1032–1034.

18. "New Data Point to the Ultimate Recovery of the Ozone Layer," *New York Times*, May 31, 1996: A14.

19. Strictly speaking, a greenhouse building stays warm because its glass walls and roof trap warm air, not radiant heat. The analogy is still helpful, however.

20. Office of Technology Assessment, *Changing by Degrees: Steps to Reduce Greenhouse Gases*, OTA-0–482, February (Washington, DC: U.S. Government Printing Office, 1991): 45; K. Caldeira and J. Kasting, "Insensitivity of Global Warming Potentials to Carbon Dioxide Emission Scenarios," *Nature*, 1993, *366*(18): 251–253.

21. Caldeira and Kasting, "Insensitivity of Global Warming Potentials."

22. Intergovernmental Panel on Climate Change, *Climate Change: The IPCC Scientific Assessment* (Cambridge, England: Cambridge University Press, 1990); D. Abrahamson, "Climate Change and Energy Supply: A Comparison of Solar and Nuclear Options," in Byrne and Rich (eds.), *Energy and Environment* (New Brunswick, NJ: Transaction Publishers, 1992): 115–140; R. Peters and T. Lovejoy (eds.), *Global Warming and Biological Diversity* (New Haven, CT: Yale University Press, 1992).

23. E. Sundquist, "Long-Term Aspects of Future Atmospheric CO_2 and Sea-Level Changes," in Revelle (ed.), *Sea-Level Change* (Washington, DC: National Research Council and National Academy Press, 1990); W. Cline, *Global Warming: The Economic Stakes* (Washington, DC: Institute for International Economics, 1992).

24. R. Cess and others, "Uncertainties in Carbon Dioxide Radiative Forcing in Atmospheric General Circulation Models," *Science*, 1993, *262*(19): 1252–1255.

25. National Academy of Sciences, *Policy Implications of Global Warming: Report of the Mitigation Panel* (Washington, DC: National Academy Press, 1991).

26. D. Lashof and D. Tirpak (eds.), *Policy Options for Stabilizing Global Climate* (Washington, DC: Climate Change Division, Environmental Protection Agency, 1991); Intergovernmental Panel on Climate Change, *Climate Change,* xviii.

27. World Resources Institute, *World Resources 1994–95: A Guide to the Global Environment* (New York: Oxford University Press, 1994): 201.

28. Environmental Protection Agency, *Inventory of U.S. Greenhouse Gas Emissions and Sinks: 1990–1994* (Washington, DC: U.S. Government Printing Office, 1995).

29. Environmental Protection Agency, *Inventory of U.S. Greenhouse Gas Emissions.* Industrial sources comprise 21 percent, residential sources 7 percent, and commercial sources 5 percent.

30. L. Lave, "A More Feasible Social Response," *Technology Review,* Nov.-Dec. 1981: 23–31; A. Manne and R. Richels, "CO_2 Emission Limits: An Economic Cost Analysis for the USA," *The Energy Journal,* 1989, *11*(2): 51–74; W. Nordhaus, "To Slow or Not to Slow: The Economics of the Greenhouse Effect," *The Economic Journal,* 1991, *101*(6): 920–937.

31. Redefining Progress, *Economists' Statement on Climate Change* (San Francisco: Redefining Progress, 1997); P. Passell, "Yawn. A Global Warming Alert. But This One Has Solutions," *New York Times,* February 13, 1997: C2.

32. W. Stevens, "Price of Global Warming? Debate Weighs Dollars and Cents." *New York Times,* October 10, 1995: C5.

33. T. Johansson, H. Kelly, A. Reddy, and R. Williams (eds.), *Renewable Energy: Sources for Fuels and Electricity* (Washington, DC: Island Press, 1993): 6.

34. Johansson, Kelley, Reddy, and Williams, *Renewable Energy,* 46.

35. Office of Technology Assessment, *Changing by Degrees,* 13–17.

36. G. Zachary, "Greenhouse Emissions Pose Tricky Problems," *Wall Street Journal,* March 10, 1997: A1.

37. G. Easterbrook, "Clinton Is Waffling on Pledges to Cut Greenhouse Gases," *New York Times,* March 12, 1997: A21.

38. V. Scheffer, *The Shaping of Environmentalism in America* (Seattle: University of Washington Press, 1991).

39. In December 1996 the U.S. Department of State produced a "non-paper" that outlined a commitment to binding, verifiable greenhouse emissions goals and outlined the U.S. negotiating position. This overview is drawn from that position paper. For further depth, see Department of State, *U.S. Climate Change Non-Paper* (Washington, D.C.: Office of Global Change, Department of State, 1996). The document is public property; therefore this section may be considered part of the public domain.

PART ONE

SENIOR-LEVEL PERSPECTIVES ON CLIMATE CHANGE

2

THE SAFE CLIMATE, SOUND BUSINESS CHALLENGE

Solutions for a Sustainable Future

Jonathan Lash

BECAUSE OF HUMAN ACTIONS the earth's climate is expected to change more rapidly in the coming decades than it has in tens of thousands of years. According to the 1995 assessment by the Intergovernmental Panel on Climate Change (IPCC), the global warming trend is "unlikely to be entirely natural in origin," and "the balance of evidence suggests that there is a discernible human influence on global climate."[1] Stopping the accelerating changes that are already under way will require ending the heavy dependence on fossil fuels that has powered the world since the industrial revolution. This in turn will require forging agreements on cooperative action among nations preoccupied with market competition in a global economy. The actions needed to address the buildup of carbon dioxide in the atmosphere are frequently characterized as major economic burdens. This need not be so. These actions also provide an opportunity to chart a more sustainable future course as individual firms and national economies become more efficient, embrace environmentally sound technologies, and accelerate the transition to a global economy fueled by renewable energy resources.

Jonathan Lash is president of the World Resources Institute.

The World Resources Institute (WRI) works to move human society to live in ways that will protect the earth's environment and its capacity to provide for the needs and aspirations of current and future generations. As the debate over global warming shifts from science to policy, the WRI is advancing policy options that will protect the earth's climate with minimal economic costs—and costs that are less than that of taking no action at all. Working in partnership with the private sector, the WRI seeks to forge the transition to a sustainable economy in the United States and globally. Because the problems associated with climate change are linked to local and regional air pollution and to U.S. national security, the WRI has focused on linked solutions to these challenges. Each of these problems is tied to our dependence on fossil fuels. A transition to cleaner energy sources will not only begin to mitigate the climate change threat but also simultaneously reduce urban air pollution and lessen U.S. dependence on foreign oil. In seeking linked solutions the WRI is designing and advancing climate policy options that are flexible and market-based, allow least-cost mitigation strategies, and are sensitive to competitiveness issues within and among nations. The WRI has also examined the true costs and benefits of climate protection, taking into account the many new business opportunities that are emerging in this area. Finally, the WRI is working with private sector partners to develop scenarios and cultivate strategies for how industry will make the transition to a sustainable economy and protect the earth's climate.

THE CLIMATE CHALLENGE

The world depends on fossil fuels for 90 percent of its commercial energy. No one country, not even the United States, which is responsible for 22 percent of industrial emissions, can successfully confront the climate change threat alone. The only way to reduce the threat of global warming is to reduce global emissions of greenhouse gases and to stabilize greenhouse gas concentrations in the atmosphere. This will require an unprecedented measure of international cooperation.

The expected impacts of global warming could affect virtually everyone on earth. Human health, water and food supplies, coastal regions, energy supplies, and the productivity of natural systems will all be affected if the earth continues to warm. Global warming could increase the range of tropical diseases like malaria and the frequency of heat-related illness and death. A rise in sea level of just nineteen inches above the 1990 level by the year 2100 (the scenario scientists consider most likely without action to slow the growth in CO_2 emissions) would threaten coastal cities and countries worldwide and could potentially submerge entire island nations. The frequency and intensity of damaging tropical storms and hurricanes could also increase in a warmer world. This possibility has spurred growing interest in the insurance industry concerning how to minimize the world's vulnerability to these potentially financially devastating storms.

To avoid the aforementioned scenarios, measures must be taken in all energy-consuming sectors of the economy: industry, transportation, utilities, and residential households. Homes, commercial buildings, and factories must become more energy efficient, reducing their fuel use for heating, cooling, refrigeration, lighting, and so on. Of utmost importance, however, are the changes needed in the power generation and transportation sectors, which together account for two-thirds of U.S. energy consumption and are the two largest sources of CO_2 emissions. Improved energy efficiency is the primary near-term solution in each of these sectors; however, energy substitution is inevitable after initial cost-effective efficiency gains are made. The only efficient way to shift economies based on cheap fossil fuels toward greater efficiency and the use of other sources of energy is to raise the price of fossil fuels through a carbon tax or similar means. A 50 percent reduction in emissions would require energy prices to more than double. Although there would inevitably be some economic dislocations in the short run, sensible phased-in measures can reduce those risks.

KYOTO

In December 1997 the third Conference of the Parties (COP-3) to the Framework Convention on Climate Change (FCCC) will meet in Kyoto, Japan, to conclude international negotiations on a formal protocol outlining future commitments by participating nations to reduce greenhouse gas emissions. The climate problem demands international cooperation, but the nations of the world see more differences than commonality of interests. Both climate change and its prevention create winners and losers among nations and industries. Countries differ based on whether they are energy importers or exporters; whether their economies rely on coal, oil, gas, or nuclear energy; whether their industries are energy intensive; and whether their geography and climate make them more or less vulnerable to climate change.

Nations have also been particularly wary of the potentially significant economic costs of climate control measures. Certain economic models seem to validate this view. Some suggest that stabilizing U.S. emissions at 1990 levels could require a tax of over $300 per ton of carbon by 2020 and could impose overall costs of nearly 2 percent of annual gross domestic product (GDP) in the same year. However, models that make such predictions are highly dependent on pessimistic assumptions about the structure and behavior of the economy and likely policy responses. Other models, based on more realistic assumptions, tell a different story: climate protection policies could actually have a modest positive impact on the economy.

In a recent report, *The Costs of Climate Protection: A Guide for the Perplexed,*[2] the WRI shows that the predicted effects of carbon reduction policies depend on what view the models take on the following key variables:

- Whether hydroelectricity, nuclear power, solar power, wind power, and other nonfossil energy alternatives will be available at competitive prices as fossil fuel prices increase

- Whether firms and consumers will reallocate their expenditures efficiently as energy prices increase, or the economy fails to equilibrate as energy prices change

- Whether nations will cooperate to take advantage of low-cost opportunities to reduce emissions by undertaking joint implementation of abatement measures or by trading carbon dioxide emissions permits internationally

- Whether revenues from carbon taxes (or, equivalently, auctioned-off CO_2 permits) are used to reduce burdensome taxes on labor and capital

- Whether reducing fossil fuel consumption will avert damage from air pollution

- Whether reducing carbon emissions will avert potential damage from climate change

Models that take an optimistic view regarding these variables (that is, those that assume availability of nonfossil fuels, efficient responses, joint implementation, cuts in taxes on labor or capital, and averted damage from air pollution and climate change) unfailingly predict more positive economic impacts than those that are less optimistic.

The WRI conducted a statistical analysis of sixteen leading economic models that have contributed to the debate on the potential costs of climate protection in assessing the economic impacts that might arise in 2020 from one much-discussed target—stabilization of carbon emissions at 1990 levels by 2010, followed by a freeze thereafter. Under the most unfavorable assumptions the models predict a decrease in GDP by 2.4 percent by the year 2020. If one assumes more favorable assumptions, then a 2.4 percent gain in GDP is projected for 2020.

Notwithstanding the economy's ability to respond to the challenge of climate change, it will take decades to replace coal and oil with other energy sources and to rebuild or re-equip homes and offices, industrial processes, and transportation systems for greater energy efficiency. By acting early, society can benefit from smaller improvements along the way. If this transition is delayed, the stock of investments in carbon-rich technologies will grow, making the adjustment more painful when it finally occurs. Furthermore, technological improvements will continue to focus on fossil fuel–based systems, at the expense of needed advances in alternative energy technologies. Decisive action at Kyoto—and thereafter—is urgently needed to provide incentives for nations and industries to act early and initiate the transition.

Such decisive action seems unlikely, however, due to the implications for specific countries, industries, and regions within countries of cutting back emissions. France and Norway, which already barely rely on coal and oil and so have smaller per capita emissions, argue that they should not have to make large future reductions. The Australians are so dependent on coal that they are reluctant to make any significant commitment to reduce emissions. By contrast, Russia and central Europe have enormous opportunities to improve energy efficiency and modernize their economies, if investment funds are available. As negotiated in the climate convention, developing countries do not yet need to make additional commitments, since the industrialized world is largely responsible for the accumulated emissions buildup to date.

The coal, oil, automobile, and other heavy industries argue that restrictions on carbon emissions and increases in energy prices would disrupt the economy, hurt competitiveness, and cost jobs. These interests collectively lobby against policies to mitigate climate change. The fear of loss rather than the hope for gain seems to be driving the response of most industries to the debate over climate policy. Many interests ignore the fact that the need to reduce greenhouse gas emissions will create significant markets for new technologies and products that agile firms with strong technological capital can exploit. The sustainable corporation does not use uncertainty as a reason for inaction; instead, it ventures ahead to innovate and stay competitive in response to change. A diverse group of industries stand to benefit from climate protection policy: natural gas and renewable energy producers, firms that sell devices and services that enhance energy efficiency, and the property insurance sector. But thus far when these sectors of the economy have advocated policies to limit climate change, their voices have been drowned out by powerful lobbies.

SOLUTIONS FOR THE FUTURE

The climate change problem is clearly too complex to deal with all at once. A solution will have to be built on successive steps as uncertainties, political conflicts, and institutional deficiencies are resolved. Successful experiences with other difficult environmental problems have shown that it is possible to tackle the challenge. A decade ago industry could not imagine giving up chlorofluorocarbons (CFCs), the chemicals that scientists discovered were depleting the earth's protective ozone layer. Firms warned that adopting substitutes would be technically impossible and disastrous for the economy. The adoption of a firm CFC phaseout goal and the use of flexible, market-based policies to implement the phaseout in the United States yielded better-than-anticipated results at lower-than-feared costs.

In many cases industries eliminated CFCs faster, or with greater technological benefits, than they had ever imagined possible. Manufacturers of large building air conditioning systems, like the Trane Company, introduced alternative systems that were more than 20 percent more energy efficient than 1990 CFC-based models. Such technology advances increased sales and saved building owners money. Electronics manufacturers, such as Nortel, redesigned production processes to eliminate the need for CFC solvents, saving millions of dollars along the way. The phaseout did not come without some cost, but with incentives in place, smart companies innovated and turned it into an economic opportunity. Fortunately the initial steps necessary to protect the earth's climate are relatively straightforward, and unlike the CFC phaseout, many technologies needed for the solution already exist.

Governments can use economic incentives to promote emissions reductions and raise productivity. These incentives include fiscal reforms to reduce subsidies to energy companies, thereby encouraging innovation and investment in new technology. The elimination of subsidies and structural improvements are sound economic policies that also have substantial environmental benefits.

Beyond such national policies it is essential that an international market for emissions reductions be created. Such an economic mechanism would allow nations with low-cost abatement opportunities to "trade" excess emissions reductions for foreign financial and technological investments that will generate more efficient growth. Another tool, joint implementation, recognizes that the party that implements an emissions reduction measure need not be the party that pays the bill for it. By allowing countries, and individual firms, to meet emissions reductions targets at the points of least cost, targets will be reached most efficiently. Joint implementation would generate large private sector capital and technology flows to developing countries. These flows could help modernize their capital stock and build a more efficient, less polluting energy sector, freeing up the developing world's own savings for other essential investments.

Even a modest beginning may be useful if national legislation provides clear economic and policy signals that will influence the decisions of investors and research and development managers. However, negotiators should also focus on the ultimate goal of stabilizing atmospheric greenhouse gas concentrations to minimize the future risks of climate change. Setting such a long-term goal would indicate clearly that the bulk of the transition still lies ahead and would establish a clear objective for further negotiations and emissions reductions targets.

To stabilize and reduce global emissions of greenhouse gases in a way that minimizes costs and economic disruption, governments would have to formulate an agreement in Kyoto that includes three elements:

- *A long-term goal.* Sensible strategies for replacing carbon-intensive capital stocks and encouraging the development of new technologies depend on setting global targets for atmospheric concentrations of greenhouse gases and a date by which they will be achieved.

- *A fair allocation of responsibility.* National governments must establish the policies that will achieve these emissions goals. Developing countries have unprecedented leverage in that global greenhouse gas concentrations cannot be stabilized without their support. These countries will be in a position to insist on an agreement that reflects their smaller cumulative contribution to the problem and their need for economic growth. Notwithstanding this reality, these nations must be bound by some commitment in the future.

- *A mechanism to encourage transnational investment in technologies that reduce emissions.* The creation of a market in emissions reductions will spur the development of the necessary technology and allow reductions to be achieved in the cheapest way possible, with allocation of costs consistent with responsibility.

Despite these imperatives, the negotiations in Kyoto are likely to focus on modest, interim abatement targets for industrialized countries. The leading U.S. proposal would stabilize national emissions at 1990 levels by 2010; Europeans have proposed a 15 percent reduction below that level. Each proposal would have difficulty being passed and implemented domestically in the United States, and developing countries are also likely to resist any such commitments.

To encourage early action toward the needed transition and to bolster private sector support for firm policies on climate protection, the WRI has launched the Climate Protection Initiative (CPI). The WRI's economic modeling work examining the costs of climate protection measures is only one element of the CPI's efforts. The CPI is also working in close partnership with corporations to define "Safe Climate, Sound Business" scenarios—technology and policy pathways that depict long-term transitions to economically affordable, climate-friendly futures. Moreover, the CPI is contributing to business strategies by developing case studies of how companies have overcome barriers to implementing carbon dioxide reduction initiatives and achieved financial and productivity benefits from them. The CPI has also sought relationships with the electronics sector, whose products could potentially play an important role in improving the U.S. economy's energy productivity. To facilitate international trade in CO_2 emissions—a critical piece of the puzzle—the WRI is working to evaluate the U.S. Initiative on Joint Implementation, a pilot program that is experimenting with different methods of carbon sequestration.

In all of its work the WRI is addressing the key concerns of its partners in industry to find an economically feasible path to a sustainable energy future. Only in this manner can society protect the earth's climate and its capacity to meet the needs of current and future generations.

NOTES

1. Intergovernmental Panel on Climate Change, *Climate Change 1995: The Science of Climate Change* (Cambridge, England: Cambridge University Press, 1996).
2. World Resources Institute, *The Costs of Climate Protection: A Guide for the Perplexed* (Washington, DC: World Resources Institute, 1997).

3

A CALL FOR COMMON SENSE

The Potential Impact of Climate Change Legislation on the U.S. Pulp and Paper Industry

Roger W. Stone

THE AMERICAN PULP AND PAPER INDUSTRY is one of our nation's largest and most significant manufacturing industries. It directly employs more than seven hundred thousand people, who work in our nation's forests, paper mills, and converting plants. Many thousands more indirectly derive their income from the industry. Our direct payroll tops $26 billion annually. Due to both its magnitude and its unique manufacturing and forest management processes, I can think of no other industry that is more qualified to speak on the issue of global climate change or has more at stake.

THE SCIENTIFIC DEBATE

Before discussing the potential impact of climate change policy on the pulp and paper industry, it is important to put the current "global warming" debate into context. Because, despite declarations by some in academic and government circles that global warming has been proven as

Roger W. Stone is chairman, president, and CEO of Stone Container Corporation.

fact beyond a doubt, it is clear that the scientific debate concerning global change is far from over—or, at the very least, it *should* be far from over. No two scientific studies can agree on either the existence of global climate change or its extent and implications. Some reports have concluded that global warming is measurable and rising; other reputable studies have concluded that global climate change to date is insignificant in the long-term context and can be traced to natural phenomena. Still others have concluded that the earth is cooling, not warming, as part of a natural climatic cycle that can be measured over centuries.

My purpose in mentioning these contradictions is not to invalidate or call into question any of these reports (although there is concern in some circles that at least some scientific reports have been intentionally slanted to advance the notion of global warming, which, if true, is unconscionable). Rather, my purpose is to demonstrate that this issue remains clouded by scientific uncertainty. To date it has not been proven beyond any doubt that industrial output plays a role in global warming—or that global warming even exists.

Therefore, to sign on to a treaty that would permanently and profoundly change the way American industry operates and would ultimately affect America's standing in the global economy is both premature and ill-advised. We in the pulp and paper industry suggest that much more study needs to be done before this theory can be accepted as fact.

THE POLICY DEBATE

That said, I should clarify this industry's manufacturing processes, its effect on atmospheric greenhouse gas concentrations, and its economic value to the nation. The pulp and paper industry affects the climate change policy debate in three distinct areas: energy use and CO_2 emissions, carbon sequestration, and international competitiveness.

Energy Use and CO_2 Emissions

The primary greenhouse gas emitted into the atmosphere by the pulp and paper industry is carbon dioxide (CO_2), which is released through the combustion of fuels. Although the pulp and paper industry is one of the most energy-intensive sectors in the country, it is also energy-efficient. It is important to note both the types of fuels this industry uses and our excellent progress in limiting CO_2 emissions. The industry uses both nonrenewable fossil fuels and biomass fuels. (Biomass fuels are the by-products of forest products activities, such as wood chips, sawdust, manufacturing scraps, and pulping liquors. They are sustainable and completely renewable and have become a primary fuel source for the industry.)

Biomass fuels used in the manufacture of pulp and paper increased to 56 percent of total fuels used for this purpose in 1995, up from 40 percent in 1972. At the same time, consumption of fossil fuels and purchased energy for this use dropped by 42 percent. Biomass fuels satisfy an even greater percentage (74 percent) of the wood products sector's energy requirements. The industry's emissions of carbon dioxide from the consumption of fossil fuels and electricity fell 8 percent between 1972 and 1995. During this same period, the industry's production rose 67 percent.

Carbon Sequestration

Lost thus far in the climate change dialogue has been the pulp and paper industry's unique and beneficial role as a carbon sink. The forest products industry favorably influences CO_2 concentrations in the atmosphere by the storage of carbon pools in both forests and wood products. It is estimated that standing timberlands in the United States contain 60 billion metric tons of carbon stored through the process of photosynthesis. Annually, total carbon stored in these forests increases a net 211 million metric tons, and another 65 million metric tons is stored in new paper and solid wood products. That adds up to 276 million metric tons of carbon stored in forests and wood products every year, compared to the 90 million metric tons that the industry emits annually. No other industry can make this claim.

International Competitiveness

Perhaps the most critical component of this issue is its potential impact on the pulp and paper industry's ability to maintain its economic viability. Some members of the current administration advocate a mandatory reduction of greenhouse gas emissions to 1990 levels by the year 2000. This would be accomplished primarily by setting caps on energy consumption, imposing new taxes on energy use and carbon emissions, imposing excessive energy efficiency standards, and perhaps placing severe restrictions on the way the industry manages timberlands.

Such draconian changes could potentially increase the industry's energy costs by as much as $100 per ton of carbon emitted, or $3 billion annually. Total manufacturing costs could rise by as much as 14 percent. If credit it not given for use of biomass fuels, direct manufacturing costs could rise by as much as 30 percent; indirect cost increases would probably be even greater.

Clearly such changes could permanently cripple this industry, causing permanent mill closures and significant job losses. Further, the industry's ability to compete internationally would be thrown into question. The pulp and paper industry's exports exceed $11.5 billion annually, representing more than 2 percent of America's exports. The simple fact is that jobs lost in the U.S. pulp and paper industry—along with its pulp and paper output—will move to developing nations that are aggressively expanding their pulp and paper manufacturing capacity, including such nations as Malaysia, Thailand, Indonesia, and Brazil. These countries are not a part of the climate change policy equation and are not required to adhere to CO_2 limitations. Nor do they all subscribe to sustainable forest management techniques, frequently cutting their virgin, tropical, or rain forests at unsustainable levels. Clearly this is not a level playing field. Much more must be done before we blindly embrace the currently proposed climate change policy.

- It is unacceptable to impose mandatory emissions reduction targets that would seriously undermine our competitiveness if many of our industry's multinational competitors are not bound by those same regulations.

- If the Intergovernmental Panel on Climate Change does move ahead with global climate change policy, it should recognize the unique role that the forest products industry plays in carbon sequestration, both in the forests it manages and the wood products it produces, and make considerations for this unique benefit. It should also note the industry's use of sustainable and renewable fuel sources and the significant CO_2 reductions that we have already made—and continue to make.

- The pulp and paper industry is one of the world's most capital-intensive businesses. It is simply not possible, or even desirable, to impose massive changes in manufacturing styles or equipment if the industry cannot implement those changes.

- Finally, a last, common-sense request: the steps that the administration and the United Nations take over the next few months could have significant economic consequences for millions of Americans. Before any decisions are made, all parties that could be affected by them should be given a voice in the process. We in the pulp and paper industry urge the administration to find the true facts behind climate change and to consider the true potential impact of its actions before committing this nation to a course of action that will have such enormous fallout.

4

CLIMATE CHANGE

The New Agenda

John Browne

FOLLOWING THE COLLAPSE of the Soviet empire at the end of the 1980s, two alternative views of the consequences for the rest of the world were put forward. Francis Fukuyama wrote a book with the ironic title *The End of History.* Jacques Delors, then president of the European Commission, talked about the "acceleration of history." In the end, history neither accelerated nor stopped. But it did change.

The world in which we now live is one no longer defined by ideology. Of course, the old spectrums are still with us—of left to right, of radical to conservative—but ideology is no longer the ultimate arbiter of analysis and action. Governments, corporations, and individual citizens have all had to redefine their roles in a society no longer divided by an iron curtain separating capitalism from communism. A new age demands a fresh perspective of the nature of society and responsibility. The passing of some of the old divisions reminds us that we are all citizens of *one* world, and we must take *shared* responsibility for its future and for its sustainable development.

John Browne is group chief executive of the British Petroleum Company, p.l.c. The text of this chapter is from a speech given by Mr. Browne at Stanford University on May 19, 1997.

We must do that in all our various roles—as students and teachers, as businesspeople with capital to invest, as legislators with the power to make law, as individual citizens with the right to vote, and as consumers with the power of choice. These roles overlap, of course. The people who work at British Petroleum are certainly businesspeople, but they're also people with beliefs and convictions, individuals concerned with the quality of life of themselves and their children. When they come through the door into work every morning, they don't leave behind their convictions and their sense of responsibility. And the same is true of our consumers. They too have beliefs and convictions, and their choices determine our success as a company.

Now that brings me to my subject in this chapter: the global environment. That is a subject that concerns us all, in all our various roles and capacities. I believe we have now come to an important moment in our consideration of the environment. It is a moment when, because of our shared interests, we need to go beyond analysis to seek solutions and take action. It is a moment for change and for a rethinking of corporate responsibility.

A year ago the second report of the Intergovernmental Panel on Climate Change (IPCC) was published. That report and the discussion that has continued since its publication show that there is mounting concern about two stark facts: the concentration of carbon dioxide in the atmosphere is rising, and the temperature of the earth's surface is increasing.

Karl Popper once described all science as provisional. What he meant by that was that all science is open to refutation, to amendment, and to development. That view is certainly confirmed by the debate around climate change. There is a lot of noise in the data. It is hard to isolate cause and effect. But there is now an effective consensus among the world's leading scientists and serious and well-informed people outside the scientific community that there is a discernible human influence on the earth's climate and a link between the concentration of carbon dioxide in the atmosphere and the increase in the planet's temperature.

The IPCC predicts that over the next century temperatures might rise by a further 1 to 3.5 degrees centigrade and that sea levels might rise by between 15 and 95 centimeters. Some of that impact is probably unavoidable, because it will result from current and past emissions. These figures include wide margins of error, and there remains much uncertainty about cause and effect and, even more important, consequences. But it would be unwise and potentially dangerous to ignore the mounting concern. The time to consider the policy dimensions of climate change is not when the link between greenhouse gases and climate change is conclusively proven but when the possibility cannot be discounted and is taken seriously by society. At British Petroleum we believe we have reached that point.

It is an important moment for us. A moment when analysis has demonstrated the need for action and solutions. To be absolutely clear, we must now focus on what can and what should be done, not because we can be certain climate change is happening but because the possibility cannot be ignored. If we are all to take responsibility for the future of our planet, then it falls to us to begin to take precautionary action now.

But what sort of action? How should we respond to this mixture of concern and uncertainty? I think the right metaphor for the process is a journey. Governments have started on that journey. The Rio conference marked an important point on that journey. So did the Berlin review meeting. The Kyoto conference scheduled for the end of 1997 marks another staging post. It will be a long journey, because the responsibilities faced by governments are complex and the interests of their economies and peoples are diverse and sometimes contradictory. But the journey has begun, and it has to continue.

The private sector has also embarked on the journey, but now that involvement needs to be accelerated. This too will be long and complex, with different people taking different approaches. But it is a journey that must proceed. As I see it, there are two kinds of action that can be taken in response to the challenge of climate change.

The first kind of action would be dramatic, sudden, and surely wrong. Actions that seek, at a stroke, to drastically restrict carbon emissions or even to ban the use of fossil fuels would be unsustainable because they would crash into the realities of economic growth. They would also be seen as discriminatory to the developing world. The second kind of action is that of a journey taken in partnership by all those involved, a step-by-step process involving both action to develop solutions and continuing research that will build knowledge through experience.

British Petroleum is committed to this second approach, which matches the agreement reached at Rio, based on a balance between the needs of development and the needs of environmental protection. The Rio agreement recognized the need for economic development in the developing world. We believe we can contribute to achieving the right balance by ensuring that we apply evenly, everywhere in the world, the technical innovations we are now developing. What we propose to do is substantial, real, and measurable; we believe it will make a difference. Before defining that action, I think it is worth establishing a factual basis from which we can work.

Of the world's total carbon dioxide emissions, only a small fraction comes from the activities of human beings, but it is that small fraction that might threaten the equilibrium among the other, much greater flows. You can think of the impact as like that of placing even a small weight on a scale that is precisely balanced. But in preserving the balance, we have to be clear about where the problem actually lies.

Of the total carbon dioxide emissions caused by burning fossil fuels, only 20 percent comes from transportation. Eighty percent comes from static uses of energy—the energy used in homes, industry, and power generation. Of the total, 43 percent comes from petroleum. We at British Petroleum have looked carefully, using the best available data, at the precise impact of our own activities. Our operations in exploration and refining produce around eight megatons of carbon. On top of that, a further one megaton is produced by our chemical operations. If you add to that the carbon produced by the consumption of the products we produce, the total goes up to around ninety-five megatons. That is just 1 percent of the total carbon dioxide emissions that come from all human activity.

Let me put that another way. As noted previously, human activity accounts for a small part of the total volume of carbon emissions, but it is that part that could cause disequilibrium. Only a fraction of the total emissions from people come from the transportation sector, so the problem is not just caused by vehicles. Any response that is going to have a real impact has to look at all emissions sources. As one company, our contribution is small, and our actions alone could not resolve the problem. But that does not mean we should do nothing. We have to look at the way we use energy to ensure that we are working with maximum efficiency, and we also have to look at how our products are used. That means ensuring our own house is in order. It also means contributing to wider analyses of the problem through research, technology, and a search for the best public policy mechanisms, the actions that can produce the right solutions for the long-term common interest of all peoples. We have a responsibility to act, and I hope that through our actions we can contribute to the much wider process, which is desirable and necessary. British Petroleum accepts that responsibility, and we're therefore taking some specific steps:

• To control our own emissions
• To fund continuing scientific research
• To develop initiatives for joint implementation

- To develop alternative fuels for the long term
- To contribute to the public policy debate in search of wider, global answers to the problem

First we will monitor and control our own carbon dioxide emissions. This follows the commitment we have already made to other environmental issues. Our overall goal is to do no harm to the natural environment. That is an ambitious goal, which we approach systematically. Nobody can do everything at once. Companies work by prioritizing what they do. They take the easiest steps first, picking the low-hanging fruit, and then they move on to tackle the more difficult and complex problems. That is the natural business process.

Our method has been to focus on one item at a time, to identify what can be delivered, to establish monitoring processes and targets as part of our internal management system, and to put in place a mechanism for external confirmation of delivery. In most cases this approach has allowed us to go well beyond the regulatory requirements. That is what we have done in the area of emissions to water and air. In the North Sea, for instance, we have gone well beyond the legal requirements for reducing oil discharges to the sea. And now, at our crude oil export terminal at Hound Point, Scotland, which handles 10 percent of Europe's oil supplies, we are investing $100 million to eliminate emissions of volatile organic compounds, which themselves produce carbon dioxide through oxidation in the atmosphere. No legislation has compelled us to take that step; we are doing it because we believe it is the right thing to do.

As well as continuing our efforts in relation to the other greenhouse gases, it is time to establish a similar process for carbon dioxide. Our carbon dioxide emissions result from the burning of hydrocarbon fuels to produce heat and power, from flaring feed and product gases, and from the process of separation or transformation. So far our approach to carbon dioxide has been indirect and has mainly come through improvements in the energy efficiency of our production processes. Over the last decade, efficiency in our major manufacturing activities has improved by 20 percent. Now we want to go further.

We have to continue to improve the efficiency with which we use energy. And in addition we need a better understanding of how our own emissions of carbon can be monitored and controlled using a variety of measures, including sequestration. It is a very simple business lesson that what gets measured gets managed. Measuring carbon emissions requires a learning process, just as with the other emissions we have targeted; but the learning is cumulative, and I think it will have a substantial impact.

We have already taken some steps in the right direction. In Norway, for example, we have reduced flaring to less than 20 percent of 1991 levels, primarily as a result of very simple, low-cost measures. The operation there is now close to the minimum flare rate dictated by safety considerations. Our experience in Norway is being transferred elsewhere—starting with fields in the UK sector of the North Sea—and that should produce further progressive reductions in emissions. Our goal is to eliminate flaring except in emergencies.

That is only one specific goal within the set of targets we will establish. Some are straightforward matters of efficient operation, such as the reduction of flaring and venting. Others require the use of advanced technologies, in the form of improved manufacturing and separation processes, that produce less waste and demand less energy. Other steps will require investment to make existing facilities more energy-efficient. For instance, we are researching ways to remove the carbon dioxide from large compressors and reinject it to improve oil recovery. That would bring a double benefit, a cut in emissions and an improvement in production efficiency.

The task is particularly challenging in the refining stage, where the production of cleaner products requires more extensive processing and there is higher energy demand for each unit of output. That means that making gasoline that is cleaner, with lower sulfur levels, takes more energy at the manufacturing stage. That is the trade-off. In each case our aim will be to establish a database, including benchmark data; to create a monitoring process; and then to develop targets for improvement through operational line management. Monitoring and controlling emissions is the first step.

The second step is to increase the level of support we give to the continuing scientific work that is necessary. As mentioned previously, there are still areas of significant uncertainty around the subject of climate change. Those who tell you they know all the answers are fools or knaves. More research is needed on the details of cause and effect, on the potential consequences of what appears to be happening, and on the effectiveness of the various actions that can be taken. We will increase our support for that work. That support will be focused on finding solutions and will be provided for work of high quality that we believe will address the key outstanding questions.

Specifically, we have joined a partnership to design the right technological strategy to deal with climate change. That partnership, which will operate under the auspices of the Battelle Institute, includes the Electric Power Research Institute and the U.S. Department of Energy. We are also supporting work being done at the Massachusetts Institute of Technology and the Royal Society in London. We are also joining the Greenhouse Gas Program of the International Energy Agency, which is analyzing technologies for reducing and offsetting greenhouse gas emissions from fossil fuels.

The third step is to encourage technology transfer and joint implementation. Joint implementation, which refers to bringing different parties together to reduce their combined net emissions, is only in its infancy; however, we believe it has great potential to contribute to the resolution of the climate change problem. It can increase the impact of emissions reduction technology by lowering the overall cost of abatement actions.

We need to experiment and to learn in this area, and we welcome additional partners. The aim of the learning process must be to make joint implementation efforts viable and legally creditable so that the concept can be included in international commitments. We have begun by entering into some specific reforestation and forest conservation programs in Turkey and Bolivia, and we are currently discussing a number of other, technology-based joint implementation projects. The Bolivian project, a program to conserve 1.5 million hectares of forests in the province of Santa Cruz, shows what can be done. It is sponsored by the Nature Conservancy and American Electric Power and is sanctioned by the U.S. government. We are delighted to be involved and to have the chance to transfer our learning from this project to other efforts. Forest conservation projects are neither easy nor simple, and the learning process is very important. Technology transfer is part of the joint implementation process, but it should go further. We are prepared to engage in an open dialogue with all parties seeking answers to the climate change problem.

So those are three steps we can all take: monitoring and controlling our own emissions, supporting existing scientific work and encouraging new work, and developing experiments in joint implementation and technology transfer. Why are we at British Petroleum doing all of these things? Simply because the oil industry is going to remain the world's predominant supplier of energy for the foreseeable future. Given that role, we have to play a positive and responsible part in identifying solutions to a problem that is potentially very serious.

The fourth step—development of alternative energy sources—is related but distinct. Looking ahead, it seems clear that the combination of new markets and new technology will shift the energy mix. The world's population is growing by one hundred million people every year. Prosperity is spreading. By the end of the century, 60 percent of the world's economic activity will be taking place in the developing world, in the areas that ten years ago we referred to as the Third World. Both these factors will create growing demand for energy. At the same time, technology moves on.

The sorts of changes we have seen in computing, with the continuing expansion of semiconductor capacity, are exceptional but not unique. I think it is a reasonable assumption that the technologies that will deliver alternative energy supplies will also continue to move forward. One or more of those alternative supplies will take a greater share of the energy market as we enter the next century. But let me be clear: "alternative" does not mean *instead* of oil and gas, it means *in addition* to oil and gas. We have been looking at alternative energy sources for a long time, and our conclusion is that one source that is likely to make a significant contribution is solar power. At the moment solar power is not commercially viable for either peak- or base-load power generation. The best solar technology produces electricity for around double the cost of conventional sources during periods of peak demand.

But the technology is advancing, and with appropriate public support and investment I am convinced that we can make solar electricity competitive for peak demand periods within the next ten years. That means that, taking into account the whole period from the time we began research on solar power until it becomes commercially viable, twenty-five to thirty years will have elapsed. For this industry that is an appropriate time scale. We are currently exploring for oil and gas in a number of areas where production would not be commercially viable at present. Thirty years ago we did that in Alaska. We take that approach because we believe that markets and technology do move and that the frontier of commercial viability is always changing.

British Petroleum has been involved in solar power for a number of years and now has a 10 percent share of the world market. The business has operations across the world, in sixteen countries. Our aim now is to extend that reach—not least in the developing world, where energy demand is growing rapidly. We also want to transfer our distinctive technologies into production, to increase manufacturing capacity, and to position the business to reach $1 billion in sales over the next decade. There will be significant investment in the United States, and we will be commissioning a new solar manufacturing facility in California before the end of 1997. The result of our efforts will be that gradually but progressively solar will make a contribution to the resolution of the problem of carbon dioxide emissions and climate change.

These are the initial steps on our journey toward the goal of averting climate change. We are examining what else we should do, and I hope to be able to announce further steps soon. Of course, as I said at the beginning of this chapter, nothing that British Petroleum can do alone will resolve the problem of climate change. We can contribute, and over time we can move toward the elimination of emissions from our own operations and a substantial reduction in the emissions that come from the use of our products. But the problem of climate change is a matter for wider, public policy to address.

British Petroleum believes that the policy debate on climate change is important. We support that debate, and we are engaged in it through the World Business Council on Sustainable Development, through the President's Council on Sustainable Development (in the United States), and in the UK, where the government is committed to making significant progress on the subject. Knowledge in this area is not proprietary, and we will share our expertise openly and freely. Our instinct is that once clear objectives have been agreed upon, market-based solutions will be more likely to produce innovative and creative responses than an approach based on regulation alone. Those market-based solutions need to be as wide-ranging as possible, because this is a global problem that has to be resolved without discrimination and without denying the peoples of the developing world the right to improve their living standards. To try to do that would be arrogant and untenable. What we need are solutions that are inclusive, cooperative, and work across national and industry boundaries.

There have been a number of market experiments already, all of them partial but many of them interesting because they show how effective markets can change behavior. For instance, we are currently working with the Environmental Defense Fund to develop a voluntary emissions trading system for greenhouse gases, modeled after the system already in place for sulfur oxides. Of course, a system that operates just in the United States is only a part of the solution. Ideally such structures should be much wider. But change begins with the first step, and the development of successful systems in the United States will set a standard that will spread.

I began with the issue of corporate responsibility—the need for rethinking in a new context. No company can be really successful unless it is sustainable, unless it has the capacity to keep using its skills and to keep growing its business. Of course, that requires competitive financial performance, but it also requires something more, perhaps particularly in the oil industry. The whole industry is growing because world demand is growing. The world now uses almost seventy-three million barrels of oil a day, 16 percent more then it did ten years ago. In another ten years, because of population growth and increased prosperity, that figure is likely to be over eighty-five million barrels a day—and that is a cautious estimate; some people say it will be more. For efficient, competitive companies, that growth will be very profitable.

But sustainability is about more than profits. High profitability is necessary but not sufficient. Real sustainability is about simultaneously being profitable and responding to the reality and concerns of the world in which we operate. We are not separate from the world; it is our world as well. I disagree with some members of the environmental movement who say we have to abandon the use of oil and gas. They think it is the oil and gas industry that has reached the end of history. I disagree because I think that view underestimates the potential for creative and positive action. But that disagreement does not mean that we can ignore the mounting evidence and concern about climate change.

As businesspeople, when our customers are concerned, we had better take notice. To be sustainable, companies need a sustainable world. That means not only a world where the environmental equilibrium is maintained but also a world whose population can enjoy the heat, light, and mobility that we take for granted and that the oil industry helps to provide. I do not believe those are incompatible goals. Everything I have said here and all the actions we are taking and will take are directed to ensuring that they are not incompatible.

There are no easy answers, no silver bullets. There are just steps on a journey that we should take together because we all have a vital interest in finding the answers. The cultures of politics, science, and enterprise must work together if we are to match and master the challenges we all face. I started by talking about the end of history. Of course it hasn't ended. It has moved on. Francis Fukuyama, who coined that phrase, describes the future in terms of the need for a social order, a network of interdependence that goes beyond the contractual—an order driven by the sense of common human interest. Where that exists, societies thrive. Nowhere is the need for that sort of social order—at the global level—more important than in this area. The achievement of that has to be our common goal.

5

AN ELECTRIC UTILITY PERSPECTIVE ON CLIMATE CHANGE

Richard Abdoo

ELECTRICITY GENERATION by fossil fuel combustion produces about one-third of the total carbon dioxide emissions of the United States. Recognizing this contribution, many U.S. electric utilities have developed voluntary greenhouse gas reduction initiatives under the Climate Challenge program, a joint project of the U.S. Department of Energy and the electric utility industry. The Department of Energy estimates that these initiatives will reduce carbon emissions by over forty-seven million metric tons in the year 2000. The experience and perspective gained from these efforts can provide a valuable resource for U.S. officials negotiating international climate change agreements. This chapter provides an electric utility perspective on what U.S. climate change policy should be and outlines the current and future activities of one electric utility, Wisconsin Energy Company (WEC), that has been active in the area of emissions reduction.

A SOUND U.S. CLIMATE CHANGE POLICY

As the administration develops the U.S. position for the third Conference of the Parties to the United Nations Framework Convention on Climate Change, to be held in Kyoto, Japan, in December 1997, it is recommended

Richard Abdoo is chairman, president, and CEO of Wisconsin Energy Company.

that any new U.S. plan to reduce post-2000 emissions include the following components.

Voluntary Efforts

Rather than imposing binding emissions caps as the next step, the administration should build on current initiatives to utilize voluntary industry efforts to achieve more reductions and should seek more partners in these efforts.

ELECTRIC UTILITY INDUSTRY. The administration should encourage implementation of a new, enhanced voluntary Climate Challenge program; recognize all voluntary actions taken by utilities, both domestically and internationally; and ensure that early participants in voluntary greenhouse gas programs are not disadvantaged compared to later participants.

OTHER SECTORS. All sectors of U.S. industry must participate in developing and implementing creative greenhouse gas reduction strategies, including a new, enhanced voluntary Climate Wise Program and new programs for the transportation sector. Electric utilities represent the largest single-point sources of carbon emissions and thus are often targeted as the potential source for the greatest emissions reductions. However, since two-thirds of carbon dioxide emissions in the United States are produced by industrial processes and transportation, and more than two-thirds of methane emissions come from landfills and agriculture, it is essential that these sectors also become involved in greenhouse gas reduction.

INDIVIDUAL CONSUMERS. Consumer behaviors have environmental impacts, including on carbon emissions. Consumer choices include the amount of energy they use for transportation, operating appliances, and home heating and cooling. Increased efforts are needed from both government and industry to provide education to consumers on the environmental impacts of their actions.

As industries continue to research and develop alternate energy technologies, consumers will have more choices:

- Affordable vehicles that run on alternate fuels, including electricity, natural gas, methanol, fuel cells, even solar power
- Vehicles with significantly improved fuel efficiency

- Increasingly efficient appliances
- Electricity produced by specific alternative (including renewable) sources

The potential benefits to the global climate of such consumer choices should be assessed in the development of any national climate action plan, which should include mechanisms to encourage cost-effective adoption of emissions-reducing, consumer-supported alternatives.

Market-Based Approaches

A national plan should include market-based approaches that allow cost-effective reductions to be shared among participants within a sector and, more important, across sectors.

Aggressive Research and Development

The U.S. government should commit to an aggressive program of research and development in energy efficiency, renewable energy, and other energy supply technologies, such as clean coal technologies and nuclear fuel storage and recycling. A variety of state and federal proposals for a Renewables Portfolio Standard (RPS) have been offered, and a few state measures have been passed. While a federal RPS could encourage the installation of more renewable-source facilities, many renewable-source technologies require significantly more development before they can become cost-competitive on a large scale. The states and the federal government should form partnerships with utilities and others to sustain the level of research and development necessary to bring these technologies to market. Since the use of renewable energy sources can provide public benefits, both environmental and economic, it is reasonable for the states and the federal government to provide research and development funding.

Despite this potential increase in lower-emissions-producing and renewable resources, it is unlikely that significant coal or other fossil fuel generation will be retired within the next twenty years. Therefore the federal and state governments should also renew their commitment to support development of cleaner coal- and oil-burning technologies to lessen the impact of these proven fuel sources. Finally, it is imperative that the U.S. government fulfill its obligation to secure a nuclear fuel storage facility so that this emissions-free, safe, and efficient energy source can remain a vital component of the U.S. energy supply well into the next century.

A Global Outlook

Since climate change is a global concern it must be addressed on a global basis, by developed and developing nations alike. Countries must be allowed to achieve emissions reductions through joint implementation (JI) initiatives and the use of voluntary, market-based means, including international emissions trading. International carbon sequestration and energy-efficiency projects can be cost-effective mechanisms for mitigating global climate change and producing measurable greenhouse gas reductions. They also provide additional environmental and sustainable-development benefits for the host countries. International emissions trading offers an opportunity to implement least-cost mitigation options flexibly without emissions caps. Emissions trading would allow both developed and developing nations to participate in greenhouse gas reductions as either a funder (buyer) or implementer (seller), and uniform trading standards would provide a level playing field for all participants.

Minimal Economic Impact

The actions proposed as part of a national plan must minimize adverse impacts on the U.S. economy. Recent studies show a variety of potential economic impacts from U.S. plans to reduce carbon dioxide emissions. Most of these studies show that if efforts to reduce greenhouse gas emissions are not conducted globally, jobs will move to states or nations with no restrictions on greenhouse gas emissions, resulting in significant economic loss. Another likely unintended result would be "leakage": an *increase* in total greenhouse gases due to the lack of restrictions and the use of less advanced technology in developing countries. Perhaps the most notable implications of these economic studies are the needs to adopt a longer-term view of this issue and to reiterate the wisdom of increasing voluntary efforts rather than imposing near-term mandates.

Beneficial Timing

The timing of emissions reduction strategies should be such that continued progress is made toward the ultimate goal of stabilized global greenhouse gas levels and minimal impact on the world's climate. Such progress would include slowing the rate of increases in greenhouse gas levels. The timing for achieving this ultimate goal should

- Be flexible, to allow reductions to be made at lowest cost
- Reflect the state of knowledge in climatic science and energy generation technology
- Consider existing transportation infrastructures
- Acknowledge the need of developing countries to improve their standard of living
- Recognize the need to develop new power generation technologies that not only emit less carbon dioxide but also are cost-effective and have sufficient generating capacity to replace existing technologies as they reach the end of their commercial usefulness

WEC'S ACTIVITIES

The appropriate method to address increases in greenhouse gas levels is a balanced portfolio of voluntary efforts in which all forms of energy use and generation are as efficient as practicable and natural vehicles for carbon sequestration (that is, forests) are retained and expanded. An example of this approach is the Climate Challenge Participation Accord drawn up by WEC. By this accord WEC commits to reduce greenhouse gas emissions by more than 16 percent, by the year 2000, from what would occur absent these actions, in the face of an almost 16 percent increase in estimated system electrical load requirements for the period 1991 to 2000. Components of the accord include the following.

Demand-Side Management

In the accord WEC offers several innovative demand-side management (DSM) initiatives that consider market forces and customer choice. These include

- Innovative financing programs for commercial and industrial customers to help them overcome the initial cost barrier to energy efficiency
- A comprehensive DSM bidding program for residential, farm, and small commercial customers that will offer a variety of energy-efficiency services based on bids received
- Continuation of load management programs offered to all customers

Efficient Energy Generation Without Greenhouse Gases

Hydroelectric and nuclear power represent two of WEC's most cost-effective means of greenhouse gas reduction. WEC and its predecessors have been using flowing river water to power generators since 1882. WEC recently signed long-term power purchase agreements with independent hydroelectric owners, as well as a landmark collaborative agreement with natural resource agencies and river advocacy groups to relicense eight of its hydroelectric facilities. At WEC's Point Beach nuclear plant, several initiatives are being evaluated that are designed to improve output and net capacity.

Other System Efficiency Improvements

WEC is pursuing a variety of heat-rate efficiency actions that will increase unit availability and capacity at our coal-fired power plants. These include equipment control and metering upgrades, feed-water heater improvements, and reduced thermal losses. Transmission and distribution system efficiency improvement projects will reduce electrical losses, since the energy that would have been lost need not be replaced by coal-fired generation. These projects include transmission system additions; high voltage distribution, conversion, and system renewal projects; application of distribution capacitors; conservation voltage deduction; and replacement of electromechanical load tap changer controls.

Waste-to-Energy Projects

WEC helps landfill gas developers select appropriate equipment and develop specific contracts, and the company purchases electricity produced by methane from five landfills. The recovery and use of methane from landfills reduces overall emissions of greenhouse gases both by replacing system-generated energy and by preventing direct release of methane into the atmosphere.

Renewable Energy Resources

In addition to hydroelectric and waste-to-energy projects, WEC is participating in initiatives with other Wisconsin utilities to investigate the use of wind energy in the state. Two state-of-the-art, low-wind-speed turbines will be installed near DePere, Wisconsin, during 1997 and will provide operating data as well as emissions-free energy to the joint utility participants. WEC is also cosponsoring a multiyear, statewide wind monitoring effort to investigate Wisconsin's wind resource.

Substitution of Fly Ash for Cement and Lime

Manufacturing cement and lime is very energy-intensive and a large source of greenhouse gas emissions. WEC utilizes over 50 percent of its fly ash as a cement replacement in concrete products or as a lime substitute for stabilizing municipal wastewater sludge. These efforts have significantly reduced the amount of fly ash deposited in landfills. WEC has also developed lightweight aggregate production facilities that use industrial by-products as well as innovative technologies to replace conventional products currently mined and manufactured by energy-intensive processes, providing net greenhouse gas reductions.

Vehicle Conversion to Compressed Natural Gas

A vehicle with dual fuel capability—the ability to run on both gasoline and compressed natural gas (CNG)—emits less greenhouse gas while the vehicle is running on CNG. WEC operates a fleet vehicles conversion program, offers technical assistance to customers wishing to utilize CNG vehicles, and provides incentives to encourage conversion of customers' and WEC employees' personal vehicles to CNG.

JI Projects

Our forestry sector JI initiative, the Rio Bravo Carbon Sequestration Pilot Project, in Belize, seeks an optimal balance between carbon sequestration, forest yield, and environmental protection while providing sustainable development opportunities for the local community. Our project in the Czech Republic city of Decin replaced inefficient, highly polluting coal-fired district heating boilers with new, state-of-the-art, natural gas–fired internal combustion engines. In addition to emissions reductions and improvement of local air quality, this technology produces both electrical power and warm water, through cogeneration, for building heat and has improved the efficiency of the warm water distribution system.

Forestation of WEC Land

WEC owns and manages approximately forty thousand acres of land in northeastern Wisconsin and the Upper Peninsula of Michigan. Currently, large portions of those lands are forested. Since 1990 steps have been initiated by WEC to obtain the data needed to ensure a sound biological basis for our comprehensive land management plans. Important aspects receiving prime consideration are sustainable timber production, biodiversity, wildlife habitat, and carbon sequestration. Wise forest management is expected to increase the carbon sequestration rate as well as the total standing crop of carbon.

FUTURE INITIATIVES

WEC will continue to seek, evaluate, and implement cost-effective opportunities for greenhouse gas emissions reductions or offsets through

- *New JI projects.* Our goal is to build a portfolio of credible, verifiable JI projects that demonstrate net greenhouse gas benefits while achieving important biodiversity protection, sustainable development, energy efficiency, and forest management objectives. WEC believes quite strongly that both carbon sequestration initiatives and energy efficiency improvements are important elements of any effort to mitigate climate change.

- *Research and development.* WEC will continue to work to enhance energy efficiency or otherwise find new ways to reduce greenhouse gas emissions on an economic basis.

- *Removal of regulatory barriers to hydroelectric and nuclear power use.* WEC recognizes the value of these emissions-free, cost-effective energy sources for our customers and shareholders and will continue to work to ensure their continued availability.

- *Increased implementation of cost-effective renewable energy sources.* WEC developed and introduced the Energy for Tomorrow Renewable Energy Program to allow customers to choose to receive their energy from renewable energy sources. The initial year of this pilot program has yielded encouraging results, and we will incorporate customer feedback into an improved, more cost-effective product that includes local renewable energy sources.

- *Development, application, diffusion, and transfer to developing countries of climate-friendly technologies.* The Decin project described previously illustrates how industrialized countries can participate in cost-effective projects that introduce improved technologies to overseas partners.

WEC remains an active participant in ongoing legislative and regulatory efforts to address the global climate change issue, taking a leading role in discussions among industry representatives, environmentalists, other utilities, government representatives, and others. Our JI projects in Belize and the Czech Republic are groundbreaking efforts that demonstrate our commitment. Through our efforts we continue to lead by example, proactively implementing no-regrets greenhouse gas reduction strategies.

6

POLICY PRESCRIPTIONS FROM THE OIL INDUSTRY

Dennis R. Parker

THE INTERNATIONAL DEBATE on the global climate change issue is a symptom of the world's failure to fully assess the impacts of proposed emissions reductions on the world economy. So far the nations of the world have focused almost exclusively on the emissions reduction targets and timetables produced at the June 1992 Earth Summit at Rio de Janeiro. Little work has been done on developing comprehensive strategies, especially for identifying and establishing incentives for both developed and developing countries to reduce their greenhouse gas emissions in a timely and cost-effective manner. The challenge is how to balance many issues. How can nations strategically limit their greenhouse gas emissions without damaging their economies? What are the most timely and cost-effective approaches? How can representatives of both the developed and the developing nations formulate climate change treaties that will be ratified by their home governments?

As a major, integrated energy company and as a subsidiary of DuPont, Conoco shares the world's concerns about potential climate change effects. We support the intent of the Rio Convention and the objectives of the International Climate Change Partnership. We also acknowledge the

---

Dennis R. Parker is vice president for safety, health, and environmental affairs at Conoco, Inc.

second assessment report of the Intergovernmental Panel on Climate Change (IPCC), which noted that concentrations of greenhouse gases in the earth's atmosphere are increasing and may contribute to global climate change.

The IPCC report also noted the scientific community's considerable uncertainty about the nature, pace, and potential impacts of climate change and, more important, the extent to which it can be attributed to human activities. We believe that at least three key issues must be dealt with in any long-term solution. First, most countries' economies, standard of living, and ability to grow depend on materials, products, and processes that contribute to greenhouse gas emissions. Second, any mandated measures to reduce these emissions would affect the world's enormous economic infrastructures and so would require time, incentives, and tremendous political will. And third, there is worldwide pressure for short-term action to advance conservation efforts and to limit the potential long-term effects of climate change.

The challenge is how to initiate scientifically sound long-term measures but avoid hasty steps that would undermine the foundations of the global economy. All nations would benefit from an assessment of the impact of emissions reduction targets and timetables on their standard of living as well as their driving habits and industrial progress. That is why all the participants attending the December 1997 climate change conference in Kyoto, Japan, should determine how proposed climate change measures will impact their nation's economy and quality of life. Since this is a global issue, it is imperative that all the nations of the world be subject to any agreements reached in Kyoto.

Developing sound global inventories of emissions, their sources, and their effects will help clarify our scientific, social, and economic understanding of the climate change issue. Unfortunately we are headed toward the Kyoto conference focused more on mandated targets and deadlines than on the strategies and details necessary to succeed in meeting our ultimate objectives.

One of those often-overlooked implementation details is incentives. Nations will find conservation progress difficult without such incentives as joint implementation and emissions credit trading programs. A good starting point is the Clinton administration's proposal to allow nations and companies to sell credits for exceeding emissions reduction targets to parties that cannot meet their goals.

A key aspect of the Clinton administration's proposal is flexibility. Different nations, industries, and even companies within the same industries will have to adapt climate change programs to their unique facilities, operations, and technologies. Of course, flaws will appear as such programs arise, but these can be managed if the programs are flexible enough. It is important that governments not negotiate in a vacuum but develop a more transparent process that involves the business community.

At the national level, developed countries and developing countries are struggling to resolve their roles in addressing global climate change. A treaty that does not include China, India, and Brazil will have little value. The developed countries may reduce their emissions, but the more populated and fast-growing developing countries will almost certainly increase their emissions, far outweighing those gains.

Perhaps part of the reason why some countries have resisted being included in any emissions reduction treaty is the lack of focus on incentives. Japan's proposal in June 1997 to provide developing countries with energy conservation and other technologies to preserve the environment is noteworthy. In fact, companies like Conoco are applying environmentally friendly technological and other assistance to current business projects overseas. Government must recognize that such direct foreign investment by private companies holds the key to effective technology transfer.

Clearly global climate change is a long-term issue that requires long-term solutions. More to the point, our world cannot afford hastily contrived mandates for emissions reductions and timetables that undermine our national economies. That is why Conoco has endorsed the call by the Business Roundtable (BRT) for a comprehensive set of policy development and implementation measures, including the following:

- Economic analysis of climate change policies and mitigation measures

- Voluntary measures to reduce greenhouse gas emissions

- Active participation in the policy development and review process

- A long-term focus, for the development of optimum strategies

- Appropriate time to develop and implement strategies for sending market signals, developing technology, and making capital investments

- Policy and long-term goals that recognize the uncertainty of the causes of climate change

- Policy and long-term goals that consider the timing and degree of their environmental and economic consequences

- Testing of the acceptability of these consequences in thorough, open public debates
- Opposition to a climate change policy that does not include all nations
- Policy flexibility, so that governments and the private sector can respond to their individual situations, with maximum emphasis on performance-based approaches rather than prescriptive measures

Conoco and other energy companies are not alone in calling for rational, holistic solutions to climate change. Insurance companies, manufacturers, and hotel and food companies have advocated through the BRT the recognition of a common responsibility to ensure that future generations will have a healthy economy and enjoy an ever-increasing standard of living. These industries also embrace equal responsibility for protecting our environment for our children and the generations that follow them. It is possible to achieve both objectives. But if we focus only on targets and timetables, we will eventually destroy the economic engines that drive healthy and growing economies. Also, our thriving economies are the sources of capital that fund new technologies, including the breakthroughs necessary to curb the growth of greenhouse gas emissions. This analytical, "life cycle" approach to emissions reductions strategies is essential to any sustainable climate change program.

The nations of the world can effectively address climate change if long-term solutions are based on improved science and well-thought-out transition plans that consider strategies, processes, costs, inventories, and incentives. The focus should be more on incentives and less on punitive measures. To reach these long-term solutions it is vital that industries, environmental groups, and government collaborate more closely. At Conoco we are dedicated to helping foster this process and to developing sustainable solutions.

THE BRT'S POSITION ON GLOBAL CLIMATE CHANGE

The official position of the BRT on the climate change issue (which forms the basis of Conoco's official position) is as follows:

> The Business Roundtable is committed to preserving and protecting the environment. We acknowledge the findings of the second assessment report of the Intergovernmental Panel on Climate Change that

the concentrations of greenhouse gases in the earth's atmosphere are increasing and that this may contribute to climate change. As stated in that report, we note that considerable uncertainty remains within the scientific community, with respect to the nature, pace, and potential impacts of climate change and, importantly, the extent to which climate change can be attributed to human activities as opposed to natural variability.

The Roundtable believes the environmental benefits and economic consequences of policy proposals, including targets and timetables for the limitation of greenhouse gas emissions, must undergo thorough analysis, review and comment. We believe that these steps are necessary before the implementation of any policies and measures which could adversely affect the economy. The Business Roundtable supports voluntary measures to reduce greenhouse gas emissions and must be an active participant in the policy development and review process.

The Business Roundtable supports efforts to address the scientific, economic and environmental challenges presented by these issues. We believe that:

- Climate change is an issue which will evolve over many decades. Optimum strategies to address global climate change should be developed with a long-term focus. Appropriate time to develop and implement these strategies is necessary to send market signals, develop technology and make capital investment. Negotiators should avoid a rush to make new commitments that could cause premature capital loss or retirements or otherwise detract from the long-term focus.

- The creation of policy and long-term goals should also recognize the scientific uncertainty and consider the associated range (timing and degree) of environmental and economic consequences (i.e., economic growth, employment, inflation, trade competitiveness and America's standard of living). The acceptability and consequences of proposed policies should be tested in thorough, open public debates.

- Climate change is a global issue which requires global response by all nations, developed and developing, in order to be environmentally effective and economically equitable. A climate policy which fails to include all nations should be opposed.

- There is a need for policy flexibility so that government and the private sector can craft individual responses to their own situations, with maximum emphasis on performance-based approaches rather than prescriptive measures. Public and private financial resources are limited, and demand that the most cost-effective, efficient approach be adopted.

Until the scientific and economic issues are better understood, there should be no rush to impose climate change policy measures, either by individual nations or collectively. Further agreements reached must include a requirement or negotiating process to bring all countries, developed and developing, into the commitment-making process. However, it is critical that an analysis and assessment of the impact on the U.S. economy be completed before any new commitments on climate change are made. Effective solutions to address climate change will require a healthy national and international economic order; hasty actions which undermine economic vitality will only defer our ability to responsibly address this issue over the longer term.

7

THE ROLE OF JUDGMENT
IN GLOBAL CLIMATE CHANGE

Max H. Bazerman, Claire E. Buisseret,
and Kimberly A. Wade-Benzoni

THE DAY BEFORE the Kellogg Environmental Research Center's Senior-Level Dialogue on Climate Change at Northwestern University, Howard Ris, the executive director of the Union of Concerned Scientists, gave an excellent talk on climate change to a group of MBA students. He was asked what it would take to get an agreement on global climate change in Kyoto. His answer was, "a very hot summer in the United States." The leader of one of the most prestigious scientific organizations in the United States was clarifying the important role of human biases on the success of one of the most important negotiations on earth. His answer highlights an underemphasized aspect of finding solutions to tough environmental problems—the decision-making processes of the actors involved, including key decision makers. Typically, decision makers and analysts tackling environmental disputes focus on the scientific facts, voluntary actions,

Max H. Bazerman, Claire E. Buisseret, and Kimberly A. Wade-Benzoni are members of the Department of Organization Behavior, J. L. Kellogg Graduate School of Management, Northwestern University. This research was supported by National Science Foundation Grant No. 9511977 and the Kellogg Environmental Research Center at the Kellogg Graduate School of Management.

and interests of the negotiating parties, who are implicitly assumed to be acting rationally. Yet, as Ris's comment suggests, a critical role is played by our unstable judgment in assessing this important societal issue.

This chapter connects Ris's comment with a vast literature on the ways in which decision makers deviate from rational thought. Ris implied one way. His implicit argument is that we tend to overrely on vivid information—in this case, the immediate sensation of a warm summer. His comment suggests that people care more about global warming when it is very hot. Yet we already know that it will be very hot some of the time, so why is it that we need this salient data to respond to this issue? The answer is that we tend to be biased by vivid data. Behavioral research on decision making has identified a large number of biases that lead judgment away from rational action.[1] This chapter highlights four of these systematic biases that are specifically relevant to the issue of global warming: vividness, overdiscounting the future, egocentrism, and the mythical "fixed pie."

VIVIDNESS

People judge the importance of an issue by its vividness. Tversky and Kahneman argue that vivid information is overly weighted in decision making.[2] This explains why people place less value on biodiversity than on saving a single specific elephant, for example, or why hunger organizations are better able to solicit funds to sponsor one child than to contribute to the broader hunger issue. General biodiversity and hunger lack the vividness that is needed to raise money. One problem facing environmentalists is the fact that people value more vivid symbols of the environment. A term exists to describe what will raise money: "charismatic mega-fauna." These are animals that strike a chord with people because of their cuteness, originality, or other appeal. The fact that these charming animals depend on diversity to survive is lost on the public.

The concept of vividness explains why Ris is probably right. When the summer is hot, global warming becomes more salient to the public, to corporate actors, and to the U.S. negotiating team. One major challenge of harnessing enthusiasm for dealing with climate change is that the costs of "solving" climate change (that is, raising gas prices, driving electric cars, meeting emissions standards, or walking to work) are vivid, whereas the benefits (improved air quality and stabilized carbon dioxide levels) are not. Like the national debt, people may agree that there is a problem, but that does not mean that they are willing to sacrifice to solve this nonvivid threat.

INAPPROPRIATELY HIGH DISCOUNT RATES

Herman Daly has been quoted as saying, "we should not treat the earth as if it were a business in liquidation."[3] We generally believe that we ought to pass on to future inhabitants the resources and systems of the natural environment in as good a state as we inherited them. However, our ongoing decisions are inconsistent with this belief. Many pollutants have already surpassed rates that are physically sustainable. For example, to take the issue of climate change, human activity contributes millions of tons of carbon dioxide into the atmosphere annually. Problems that are in the distance, such as the potential effects of global warming, are often given insufficient attention.

This "discounting of the future" can be disadvantageous both in terms of individuals' self-interest and also from an intergenerational, global, or environmental perspective,[4] yet research shows the use of extremely high discount rates.[5] For example, even when they would actually make back the extra costs in less than a year, many homeowners skimp on the amount of insulation they put in their attics and walls and do not buy more expensive, energy-efficient appliances.

Large organizations also exhibit dysfunctionally inappropriate discount rates. For example, one of the best-known, most highly esteemed universities in the United States made the decision to embark on improving its infrastructure. Due to budget limitations, however, builders and planners failed to use the most long-term cost-efficient products.[6] Because a very high implicit discount rate was used to make construction decisions, present benefits (reduced costs) were obtained at the expense of future costs (increased energy consumption). In this way the investment group of the university lost future returns because of the shortsightedness of the construction process. This behavior was also myopic in an environmental sense, because the discounting resulted in greater energy consumption and thus greater environmental degradation.

Confronting global warming will involve paying increased costs now to avoid much larger (but currently nonvivid) costs in the distant future. Addressing the problem is likely to benefit future generations more than ourselves. Yet it is easier for us to spend resources that afford our children immediate benefits (such as providing them with cars, clothing, and toys) than to deny them these resources in order to deal with an enormous issue like global warming, an issue that is truly central to the interests of future generations. Providing immediate tangible benefits for our children allows us the illusion of caring about future generations. The unfortunate result of inappropriately discounting the value of future benefits is our failure as a society to act on global climate change.

EGOCENTRISM

Negotiations over climate change and environmental issues in general are particularly vulnerable to egocentrism. Egocentric interpretations of fairness are judgments that are biased in a manner favoring the individuals making the judgments. Egocentrism exists to the extent that subjects differentially interpret what is fair in ways that serve their own interests. Thus if two people dividing a limited pool of resources are each asked to assess the percentage of the resources that they deserve—and the two percentages exceed 100 percent—their perceptions are egocentric.[7]

The problem of reaching consensus on what is fair is a common obstacle to the resolution of environmental conflict. Environmental conflict and resource allocation are often characterized by highly complex issues, insufficient scientific information, and technological uncertainty. These qualities make egocentrism likely and conflict resolution particularly difficult.[8]

In the allocation of environmental resources, most people attempt to obtain benefits for and avoid burdens to themselves. Yet they also want to preserve their positive self-image as someone who is concerned about issues of justice and has contributed his or her fair share to the common good. Thus when considering responsibility for global warming the developed world blames the developing world for destroying the rain forests, and the developing world blames the developed world for overconsumption. In another example, consumers blame corporations for pollution without accepting that their consumption creates the demand the corporations are meeting. Egocentric interpretations of fairness create a potential obstacle to the resolution of environmental conflict by allowing for a convenient reconciliation of two apparently conflicting goals: individuals can have what they want, do what they want to do (seize a larger share of a limited desirable resource or bear a smaller share of an undesirable burden), and still believe that their actions are fair and in line with what they should do (because they practice self-restraint in the use of the resource, for example, or take at least partial responsibility for shouldering the burden).

Uncertainty, which is common in connection with long-term environmental issues, compounds the problem by allowing individuals to further reconcile the two goals of self-interest and fairness. There are no clear guidelines governing what and how much human beings should or should not do environmentally; furthermore, the scientific evidence is often unclear or outright conflictual. This uncertainty enables the formation of egocentric interpretations of fairness, granting individuals the illusion of consistency between an attitude of concern for the environment and behaviors that contradict this concern[9] and are detrimental to the health and sustainability of the natural environment. For example, since it is unclear which behaviors are most important to solving environmental problems, egocentric biases may allow people to believe that their positive contributions to solving environmental problems are more important than the contributions of others. Similarly, individuals can perceive their own negative contributions to environmental problems as less significant, allowing them to dodge blame and instead point the finger at others as the primary villains. In sum, uncertainty compounded by egocentric biases permits people to avoid responsibility for contributing to environmental problems and for modifying their behavior to help solve these problems.

In terms of global climate change, we can see how different parties can egocentrically, yet sincerely, develop different views. The issue is complex—economically, politically, and environmentally. There is also scientific uncertainty surrounding the extent of the danger from climate change, and in some cases whether it is occurring at all. The parties are likely to have egocentrically biased views of who is responsible for the current condition, what is the magnitude of the problem, and who should pay to solve the problem. A critical point to realize is that parties will honestly have different answers to these questions as a result of egocentrism.

MYTHICAL "FIXED PIE"

Discussions of environmental issues are often highly partisan, with the analysts on one side arguing that environmental protection is costly[10] and those on the other side arguing that such protection is essential. Full acceptance of either view results in the mythical "fixed pie," the idea that there is a limited set of outcomes, possibilities, or resources. Most often negotiators fail to reach optimal outcomes because they do not look for integrative trade-offs that can enlarge the pool of resources to be distributed.[11] Instead they approach the negotiation with a fixed-pie assumption, which creates a competitive situation, hinders cooperation, and masks potential trade-offs or creative opportunities that will improve the overall quality of the agreement. Not that environmental conflicts often have simple win-win solutions, but there are often trade-offs that can enhance the attractiveness of the solutions for all sides.[12]

Furthermore, when both sides assume that the other side's gain is their loss, reactive devaluation is likely to accompany the mythical fixed pie. In reactive devaluation, negotiators believe that if a deal or proposal is acceptable to their opponent, then it must be bad for them.[13]

In the climate change debate there are potentially several partisan groups fighting over the fixed pie: developed versus developing countries, industry versus environmental groups, industry versus the government. Each of these groups has different interests and potentially views these interests to be in opposition to another group's, thus perceiving the climate change situation to be a fixed pie.

The Senior-Level Dialogue on Climate Change emphasized the need to avoid fixed standards in responding to global climate change, to allow corporations the opportunity to creatively respond to the problem. We agree with the need for flexibility. However, corporations should not view this as an opportunity for shirking but rather as an opportunity to show how well they can respond environmentally when allowed to figure out a creative solution.

CONCLUSION

Humans can be so impressive yet so incompetent in responding to major problems facing society. As Nisbett and Ross[14] wrote,

> One of philosophy's oldest paradoxes is the apparent contradiction between the greatest triumphs and the dramatic failures of the human mind. The same organism that routinely solves inferential problems too subtle and complex for the mightiest computers often makes errors in the simplest of judgments about everyday events. The errors, moreover, often seem traceable to violations of the same inferential rules that underlie people's most impressive successes. . . . How can any creature skilled enough to build and maintain complex organizations, or sophisticated enough to appreciate the nuances of social intercourse, be foolish enough to mouth racist clichés or spill its lifeblood in pointless wars?

How can a species talented enough to identify the pattern of global climate change also allow this dysfunctional pattern to continue? Our answer is that even the brightest humans fall victim to a variety of systematic and predictable cognitive errors. We believe that teaching our citizens, leaders, and negotiators to be aware of these errors is central to the negotiation of a global climate change solution.

NOTES

1. M. H. Bazerman, *Judgment in Managerial Decision Making,* 4th ed. (New York: Wiley, 1988).
2. A. Tversky and D. Kahneman, "Judgment Under Uncertainty: Heuristics and Biases," *Science,* 1974, *185:* 1124–1131.

3. Cited in A. Gore, *Earth in the Balance* (Boston: Houghton Mifflin, 1993): 191.

4. K. A. Wade-Benzoni, "Intergenerational Justice: Discounting, Reciprocity, and Fairness as Factors That Influence How Resources Are Allocated Across Generations" (Ph.D. diss., Northwestern University, 1996).

5. G. Loewenstein and R. Thaler, "Anomalies: Intertemporal Choice," *Journal of Economic Perspectives,* 1989, *3:* 181–193; D. Gately, "Individual Discount Rates and the Purchase and Utilization of Energy Using Durables," *Bell Journal of Economics,* 1980, *11:* 373–374.

6. M. H. Bazerman, K. A. Wade-Benzoni, and F. Benzoni, "A Behavioral Decision Theory Perspective to Environmental Decision Making," in D. M. Messick and A. E. Tenbrunsel (eds.), *Ethical Issues in Managerial Decision Making* (New York: Russell Sage Foundation, 1996).

7. K. Diekmann, S. Samuels, L. Ross, and M. H. Bazerman, "The Descriptive and Prescriptive Use of Previous Purchase Price in Negotiation," *Organizational Behavior and Human Decision Processes,* 1997, *66:* 179–191.

8. Bazerman, Wade-Benzoni, and Benzoni, "A Behavioral Decision Theory Perspective."

9. Bazerman, Wade-Benzoni, and Benzoni, "A Behavioral Decision Theory Perspective."

10. N. Walley and B. Whitehead, "It's Not Easy Being Green," *Harvard Business Review*, May-June 1994: 46–51; K. Palmer, W. Oates, and P. Portney, "Tightening Environmental Standards: The Benefit-Cost or the No-Cost Paradigm?" *Journal of Economic Perspectives,* 1995, *9*(4): 119–132.

11. M. H. Bazerman and M. A. Neale, *Negotiating Rationally* (New York: Free Press, 1992).

12. A. J. Hoffman and others, "A Mixed-Motive Perspective on the Economics Versus Environment Debate" (Working paper, Center for Dispute Resolution, J. L. Kellogg Graduate School of Management, Evanston, IL, 1997).

13. C. Stillenger, M. Epelbaum, D. Keltner, and L. Ross, "The 'Reactive Devaluation' Barrier to Conflict Resolution" (Working paper, Stanford University, 1990).

14. R. E. Nisbett and L. Ross, *Human Inference: Strategies and Shortcomings of Social Judgment* (Englewood Cliffs, NJ: Prentice Hall, 1980): xi–xii.

8

THE IMPORTANCE OF FLEXIBILITY IMPLEMENTED THROUGH VOLUNTARY COMMITMENTS TO REDUCE GREENHOUSE GAS EMISSIONS

Patrick J. Mulchay

INTERNATIONAL NEGOTIATIONS will continue in December 1997 at the third Conference of the Parties (COP-3) in Kyoto, Japan. For developed countries the United States supports verifiable, binding medium-term (2010 to 2020) targets that are realistic and achievable and are designed with maximum flexibility. It is imperative for the developed world that the agreement include specific provisions that advance the implementation of commitments by developing nations. There are two outstanding issues of importance for the electric utility industry that are not adequately addressed in the U.S. position paper. Utilities are urging that the U.S. protocol include "where" flexibility (that is, acceptance of projects undertaken jointly between countries) and "when" flexibility (that is, recognition and credit for early reductions of greenhouse gas emissions and phased commitments in the future).

Patrick J. Mulchay is executive vice president and COO of Northern Indiana Public Service Company.

"WHERE" FLEXIBILITY

The U.S. Initiative on Joint Implementation (USIJI) encompasses twenty-five pilot projects between nations. Joint implementation (JI) works on the principle outlined by Peter Passell in a February 13, 1997, *New York Times* article[1]—national targets for containing emissions will be very expensive to meet in the rich industrial economies, but allowing these already rich countries to pay the emerging economies to use less energy and less carbon-intensive fuels as they develop offers a double dividend. Besides reducing emissions immediately, it would also create a pool of capital to be used as an incentive to push emerging economies toward environmentally benign growth. The U.S. proposal for a protocol framework defers the adoption of criteria for JI projects to a later negotiating session. If the USIJI is to move beyond the pilot phase, future investors must be assured of receiving credit for their projects.

An example of a USIJI project is the Binov district heating pilot project that Northern Indiana Public Service Company (NIPSCO) and two other midwestern utilities are undertaking in the Czech city of Decin. Each utility contributed $200,000 in the form of an interest-free loan, and each will receive one-third of the emissions reductions realized in the lignite-to-natural-gas conversion. Assuming a twenty-year life, the cost to NIPSCO of carbon dioxide emissions reductions at the Binov plant is approximately $0.20 per ton. In comparison, NIPSCO's rural tree plantings sequester carbon dioxide at a cost of $58.50 per ton, and biomass cofiring (assuming a fuel cost of $1.20 per ton) would offset carbon dioxide emissions at a cost of $1.70 per ton. As a participant in the Decin pilot project, NIPSCO urges the inclusion of JI criteria, including methodologies for calculating credits, as an integral component of any protocol adopted at COP-3.

"WHEN" FLEXIBILITY

In addition to "where" flexibility, the U.S. position should promote "when" flexibility to further balance economic impact and expected environmental benefits. Significant cost savings may be realized through a delay in emissions reductions to allow orderly capital stock turnover and development of new technologies. Although the administration has assured the Edison Electric Institute that utilities that take early action will receive credit toward future targets, the U.S. proposal for a protocol framework does not provide for credit for early actions. The electric utility industry is making early, significant, voluntary reductions under the assumption that these efforts will be recognized in any future regulatory framework. It is important for continued and future good-faith efforts on the part of business and industry that the administration fully recognize these efforts.

Support for additional research and development is critical for cost-effective greenhouse gas emissions reductions in the future. Approximately 93 percent of our reductions have resulted from residential, commercial, and industrial energy-efficiency programs. NIPSCO's experience shows that increased use of electrotechnologies are essential to cost-effective greenhouse gas emissions reductions. NIPSCO supports continuing efforts to develop and implement electrotechnologies in the marketplace. Technology development is key to cost-effective reductions. Presently there is no work under way to develop a technology strategy within a global, public-private partnership. NIPSCO encourages the Electric Power Research Institute in their efforts to initiate such a partnership.

BALANCING EMISSIONS REDUCTIONS AND COMPETITIVENESS

A U.S. Department of Energy study analyzed the potential economic impacts of increased energy prices on energy-intensive industries, assuming that new greenhouse gas control policies will constrain only industrialized countries and that any emissions control mechanism—from new energy taxes to emissions standards and tradable emissions permits—will drive up energy costs to some degree. According to the study, rising energy prices driven by new climate commitments could have a crushing effect on six U.S. industries: paper and allied products, iron and steel manufacturing, petroleum refining, aluminum production, chemical manufacturing, and cement manufacturing.

Increased energy costs from emissions mandates could devastate the U.S. steel industry (which has already invested heavily in energy efficiency and pollution control technologies), without bringing a significant decrease in worldwide energy-related emissions from steelmaking. Production will simply be shifted to developing countries and may possibly lead to *higher* levels of overall pollution due to lower standards in those countries. This issue highlights the necessity for the thoughtful application of binding agreements for all nations—developing and developed.

Energy costs account for approximately one-third of the cost of making steel. Almost half of the electricity NIPSCO generates is delivered to the steel industry. Steelmaking facilities in northern Indiana have invested substantially in the past decade to improve their efficiency, both in production and in energy use. Primary Energy, a subsidiary of NIPSCO Industries, is developing cogeneration projects with several of our steelmaking customers. These projects will contribute significantly to NIPSCO's greenhouse gas reductions. In 1998 three Primary Energy cogeneration projects will go on-line at Inland, U.S. Steel, and National Steel, displacing nearly one million metric tons of NIPSCO's carbon dioxide emissions.

Sensible decision making on the greenhouse gas issue should involve a careful balancing of costs and benefits. However, this is complicated by the global effects of greenhouse gas concentrations in the atmosphere, the long-term consequences and short-term costs associated with the issue, and the global economy and tension between developed and developing nations.

NIPSCO'S COMMITMENT TO THE ENVIRONMENT

Northern Indiana Public Service Company (NIPSCO), a subsidiary of NIPSCO Industries, Inc., is the second-largest electric company and the largest gas distribution company in Indiana. We serve the northern third of Indiana, including the densely populated southern shore of Lake Michigan, where steel mills coexist with the Indiana Dunes National Lakeshore. NIPSCO's electric operations include four coal- and gas-fired generating stations with modern pollution control equipment and two small hydroelectric plants. Our gas facilities include an underground storage field and a liquefied natural gas plant.

NIPSCO is publicly committed to environmental stewardship and proactive environmental performance and has made significant investments in environmental programs and pollution control equipment. We support environmental programs and investments in greenhouse gas mitigation, environmental auditing, natural resource enhancement, pollution prevention practices, environmental management systems, performance targeting, proactive land investigations, and community outreach.

NIPSCO Industries believes that business and industry have significant roles to play in the protection, preservation, and enhancement of the environment by taking a proactive, leadership role that goes beyond simply complying with regulations. We understand the importance of environmental issues on communities in our service territory and position our environmental efforts in the direction most appropriate to our business and the communities we serve.

In March 1997 NIPSCO became the first utility in the United States to have major facilities, including a generating station, certified under the international environmental management system (ISO 14000). One element of the U.S. ISO 14000 standard requires that facilities identify their environmental impacts. Greenhouse gas emissions are identified as a significant environmental impact. NIPSCO is taking steps to reduce greenhouse gases, even though there is continued scientific and political debate regarding the certainty of climate change.

NIPSCO's approach to greenhouse gas reduction includes our participation in the Climate Challenge program. NIPSCO Industries recognizes that the potential impacts of climate change on natural systems, the economy, and the quality of life of future generations is significant. Scientific evidence suggests that climate change would be detrimental to human health, ecosystems, food security, and water resources. The science, although still developing, provides a compelling basis for action to address climate change. We support a national commitment with enough flexibility to respond to the developing knowledge of climate change.

The electric utility industry is a world leader in addressing greenhouse gas emissions. The Climate Challenge program, a voluntary partnership between the electric utility industry and the U.S. Department of Energy, is the flagship program of the administration's Climate Change Action Plan and is the world's largest and most successful voluntary initiative on global climate change. In support of the U.S. policy approach to climate change, NIPSCO Industries and approximately seven hundred other electric utilities have demonstrated that significant reductions in carbon dioxide emissions are possible through voluntary action. In the year 2000 the electric utility industry will collectively reduce, avoid emitting, or sequester nearly 169 million metric tons of carbon dioxide and equivalent greenhouse gases.

In February 1994 NIPSCO Industries joined the Climate Challenge program as a charter member and voluntarily committed to reducing its greenhouse gas emissions through twenty-one specific projects and by participating in two industry initiatives. In 1995 NIPSCO reduced its emissions of greenhouse gases by 1.27 million metric tons, or 6 percent of our total CO_2 emissions. We reported greenhouse gas reductions from twenty projects and documented an additional five projects under way that will show reductions in future years: a JI project in the Czech Republic, a biomass cofiring feasibility study, and three cogeneration projects with local steel mills.

NIPSCO Industries' 1995 report to the program is summarized below. We reported greenhouse gas reductions in nine of ten reporting categories. For the electricity generation, transmission, and distribution category, for example, we reported that pole-mounted transformers are periodically being replaced with new, more efficient models with lower electric losses. New capacitors added to the company's distribution and transmissions systems are providing voltage improvements, power factor improvements, loss reductions, system capacity releases, and energy savings.

NIPSCO's greatest reductions were realized in the energy end-use project category. Although NIPSCO does not have a formal demand-side management program, our demand-side management focus and our efficiency-improvement marketing activities target both electric and gas customers in the residential, commercial, and industrial sectors. Greenhouse gas reductions were reported for those specific company programs designed to influence consumer behavior in favor of energy efficiency.

NIPSCO's activities in the transportation category include support for natural gas– and electric-powered vehicles and participation in a pilot program to field-test the Employee Commute Option requirements of the 1990 Clean Air Act amendments. We operate one of the country's largest fleets of natural gas–powered vehicles. GreenFuels, a subsidiary of NIPSCO Industries, is a leader in utilizing and marketing natural gas vehicle (NGV) technology and is increasing the number of NGVs operating throughout our service territory by working in partnership to provide a highly reliable fueling infrastructure and by developing strategic alliances with educational, governmental, and social organizations to promote NGVs. We project that by the year 2000 there will be approximately 1,750 NGVs operating in our service territory.

In the waste treatment and disposal category, NIPSCO reported greenhouse gas reductions associated with electricity generated from landfill gas at two sites. A third landfill gas–to-energy project is under development.

In the natural gas systems–methane category, NIPSCO initiated a project to replace the North Trenton pipeline gathering system (approximately twenty miles of pipe), significantly reducing the amount of natural gas released to the atmosphere from the system. The company is participating in the Environmental Protection Agency's voluntary Natural Gas Star Program to replace old cast-iron and unprotected steel gas mains with durable, corrosion-resistant plastic mains; to replace old pneumatic control devices with new low-bleed devices; and to inspect and repair high-pressure regulator and metering station equipment.

NIPSCO is involved in three local carbon sequestration projects and is a member of UtiliTree, an electric utility initiative developed in response to the Climate Challenge program. As the owner of a number of large tracts of rural land, NIPSCO has the opportunity to undertake two reforestation projects on approximately fifty acres at our Schahfer generating station. Our urban tree-planting program is designed to demonstrate to customers that trees and utilities can coexist if attention is given to planting the right tree in the right place. Compatible, low-growing species are planted beneath our lines, and shade trees are planted away from the lines. NIPSCO is participating in the Rio Bravo Carbon Sequestration Pilot Project (part of the USIJI) through the UtiliTree Carbon Company.

In the ozone-depleting chemicals category, NIPSCO reported to-date progress on the company's efforts to complete phaseout of our ozone-depleting chemicals and products by 1996.

NIPSCO has committed to coal combustion by-product utilization by pursuing markets for 50 percent of the company's Class C ash output by the year 2000, greatly reducing carbon dioxide emissions associated with the traditional production of cement.

Projects reported in the other emission reduction projects category include the company's recycling program (which includes waste paper, glass, aluminum, corrugated cardboard, wood pallets, wood reels, and used oil) and our employee training program. In 1995 NIPSCO's training facilities provided over 7,800 student days of training, many of which were in technical areas that have a direct effect on greenhouse gas emissions.

Because NIPSCO's system is predominately coal-fired, we are limited in the scope of the generation projects we can undertake internally to reduce greenhouse gas emissions. This has not restricted our pursuit of external opportunities and unique internal applications, however. For example, NIPSCO is conducting a biomass test burn (10 percent urban wood waste, 90 percent Powder River Basin coal) to scope the feasibility of expanding our energy supply portfolio to include a small percentage of renewables.

NOTE

1. P. Passell, "Yawn. A Global-Warming Alert. But This One Has Solutions," *New York Times,* February 13, 1997: C2.

9

AN ARGUMENT AGAINST FLEXIBILITY

A 2000 Start Date and Short Budget Periods
Provide Benefits to the Environment and Industry

Terence H. Thorn

AS THE NATIONS OF THE WORLD address the setting of targets and timetables for the control of greenhouse gases, one of the most important issues with which delegates will grapple is the setting of an appropriate start date for a real carbon control program and the length of so-called budget periods. These questions will determine how fast we reduce carbon, the cost of carbon reductions, and the rate of innovation in carbon-reducing technologies.

First, the question of *when* a carbon control program should be started is at the heart of the current debate on climate change. While some countries see the need to begin a carbon control program sooner rather than later, other countries are proposing programs that would not start until between 2005 and 2010 or even 2020. If a serious carbon mitigation program is delayed until 2010 or 2020, the environmental and economic benefits touted by advocates of carbon control regimes will surely fail to materialize. The benefits derived from a start date in the

Terence H. Thorn is senior vice president of environmental and international government affairs at Enron Corporation.

year 2000 include establishing good regulatory habits, sending the right signals to the marketplace, providing industry with more certainty, and leveling emissions growth.

Second, *how* companies approach their carbon control obligation is critical to the generation of new and better energy technologies. Currently some countries are discussing the concept of long-term emissions budget periods (such as five to ten years) in the context of setting targets and timetables for the control of greenhouse gases. This would mean, for example, that each country or source would get an allocation of emissions allowances for a five- or ten-year period and that the reckoning of who met or exceeded their allocation would not come until the end of the period. According to this logic, three-year budgets are better than one-year budgets, ten-year budgets are better than three-year budgets, and thirty-year budgets are better still. On the contrary, short time periods are good for the environment and good for promoting green technologies.

This chapter synthesizes the work of other authors into a coherent regulatory approach calling for carbon control action based on the "polluter pays" principle, the creation of a price signal, and the promotion of regulatory certainty under a regime that incrementally rolls in new and more stringent programs over time.[1] It is premised on two notions: an international carbon credit trading regime (based on joint implementation or allowance-based approaches) will also exist, and a modest regulatory program (one that has small reductions rolled out over time, such as a 1 percent per year net reduction in CO_2 emissions) is simpler, easier to implement, and more likely to achieve reductions both in the short run and in the long run.

REASONS TO BEGIN A REGULATORY PROGRAM SOONER RATHER THAN LATER

There are many reasons why a carbon control regime should start as soon as possible, and there are few, if any, reasons to postpone it. First, starting a regulatory regime during the next few years, however modest that regime might be, would create good habits: starting regulatory programs sooner rather than later gets both regulators and industry into the habit of accounting for carbon emissions. Second, even a modest regulatory program will send a price signal, and sending the right signals to environmentally friendly technology producers indicates that markets for their products are real and viable in the near term. Such price signals, therefore, will make additional investments in facilities that produce environmentally friendly technologies justifiable. Third, establishing regulatory certainty is important since actions that are planned to go into effect sooner rather than later are more likely to be implemented. Finally, starting a regulatory program sooner instead of later will slow emissions growth painlessly; contrariwise, allowing emissions to continue to increase before reductions are begun will only jeopardize the start of a "safe-landing" decline in emissions. These points are expanded upon in the paragraphs that follow.

1. *Shorter budget periods will get people into the habit of accounting for carbon emissions.* There is great value in developing good habits; it is good for people, the government, and the private sector. Accounting for carbon emissions in energy and transportation planning is a habit that we should encourage. Furthermore, whereas *planning* regulatory programs focuses staff attention, *implementing* regulatory programs, however modest, will lead to even more care and attention and a more concerted effort by industry to anticipate possible outcomes of emissions-related actions.

Forming good habits early is just as important as reversing bad habits sooner rather than later. Even small actions taken in early years will begin to change attitudes and prices in a way that no amount of discussion, persuasion, or good intentions can match. The result of getting near-term reductions will compound over time, just like financial investments, and can only be of benefit in the long term.

2. *Real reductions are more important than promised reductions.* Although voluntary programs have had some modest effects to date, these programs have not succeeded in slowing emissions growth. No one believes that voluntary carbon control programs will lead to large reductions of atmospheric carbon. While some people continue to support voluntary measures to control greenhouse gases, little evidence has been found that voluntary measures alone achieve very much in the way of environmental results. This was the observation of U.S. Undersecretary of State for Global Affairs Timothy Wirth, who noted in Geneva that the current voluntary structure for getting carbon reductions has failed. This result has also been confirmed in a study conducted by Dr. Terry Davies, director of resources for the Future's Center for Risk Management. His report concluded that voluntary programs usually do not achieve very much beyond good intentions and are actually peripheral to solving any problem at all.[2]

Instead of debating the consequences of one static program design versus another, action should be taken now to develop a modest regulatory program that mandates carbon mitigation on a slow and steady slope. This would provide real-world evidence that will overwhelm any oratory. Two years of real emissions reductions would provide more information on the cost of carbon control than a thousand simulation models. Two years of real emissions reductions would also create more procedures within industry and government bodies than a thousand conferences or a thousand newsletters. There is no substitute for experience.

3. *Price signals must be sent to environmental technology producers.* All stakeholders want to promote the development of more technologies that are both cheap and yield good environmental results. If one is to harness the creative energies of the technology community and foster the emergence of new, greener technologies, there must be a direct payoff— in this case, revenues. By delaying the revenue stream, governments only freeze the development and promotion of technology and retard the decline in prices of carbon-reducing technologies.

Contrary to common belief, the necessary green technologies exist today, and more are on the drawing boards. Yet without the prospect of real demand and sales, these technologies will not reach the market and will never be accepted, regardless of how long we wait for them. The smallest commitment to real, near-term action, however, will realize an immediate response from the green technology industry.

4. *Early actions* do *happen; delayed action* may *happen.* An affirmative, action-oriented plan that goes into effect sooner rather than later will have a much greater likelihood of being implemented. In today's global marketplace, companies are looking increasingly to the near-term development of business. Take, for example, the issue of restructuring in the electric utility industry, where without a regulatory regime in place the future is too uncertain for some companies to develop their long-term investment strategies. History has proven that without a near-term goal or mandate in place, industry will not take any action.

5. *Steep reductions for carbon emissions make no sense.* We know it is difficult to reduce carbon emissions. Even with better technology, there will be no simple, cost-free remedy. The buildup of infrastructure in our societies has created an inertia of enormous proportions that cannot be quickly defeated. Delaying implementation of some type of regulatory regime only increases this mass and steepens the slope of change that must take place at some future time. Further, any attempts to move this huge mass up a steep slope can only result in a crash landing. Instead we must plan on a more gradual, safe-landing path that achieves our eventual goal of reducing carbon emissions. Such an achievement can only be realized if we start early.

HOW TO GET RESULTS: WHY SHORTER
BUDGET PERIODS MAKE MORE SENSE

As noted previously, some countries (such as the United States) are now discussing the concept of long-term emissions budget periods, with reckonings of who met or exceeded their emissions allocations delayed until the end of each period. Clearly this makes compliance easier for regulated organizations, since the costs of compliance can be pushed off until a later date. Long emissions budget periods are bad for the environment, however, and bad for developing technologies. And, as already mentioned, short budget periods are good for the environment and good for promoting green technologies. Short-term budgets will enable us to begin reducing emissions slowly and steadily while at the same time responding to fluctuations or variations in emissions levels. First of all, carbon emissions come from almost all sectors of the economy. In any country, the diversity of carbon sources tends to even out fluctuations in emissions levels. Factors that may increase emissions in one sector may not affect or may even depress them in another sector. Emissions trading allows one sector to offset another and smooth out total emissions reductions. Even if all sectors in one country have a high year, carbon credit trading with other countries provides another safety valve to protect the emitting community.

Beyond these factors that reduce emissions volatility, the concern that emitters will be caught unprepared presumes that companies are stupid and lack foresight. On the one hand, if regulated companies are risk takers, they will make every endeavor to comply; and if they fail to control enough of their carbon emissions, they will pay their penalties and should not complain. On the other hand, if regulated companies are risk-averse, they will seek to protect against a potential shortfall of carbon reductions. Thus risk-avoiding companies will either get some kind of insurance for carbon emissions reductions or overcontrol their carbon emissions beyond what is required in the given time period. Either action would yield an acceptable outcome in current and future time periods.

If we believe that an active carbon trading market will develop, we must also acknowledge that the marketplace will lead to the provision of risk management products like carbon options, carbon reduction insurance, and the like. Risk management products have been developed to manage all kinds of risks associated with gas trading, electricity trading, and even sulfur dioxide permit trading. There is no reason to think that companies like Enron and other traders will fail to provide risk management products to manage emissions risks.

In the event regulated companies do not protect themselves by buy-ing insurance, companies can still overcontrol their emissions at one fa-cility and use those "extra" emissions reductions to meet their carbon control obligations at another facility (or sell them to other companies who need them). In short, it is fair to say that industry can look out for itself by protecting its financial interests in traditional ways.

The other argument for long-term budget periods is that we must allow time for the market's invisible hand to point to the most cost-effective solution through the turnover of capital stock and its replace-ment with improved technology. This argument neglects the fact that there are already many improved carbon-reducing technologies avail-able that are not being utilized because there is no incentive for indus-try to control carbon emissions. There are many more potential technologies that could be developed but are languishing for lack of a perceived market. Stalling the achievement of carbon reductions will re-tard the development of green energy technologies such as fuel cells. Far from encouraging their use, long-term budget periods delay the point at which they will start to be introduced or even developed.

BENEFITS OF SHORT-TERM DECLINING CAPS

To reverse this trend we must implement budgets with short-term de-clining caps that require continuing results and provide the impetus for technology development and implementation. *The cap does not have to decline quickly, as long as it starts early and continues on a regular basis.* A very small decline, such as a 1 percent per year net reduction, will send the required signal.

Simplicity

A one- or two-year declining cap is easy to understand and easy to es-tablish. The simple reality of the system will encourage companies to meet their carbon control obligations by investing in streams of low-cost reductions or by getting certifiable excess reductions from other Annex 1 countries. Being risk-averse, companies are likely to overcontrol emis-sions, thus providing an environmental dividend. Those companies not wanting to overcontrol may buy carbon credits instead, and the value established for the reductions will provide the needed impetus for the development and application of new technologies.

Stringency

Protecting the environment should be the ultimate goal of any environmental program. If a lax regulatory standard is established and becomes the status quo, creating a more stringent standard later will be difficult if not impossible. The opposite, however, is not as problematic. Starting with too strict a standard can lead to a strong signal for developing new technologies and eventually to the new technologies themselves. Moderating a strong standard is easier than strengthening a lax standard. Of the two risks—of setting a standard that is too stringent or too lax—many would prefer leaning on the side of overcontrol, of greater environmental protection and stronger signals to technology producers. It is easy to envision the difficulty of starting even a mild carbon control program, even with substantial scientific and political support. Accordingly, imagine how difficult it will be to make the budget period shorter (down to two or three years from five or ten) if and when longer periods are shown not to succeed in achieving promised outcomes.

Less Passing Off to Unseen Successors

Long budget periods give individuals within companies the opportunity to pass off compliance investments to unseen and unknown successors. This problem is especially important during periods of restructuring and liberalization within the energy sector, when companies are especially reluctant to make investments that might not be beneficial under some new, not yet well defined regulatory regime. It is easy to pass off environmental problems to the future. Thus one role of regulators is to make sure that problems are treated today.

Support for New Technologies

The carbon-reducing technologies that will allow us to reach stabilization must have an adequate market to become economically viable. This applies to research, development, and production propositions. The cost-effectiveness that is derived from many so-called new technologies is really derived from mass production. Although the basic technology may already have been invented and applied, costs rapidly decline in going from small-scale implementation to mass production. This was true in the case of the automobile, the computer, and the VCR, and it applies for almost all other technologies. The lesson learned is obvious—mass production lowers costs. By postponing demand to some further time period, regulators could deprive the marketplace of the demand that is necessary to drive prices down and bring green technology to the marketplace.

CONCLUSION

Clive Bates, who is with the International Institute for Energy Conservation in London, has written on the issues of "when," "where," and "which" kind of flexibility, and his thoughts justify repetition here. He writes,

> There are really three types of flexibility. . . . "Where" flexibility allows a party to meet its targets by buying reductions in other parties if the cost of reductions is lower—either through emissions trading or, where it can be made to work, between parties with emissions targets, through Joint Implementation. . . . "When" flexibility, however, allows the party to decide when it will make reductions. The three most contentious elements of "when" flexibility are: a late starting date for targets (say 2010); long budget periods (say 10 years); and the ability to borrow from a future budget period. . . . "Which" flexibility allows the parties to decide which greenhouse gases to reduce to meet an overall greenhouse gas reduction and may include netting sources such as fossil fuel burning against sinks such as growing trees.
>
> "Where" flexibility has a number of advantages, which could have good implications for the climate. "Where" flexibility creates a market price signal incentive to reduce carbon because carbon emitters will make reductions as long as these are less than the price of permits on a trading market; this will flush out "no-regrets" potential and have the same effect on behavior as a carbon tax. It should achieve the lowest global cost reduction across those participating in trading or JI—thus creating a rationale for more ambitious targets. It eases the burdens of the common 1990 baseline for some parties since those companies that find reductions most expensive can purchase cheaper emissions from elsewhere. It exposes the costs of responding to climate change, and these are likely to be low. Lastly, it creates a compliance mechanism since parties will have to buy enough permits to meet their targets.
>
> "When" flexibility has many disadvantages and is plain bad for the environment. "When" flexibility blurs the signal to investors, manufacturers and consumers to take action to reduce CO_2 since investors will never be sure when there will be a political commitment to reduce greenhouse gases. Who will ever move into the green technologies if the market is so vague? "When" flexibility also allows

greenhouse gas reduction burdens to be passed to future generations and infringes upon the principles of sustainable development. Borrowing allows emissions debts to be run up and never be repaid. It is an invitation for a political default by future non–environmentally friendly governments, and most of all, "when" flexibility will stop the development of "where" flexibility such as emissions trading. Which country will go to the market to buy emissions when it can push off carbon reduction obligations to future generations? How will a market ever form if budget periods are 10 years long and the only pressure to trade is at the end of the period? Banking is less problematic, as it encourages initial over-compliance and facilitates the use of short budget periods.

"Which" flexibility is ugly and awkward, particularly where sinks such as forests are concerned. Many other greenhouse gases inventories are known with much less certainty than CO_2, and this could weaken the whole regime—a chain is only as strong as its weakest link, and CO_2 emissions increases may be hidden behind bogus non-CO_2 reductions. Growing forests is qualitatively different [from] reducing CO_2 from fossil fuels. Carbon drawn into forests remains within the rapidly circulating carbon cycle and will quickly be returned to the atmosphere, whereas carbon released through fossil fuel burning is a net addition to this cycle from reservoirs laid down over geological time. Separate targets and/or policies and measures for each gas are a much better idea. Stopping deforestation is justified in its own right under the FCCC and Biodiversity Convention.

So flexibility is good, but only as long as it is forcing sound economic decisions and creating incentives for a greenhouse gas mitigating investment. If flexibility is encouraging delay, inaction, or statistical fudging, there is no room for it in the climate convention.[3]

Those people and companies that are interested in developing cost-effective solutions to excess carbon emissions, want to develop a carbon credit trading regime, want to start sooner instead of later to protect the planet, and are interested in regulatory integrity will support this thesis: starting sooner is better; smaller budget periods are better; and "where" flexibility (in promoting JI) is better.

Emissions reduction borrowing, delay, and long budget periods must be rejected. They serve no purpose other than to delay the day of reckoning. In America there is a saying: "You either pay now or pay later." The cost of delay in this case, however, could be the permanent handicapping of regulatory programs and the retardation of technological progress in carbon-controlling technologies.

NOTES

1. See F. Grant and J. Palmisano, "Discussion Paper I: Starting a Carbon Control Program in 2000 Makes Sense for Industry and the Environment," and "Discussion Paper II: Why Short Budget Periods Are Good for Industry and the Environment," Enron Europe, London, March 1997.

2. T. Davies, *Industry Incentives for Environmental Improvement: Evaluation of U.S. Federal Incentives* (Washington, DC: Resources for the Future, 1996).

3. C. Bates (1997, March 12), "Where Flexibility Is Good, When Flexibility Is Bad and Which Flexibility Is Ugly," *Climate Change Economics and a Joint Implementation Fortnightly Update*, 1997, no. 15: 1–2.

10

THE UNIQUE ROLE OF THE
U.S. FOREST PRODUCTS INDUSTRY
IN MITIGATING CLIMATE CHANGE

The Honorable W. Henson Moore

THE ISSUE OF GLOBAL CLIMATE CHANGE has significant implications for the world ecosystem, the world economy, and the continued international competitiveness of the U.S. forest products industry. The U.S. government is involved in United Nations negotiations pursuant to the Berlin Mandate for an amendment to the treaty on climate change signed at Rio. The Rio treaty committed the United States and other nations to voluntarily stabilize their carbon emissions at 1990 levels by the year 2000. Current negotiations are aimed at imposing mandatory (versus voluntary) reductions to below 1990 levels thereafter.

Under the Berlin Mandate only the United States and other developed countries will assume legally binding emissions reduction commitments. The developing countries have refused to take on mandatory commitments. As a result there will be no meaningful worldwide effort to stabilize atmospheric concentrations of carbon dioxide, and U.S. industry in general and the U.S. forest products industry in particular will be put at a severe competitive disadvantage. For this reason great caution and

---

W. Henson Moore is president and CEO of the American Forest and Paper Association.

careful consideration of the issues before the U.S. government and the international community are essential.

This chapter addresses the current uncertain state of the science on the effects of greenhouse gas emissions; the potential economic impacts of climate change policy on the U.S. forest products industry, with particular emphasis on the industry's global competitiveness; and the unique role of the U.S. forest products industry in relation to this issue.

THE UNCERTAINTIES OF CLIMATE SCIENCE

Despite years of debate scientists are still unsure of the effects, if any, that increased emissions of so-called greenhouse gases (primarily carbon dioxide) will have on the global climate. Although most experts concede that emissions of carbon dioxide have been increasing for several decades, the relationship of this phenomenon to global warming is considerably less than certain. Part of this uncertainty is attributable to the untested assumptions of climate change models. It is projected, for instance, that increases in carbon dioxide will yield only a one-degree increase in surface temperatures. To predict higher rates of warming, climate modelers must assume feedback mechanisms that amplify the warming effects of carbon dioxide. As an example, they assume that warming caused by carbon dioxide will increase evaporation rates and thus increase water vapor concentrations in the atmosphere. Like carbon dioxide, water vapor is a greenhouse gas that traps heat near the surface. High concentrations of water vapor also promote cloud formation, however, and the net result of increased cloudiness could be a net reduction in heat load, offsetting the warming effects of carbon dioxide.

In 1988 the United Nations established the Intergovernmental Panel on Climate Change (IPCC) to provide a "consensus" scientific perspective on global climate change and to provide scientific information to guide the decisions of policymakers. Although the second assessment report of the IPCC concluded that "the balance of evidence suggests a discernible human influence on global climate," the report also presents data that bring into sharp question whether carbon dioxide emissions in fact have any negative environmental effects.

In light of these uncertainties, prudence demands that, at a minimum, policymakers defer the imposition of mandates and timetables until a better understanding of the interaction between greenhouse gases and atmospheric temperature is achieved and more cost-effective technologies to address the phenomenon of global warming, if indeed it exists, are developed. The unique role of the forest products industry as a potential mitigator of increases in greenhouse gas emissions also must be recognized in all international agreements and in subsequent U.S. climate change policy.

This lack of consensus also suggests that the U.S. government should support those technological advances that have multiple purposes. For instance, there are emerging technologies (discussed in more detail later) that can reduce carbon dioxide emissions—should that objective prove important—but that also have the potential to accrue benefits to the country, as well as the forest products industry, in enhancing its global competitiveness. These potential benefits would result from the renewable resource base that is at the heart of the forest products industry. The new technologies have the potential to provide us with much higher energy efficiency and thereby offset the need for increased electrical power generation.

POTENTIAL IMPACTS OF U.S. CLIMATE CHANGE POLICY ON INDUSTRY COMPETITIVENESS

The U.S. forest products industry has many important assets: a productive workforce, an abundant and expanding domestic fiber base, modern plants and equipment, and cutting-edge technology. The costs of producing pulp, paper, and paperboard in the United States, for instance, have been kept in check as a result of high investment in new equipment, productivity improvements, new technologies, and gains in energy efficiency. Between 1989 and 1995 capital investment totaled $60 billion in the industry. As a result the U.S. pulp and paper industry is the world's largest producer and remains a strong, competitive industry with growth potential in both domestic and export markets.

Exports are an important component of the U.S. paper industry's success. As domestic sales increased at only a modest rate, U.S. producers expanded their sales efforts in foreign markets. In the past decade alone exports have increased at a 10.6 percent annual rate, compared to an overall increase in production of 2.7 percent. Most of this increase has come from higher exports to Canada, Mexico, the Far East, and South America. At the same time, however, the U.S. industry is subject to increasing competition for domestic and global market share. Traditionally Canada and the Nordic countries have presented the most significant competitive threat, by capitalizing on their readily available timber, inexpensive energy supplies (such as hydropower), and well-developed marketing networks.

In recent years, however, a number of developing countries with extensive forest resources (such as Brazil, Chile, Indonesia, Malaysia, and

Thailand) have decided that their forest products industries are strategic industries in which investment should be encouraged. Many of these governments provide incentives in the form of grants, tax breaks, higher tariffs, and the imposition of nontariff barriers. As a result there is a growing threat to the U.S. industry from developing countries in which pulp and paper companies enjoy government subsidies, cheap fiber, low-cost labor, and state-of-the-art manufacturing facilities.

Any contemplated actions that will further enhance the position of these competitors must therefore be seriously weighed and their likely impact on the U.S. industry thoughtfully measured. Based on a U.S. Department of Commerce study, to stabilize emissions at 1990 levels energy costs could increase by as much as $100 per ton of carbon emitted. This increase would cost the U.S. forest products industry $3 billion annually on fossil fuel–generated energy alone.

The impact of this additional cost must be viewed in light of the conclusions of a recent study by the U.S. Department of Energy (DOE). The DOE study showed that the delivered variable cost of pulp today from U.S. manufacturing facilities already can be as much as 30 percent higher than pulp from developing countries. If proposed treaty provisions are not imposed on developing countries as well as the developed nations, their competitive advantage could increase even further.

As noted previously, the U.S. forest products industry has succeeded in spite of competition from foreign firms that receive subsidies from their governments, have access to cheap fiber, and pay less to their workers. It would be wrong to conclude that the U.S. industry could survive the introduction of still another obstacle to maintaining its position in the global marketplace, especially one of the magnitude contemplated by the Berlin Mandate. Indeed, it is entirely likely that U.S. companies will seek cheaper energy, cheaper fiber, and cheaper labor by moving offshore to countries exempted from greenhouse gas emissions reduction requirements. The ironic result of this move, of course, is that there will be no net reduction in atmospheric greenhouse gas concentrations and perhaps even a net increase in the emissions that the Berlin Mandate seeks to reduce.

THE INDUSTRY'S UNIQUE ROLE IN MITIGATING CLIMATE CHANGE

It is clear that the uncertainties of the science and the potential for devastating economic impacts argue against precipitous or prescriptive action by the world community. What is less widely recognized, however, is that it is equally important for that community to recognize the important role the forest products industry plays in mitigating the impacts of greenhouse gas emissions. Recognition of this role must be included in all future discussions of the issue.

Carbon Stores

Forests play an integral role in the global carbon cycle. Through photosynthesis, trees absorb carbon dioxide from the air and then release oxygen. This carbon sequestration effect should be acknowledged in mitigation strategies to offset emissions. U.S. forests have a current standing inventory of sixty billion metric tons of forest-sequestered carbon.[1] (To put this into perspective, this represents forty years of total U.S. emissions at 1.5 billion metric tons per year.) The total carbon in forests increases by a net two hundred million metric tons annually.[2] Paper and solid wood products such as housing and furniture continue to store carbon for decades after harvest. The total carbon content stored in paper and solid wood products is approximately sixty-five million metric tons per year.[3]

This long-term carbon sink and the net benefit of carbon storage is currently unrecognized by the IPCC. The U.S. forest products industry believes that all international organizations and domestic agencies must accept the role of carbon sequestration by forests and long-term storage in wood products as an offsetting and mitigating factor when considering emissions from manufacturing facilities. The U.S. government should also ensure that other countries adopt reporting mechanisms sufficient to gather the data necessary to demonstrate these effects.

Biomass Fuels

Biomass fuels, consisting of forest industry and wood products manufacturing by-products, are renewable and sustainable energy sources that can substitute for fossil fuels. The forest products industry utilizes biomass fuels as a primary energy source in its manufacturing processes. Wood wastes (wood chips, bark, sawdust, and manufacturing scraps) and pulping liquors recovered from the manufacturing and harvesting processes are the dominant sources of biomass fuels.

Wood products manufacturing derives 74 percent of its energy requirements from biomass. The use of self-generated biomass fuels in pulp and paper manufacturing increased from 40 percent of the total in 1972 to 56 percent in 1995, while fossil fuel and purchased electricity consumption decreased by 42 percent per ton of production. In the same time period emissions from fossil fuels and purchased electricity decreased by 8 percent, while total pulp and paper production increased by 67 percent.[4] Because of the continuous growth, regeneration, and sustainability of U.S. forests and the importance of biomass energy to the U.S. forest products industry's continued vitality, biomass energy must continue to be treated as a net zero emitter of carbon dioxide.

Voluntary Industry Research

Much of the decrease in carbon dioxide emissions from the U.S. forest products industry is due to the voluntary application of new technologies that have been implemented over a long period of time (a span approximately equal to the industry's investment cycle, which is estimated to be between twenty and thirty years). Recently the industry, in cooperation with the DOE, launched a joint effort to ensure that this sort of technological evolution continues. In 1994 the industry developed its "Agenda 2020," a powerful vision for the future that articulated a far-reaching set of goals and identified which technology gaps need to be filled to attain those goals by the year 2020. Among the agenda's objectives is the development of mills that operate with greater energy efficiency and in increasing harmony with the environment. Another project of particular interest is an effort to increase the recycling and reuse of black liquor, a by-product of pulp manufacturing, as a replacement for fossil fuels. The potential for the development of innovative technologies such as this provides still another reason for the world community to refrain from hastily mandating less efficient, more expensive emission controls that will impede the continued economic growth of the U.S. forest products industry and cost Americans jobs.

CONCLUSION

For the U.S. forest products industry to maintain its leadership in the world market, U.S. policy with respect to global climate change must reflect the following basic principles:

- No commitments to mandatory emissions reductions targets or timetables should be made until more research is completed to resolve the ongoing scientific debate on the effects of greenhouse gas emissions.
- The United States must insist on the inclusion of developing countries before signing on to any international treaties.

- The role of carbon sequestration in forests and long-term carbon storage in wood products must be recognized as an offsetting and mitigating factor in setting emissions standards for manufacturing operations, and to that end the United States must ensure that other countries have sufficient mechanisms in place to record carbon sequestration and storage data.

- Biomass fuels must continue to be treated as net zero emitters of carbon dioxide.

- Precipitous action should be avoided to allow time for the development of cheaper, more efficient means of controlling greenhouse gas emissions.

NOTES

1. American Forests, *Forests & Global Change* (Washington, DC: American Forests, 1996).
2. U.S. Forest Service data.
3. American Forests, *Forests & Global Change*.
4. From a 1995 American Forest and Paper Association energy survey.

11

AN INSURANCE INDUSTRY
PERSPECTIVE ON CLIMATE CHANGE

Eugene L. Lecomte

IF THERE IS ONE THING that underwriters abhor, it is uncertainty. Therefore, in light of all the conflicting information, ongoing debate, and continued uncertainty regarding "global warming," it should not come as a surprise that insurers in the United States are reacting with caution before embracing any one position.

On the one hand, the Intergovernmental Panel on Climate Change (IPCC) of the United Nations contends that global warming is occurring and that the earth's inhabitants are having a "discernible" impact on the planet's climate. Those associated with the IPCC, including many European insurers and reinsurers, contend that "natural catastrophes are linked to global warming" and are "alarmed about the potentially devastating financial losses linked to a long list of environmental issues, ranging from climatic changes to risks of contaminated landfills."[1]

These concerns were also articulated in a position paper of the United Nations Environment Programme (UNEP) Insurance Industry Initiative:

> Based on the current status of climate research and on their experience as insurers and reinsurers, the member companies of the UNEP-Insurance Industry Initiative conclude that "human activity is already

---

Eugene L. Lecomte is president emeritus of the Insurance Institute for Property Loss Reduction.

affecting climate on a global scale" (e.g., through the enhanced greenhouse effect). According to the IPCC, "the balance of evidence suggests a discernible human influence on global climate." Man-made climate change will lead to shifts in atmospheric and oceanic circulation patterns. This will probably increase the likelihood of extreme weather events in certain areas. Such effects carry the risk of dramatically increased property damage, with serious implications for property insurers and reinsurers. Potentially, there could be large implications for investment activities as society plans for, and adapts to, the new climate regime.[2]

Again, it should be noted that most of the insurers and reinsurers who are signatories to the UNEP Insurance Industry Initiative are from Europe and Asia.

A leading proponent of scientific certainty concerning global warming is Dr. Jeremy Leggett, former director of Greenpeace International and now director of The Solar Century. Dr. Leggett strongly supports the contention that "scientific research since 1989 has shown, beyond reasonable doubt, that heat-trapping greenhouse gasses—mostly produced by coal-burning, oil and gas—are in the process of slowly overheating our planet, risking climatic extremes and, indeed, catastrophic destabilizations of the climate system."[3]

On the other hand, Dr. William M. Gray, an atmospheric scientist at Colorado State University, has repeatedly expressed opposition to the theory of global warming. Dr. Gray forecasts hurricane activity based on his analyses of El Niño, sea surface temperatures, and monsoon conditions in the Sahel.[4] Dr. Gray is supported in his opposition to the global warming theory by numerous earth scientists, including Dr. Robert F. Giegengack, professor of geology at the University of Pennsylvania. Dr. Giegengack contends that the global warming currently taking place is a cyclical event. He declares that "more and more, we are convinced that the variation in climatic change, that we observe from many different criteria, directly follows solar behavior with the following periodicities: a hundred thousand years, forty-one thousand years, twenty-three and eighteen thousand years, and a hundred and eleven years—based on the sun spot cycles."[5]

Adding to the uncertainty is a statement in the November 1995 Leipzig Declaration, signed by dozens of the world's top scientists, which declared, "There does not exist today a general scientific consensus about the importance of greenhouse warming from rising levels of carbon dioxide."[6]

It is against this backdrop of conflicting information, statements, and data that primary insurers in the United States have chosen to avoid, for the present, engaging in the debate regarding global warming. In arriving at this conclusion, insurers agree that they are a stakeholder in matters and issues associated with climate and climate change. Insurers opine that they must become more knowledgeable and inquisitive about climate issues. Further, they believe that underwriters must become knowledgeable of the atmospheric sciences so that they can effectively discharge their responsibilities, raise pertinent questions, recognize when loss attributable to climate is a certainty, and do these things without engaging in scientific aspects of the debate that they are ill-equipped to tackle.

It is appropriate to list some of the factors that influence the decision of primary insurers in the United States not to become aggressively proactive regarding climate change issues. In part, insurers' attitudes and actions are shaped by the following facts:

- There are some six thousand licensed insurance companies of all kinds (property-casualty, surety, health and accident, life, and so on) operating in the United States, which function independently and competitively. About four thousand of these are property-casualty insurers (monoline and multiline; single-state, regional, and national), and the remaining two thousand are life and health insurers.

- It is difficult if not impossible to gain consensus among these companies, particularly on matters relating to earth sciences and even more so when there is disagreement in the scientific community on these issues.

- Although there is growing scientific evidence to support global warming theories, there has been no scientific evidence that global warming will result in more frequent or severe weather-related events.

- Primary insurers are confronted with a myriad other issues, including earthquakes, Superfund claims, asbestosis, lead paint, wildfires, crime (thefts and burglaries), automobile losses, worker compensation, general liability claims, physical and cyber threats, the rising costs of medical care, and so on.

- Primary insurers are troubled by inadequate rates for and high cost of catastrophe reinsurance, a growing and aging population, expanding exposures, and the need to remain competitive.

- Insurers continue to face losses from weather-related causes and events (hurricanes, tornadoes, flooding, hailstorms, precipitation, and erosion), some of which are catastrophic.

The foregoing litany, while not complete, certainly demonstrates the full plate of issues confronting primary insurers. This in turn explains why insurers turn away from subjects that are beyond their direct control or area of expertise. The above itemization does not include issues associated with insurers' administration and support of residual market mechanisms or with the operation of guarantee funds. Neither does it reflect the burdens of the federal tax code, which prohibits reserving for unincurred events. State regulation, which imposes costly operational and coverage requirements on insurers, should also be considered. In view of all this, and in an era in which insurance is viewed as an "entitlement," insurers are not prone to voluntarily assume any uncertain obligations that would carry with them losses and additional costs.

At the outset I indicated that underwriters abhor uncertainty and seek to avoid it wherever possible and practical. They seek to avoid the uncertainties of climate, building codes and code enforcement, demographic shifts, sudden expansion of real and personal property values, land-use measures that permit people to be directly in harm's way, and the attitude "it won't happen to me."

Before discussing the Insurance Institute for Property Loss Reduction (IIPLR) and its strategic plan, I will set the stage with the following catastrophe loss review. In the quarter century preceding the period 1991 to 1995, U.S. property-casualty insurers had virtually escaped the wrath of catastrophic losses. From 1965 to 1990 catastrophic losses from all causes amounted to $31 billion, or an average of $1.2 billion per year. In the period 1991 to 1995 catastrophic losses only from weather-related causes were $37 billion, or an average of $9.25 billion per year. Losses from all causes were $51 billion, or an average $10 billion per year.[7]

During the interval (1965 to 1990) of relative freedom from severe wind catastrophes, insurers were lulled into a false sense of security and misread their rate level needs for long-term adequacy in the Southeastern Atlantic and Gulf Coast areas. In addition, insurers failed to recognize the magnitude of the demographic and exposure changes taking place in the Sunbelt region. For instance, the following 1996 data[8] demonstrate the extent of the demographic growth in Florida, California, and Texas. Florida's population density rose from 18 persons per square mile in 1920 to 180 persons per square mile in 1980 and 250 persons per square mile in 1994. That represents an increase of 1,333 percent, and a 43 percent increase between 1980 and 1994. In comparison, California's population density rose by 814 percent from 1920 to 1994. Texas's population rose by 289 percent over the same time period.

Insurers were not alone in failing to assess what was happening as a result of these demographic shifts, including exposure growths and code enforcement situations. Federal, state, and municipal emergency planners were also lethargic in the absence of catastrophic events. This began to change with the wake-up call from Hurricane Hugo, which struck Charleston, South Carolina, in 1989, and momentum grew when Hurricane Andrew ravaged Dade County, Florida, in 1992. The Great Flood of 1993 increased insurers' sensitivity to catastrophic loss, even though most flood insurance is provided by the federal government. The Loma Prieta earthquake of October 17, 1989, and the Northridge earthquake on January 14, 1994, further elevated insurer anxieties. The latter event proved to be a major financial drain, with insured losses exceeding $12.5 billion. Adding to insurer uneasiness have been Hurricane Opal (October 4, 1995) and Hurricane Fran (September 6, 1996); a number of severe snowstorms, hailstorms, tornadoes, and wildfires have left their imprint as well, to say nothing of the floods of 1997.

Data compiled for 1996 by Munich Reinsurance[9] disclose that the drumbeat of natural catastrophes and the accompanying financial drain continues. According to these data, in the United States there were 195 events (earthquakes, windstorms, floods, and so on), or 32 percent of the events worldwide that year. These caused 1,020 deaths, or 8.6 percent of the worldwide total, and resulted in $21.3 billion in economic losses, or 35 percent of economic losses worldwide. Of this amount, $7.5 billion was in insured losses, or 81 percent of the worldwide total of insured losses. This data graphically reveals why U.S. insurers have a stake in the solution to the problems under discussion.

IIPLR was conceived because insurers recognized the need to eliminate from the insurance system as many losses caused by earthquakes, severe windstorms (including hurricanes and tornadoes), hailstorms, floods, and wildfires as possible. IIPLR does its job by vigorously working in the following six areas: public outreach; community land use; construction of new buildings; retrofitting of existing structures; collection, analysis, and dissemination of information; and acquisition of resources.[10]

By working to reach out to the public, IIPLR ensures that all stakeholders (policymakers and decision makers, insurers, businesses, emergency planners, lenders, designers, builders, and the general public) are aware of natural hazards, understand the associated risks, know how to reduce those risks, and know how to take action to reduce the level of risk to which they are exposed. The major components of this program are public relations, education, and articulation of response and recovery issues.

By working on community land-use measures, IIPLR encourages responsible decisions about the density, type, and location of structures and creates incentives to reduce development in high-risk areas subject to natural hazards. By working for stronger building codes, IIPLR assists in ensuring that all new structures are designed, engineered, and constructed using up-to-date techniques and materials.

In its efforts to secure stronger structural building codes, IIPLR will, where practical, lend its support to all codes as a part of its ongoing efforts to construct lower-risk buildings. For instance, IIPLR recognizes that many energy-efficiency technologies (and, in turn, energy codes) have direct property loss reduction benefits (for example, attic insulation and ventilation can reduce ice-damming problems; wall and floor insulation can prevent frozen pipes; and double-glazed windows can reduce losses from fire, wind, and theft). IIPLR also believes that energy-efficiency requirements in building codes are cost-effective in their own right. That means that even if climate change does not prove to be as great a risk as some predict, homeowners and the economy will be better off with the improved codes.

Further, IIPLR believes that code, code enforcement, and land-use measures will, when coupled with an effective public education program, provide a safer future for all Americans while concurrently helping to ensure the availability and affordability of property insurance. By promoting the retrofitting of existing structures, IIPLR participates in the reduction of potential deaths, injuries, and property damage.

Finally, IIPLR recognizes the need for credible data to provide the cost justification for mitigation initiatives. Therefore IIPLR has undertaken the development of an insured "paid loss" database for catastrophic events, to be followed by a second phase that will begin to look at other items, such as specific damages to differing classes of structures and types of materials. IIPLR believes that ultimately this database will render valuable information and contribute to the reduction or elimination of losses.

The work of IIPLR will reduce deaths, injuries, economic loss, and property damage from catastrophic natural disasters. All the stakeholders need to work together, however, to identify and understand the myriad associated problems, to understand their impacts on us individually and collectively, and to work in harmony to bring about solutions. This type of commitment means that provincial and parochial attitudes must be set aside. The Kellogg School's Senior-Level Dialogue on Climate Change provided an excellent stepping-off point for the parties to build bridges of confidence and trust on which understandings can be formulated and future actions initiated. Together we can begin to reduce the uncertainties.

NOTES

1. K. Fossli, "Environment Conference: Insurers Turn Eco-Friendly," *Financial Times,* European edition, March 30, 1995, p. 3.
2. From the *UNEP Insurance Initiative Position Paper,* Geneva, July 9, 1996.
3. J. Leggett, *Climate Change and the Financial Sector: The Emerging Threat—The Solar Solution* (Munich: Gerling Akademie Verlag, 1996).
4. W. Stevens, "Storm Warning: Bigger Hurricanes and More of Them," *New York Times,* June 3, 1997: C10.
5. R. Giegengack, "The Global Warming Phenomena: Man-Made or a Natural Process?" in *Natural Disasters: Local and Global Perspectives* (Boston: National Committee on Property Insurance, 1993): 18.
6. F. Seitz, Letter to the editor, *Journal of Commerce,* May 5, 1997: 10A.
7. R. J. Roth, Sr., address to the annual meeting of the American Meteorological Society, February 6, 1997, Long Beach, California.
8. From a 1996 Florida legislative working group on property insurance markets.
9. Munich Reinsurance, "Annual Review of Natural Catastrophes," *Topics,* 1996.
10. Insurance Institute for Property Loss Reduction, "A Blueprint for Achievement," in *IIPLR Strategic Plan* (Boston: Insurance Institute for Property Loss Reduction, 1996).

12

FINDING NEW WAYS TO THINK ABOUT THE ENVIRONMENT AND ECONOMY

Magalen O. Bryant and Chandler Van Voorhis

EVERY NOW AND THEN an issue or event comes along that requires us to move from the logical and the conventional to a new way of thinking. The global climate change problem is that type of issue. We must look for new ways to solve a problem of grave importance. Finding common ground among governments, industries, and environmental organizations will require us to venture on to new frontiers. To do so we must be willing to admit the limitations of our conventional thinking.

One of the core challenges at the National Fish and Wildlife Foundation is to keep in tune with global changes. We do this by seeking and creating new alliances that break down communication barriers and leverage ideas by piecing together common interests. If we don't make waves now to solve these challenges, we may drown in their undercurrents later.

Magalen O. Bryant is chairperson of the board of the National Fish and Wildlife Foundation. Chandler Van Voorhis is CEO of GreenWave, a weekly radio talk show dedicated to those businesses, organizations, and individuals dedicated to solving our world's environmental problems.

The global marketplace is remapping the world's boundaries, yet we insist on operating within the old lines. This is how we are approaching the issue of global climate change. It is accepted that the optimum goal of global climate change policy is to achieve worldwide carbon dioxide emissions reductions. Such policy should ensure the safety of the world population, with limited economic repercussions, and be achieved by agreement of all participating nations.

But how are we to draft and approve a legally binding global instrument when we do not have the proper global structure to do so? How are we to seek a world of interdependence when we have yet to accomplish worldwide independence? How are we to achieve a level economic playing field when the political field is fraught with infighting, with ideological and religious differences? We must revert to thinking like a beginner, shaking away the layers of traditional knowledge that ensnare our every move.

NEW WAYS OF THINKING ABOUT ENVIRONMENTAL PROBLEMS

One of the core problems behind the global climate change issue is that we are continuing to follow the very steps that got us to this point. We see a solution through binding legal agreements among nations. Nations will agree to a series of set goals and caps that will apply to all industries. These goals and caps will be uniformly set and undiscriminating in nature. To achieve an effective agreement requires total participation, which means that political ideology and religious differences must be set aside. In other words, the political playing field must be made level; and that is a difficult aspiration, at best.

But shouldn't the object really be to level the economic playing field, in this global economy? If this is so, then why are negotiations proceeding strictly among political entities? For instance, why don't we gather all the members of the global automotive industry together and let them seek agreement on carbon dioxide emissions caps that would apply equally throughout their industry? This would help to alleviate businesses' fears that their competitors will gain an economic advantage as a result of global climate change policies. The United Nations could sanction admittance to the global marketplace for companies that enter into industry-wide agreements it approves. For those that choose not to enter into such agreements, admittance to the international marketplace would be denied.

Think about it: if we act through nations, then each member of each industry must be assured that their competitors' governments are entering into the agreement also; otherwise they will be at a competitive disadvantage. But if, for example, carbon dioxide emissions caps for the auto industry were to be set by the industry itself, using its own scientists and economists, it would allow the industry to find the optimum caps that would achieve real results with minimum economic repercussions and built-in incentives. The caps would be unique to the industry. But more important, this process would empower industry members to reach a consensus that would level the industry's playing field, allowing no competitive imbalances, while making significant strides toward alleviating the climate change problem through emissions reductions and technological innovations.

This approach could be used for every industry. However, it might prove both prudent and more momentous to start with the automotive industry, considering that 40 percent of carbon emissions come from automobiles. To tackle the global climate change problem we must take a fresh approach bound only by our imagination. Over the past twenty-five years of the environmental movement we have learned a lot. But the most important lesson has been the realization that the world's resources are limited. For industry this realization has added an important variable to the business equation.

NEW WAYS OF THINKING ABOUT ECONOMIC PERFORMANCE

It has been this realization that has forced businesses to look at pollution in a whole new light. No longer can businesses afford to waste raw materials: that would mean putting the company in jeopardy in the future. To the businessperson, pollution means inefficiency in the product, which equals an economic loss. The price of pollution is typically buried somewhere within the life cycle of the product, and the consumer usually pays for it, directly or indirectly. So one way for a company to gain a competitive advantage is to make the process by which its product is produced more efficient. Another way is to reinvent the product. This has been done by developing closed-looped systems where pollution or waste is recaptured, broken down into its original components, and reused. This enables the business to both lower its pollution output and reduce its materials costs. The bottom line is that pollution hurts a company's ability to be competitive in the global marketplace. Not only can pollution have a negative effect on a company's bottom line, it can also directly affect the value of its stock.

Recently ICF Kaiser conducted a study analyzing whether improving a company's environmental management systems and environmental performance would yield a higher stock price. The study gathered data from three hundred of the largest U.S. companies and found that those that had an environmental management system in place and sought to improve their environmental performance enjoyed 5 percent higher stock prices. Why? For one thing, companies that effectively lower their risk of an environmental mishap lower their potential liability, which makes investing in them more attractive. Also, if companies raise their product yield (which is to say, if they lower the waste they produce), they are operating leaner, which reflects favorably to the outside investor and states that they are looking for an opportunity at every turn.

In another study Duke University's Professor Doug Lober compared unscreened stock portfolios with environmentally screened portfolios. He found that the environmentally screened portfolios outperformed the unscreened ones by about 3 percent over a three-year period, 5 percent over a five-year period, and 1.7 percent over a ten-year period. This shows the importance of the environment in our economic system. Acting on this premise, Winslow Management and their Green Century Balance Fund screens companies on the basis of their financing and environmental record. This screen includes information on water pollution, the number of brown fields, and so on. The results are calculated into a score to determine if the companies are worthwhile investments.

But more than that, there is a promising new generation of businesses on the horizon that will help usher in a new way of doing business, and this will ultimately lower the level of carbon dioxide emissions. Some of these businesses are information-based. Others are solution-oriented businesses, like Thermo-Fibergen, which takes the sludge from paper mills and recycles 15 percent of it back into long-grain fibers. The remaining 85 percent is made into a variety of other products.

What all of this means is that processes are becoming more and more efficient and products are being reinvented. We need to use global climate change as a springboard issue for further innovation, not restraining regulation that mirrors how we do things in our own countries. We need to seize the opportunity to be different and to set sail in a new direction.

Regulations and binding agreements resemble a partially engaged parking brake on a car rather than a guiding force or helping hand. A car with its parking brake partially engaged risks burning out its engine, and that can be the most expensive in the long run. Conversely, if regulation or binding agreements are constructed in such a way as to spur and channel innovation, then a win-win situation prevails and the zero-sum model can be thrown aside.

NEW WAYS TO MEASURE NATURAL CAPITAL AND ECONOMIC GROWTH

The approach we take to mitigating global climate change will directly affect the success of our efforts. One emerging trend is to place value on our natural systems. Recently a group of scientists valued our global natural systems at $33 trillion, a number that is hard to fathom. And this is still far below the intrinsic value of our natural systems in a world that has yet to perceive scarcity. Imagine the value when and if it does. One example of how to value natural systems involves New York City and its investment in its watershed. To protect its water supply in the Catskills the city invested around $1.5 billion in watershed protection, thereby saving the city from having to build a water filtration facility at a capital cost of $6 to $8 billion and with $300 million in annual operating costs.

There is a valuable lesson here. Each country, each entity, each business can do something about the global climate change problem by building carbon sinks. A grassroots approach is just one of a few ways to effectively accomplish this. It is a cost-effective approach to stabilizing the situation. The National Fish and Wildlife Foundation is working on a carbon sequestration program in Costa Rica, helping to purchase 4,800 acres of lowland rain forest in the Esquinas Forest National Park. Many companies are already buying forests with added value beyond carbon sequestration—such as sustainable timber production, biomining, and ecotourism, which is predicted to surpass oil and gas in revenue by the year 2000.

On a deeper level, changing the way we measure economic growth could help free us to initiate more concerted actions to protect the global climate. In the United States the gross domestic product (GDP) is our standard measure of economic growth. Whenever money changes hands, GDP goes up. There is no mechanism for accounting for positive versus negative inputs. For example, pollution is counted at least three separate times in figuring our GDP: once when it occurs, again when it is cleaned up, and yet again in increased health costs.

How good are our economic indicators when pollution of our air and water is counted toward positive economic growth? Our system of measuring economic growth is not bound or grounded to progress or quality of life but rather to the number of times currency moves among us.

It is time to adopt a new way of counting economic prosperity that is linked to social progress and the environment.

New economic indicators must be grounded on the relationship between our natural and economic systems. Our economy and our environment are not in an "either-or" relationship. Each draws its essential energy from the other. As John Muir once said, "when we try to pick out anything by itself, we find it hitched to everything else in the universe."[1] To find the common ground among industry, governments, and environmentalists, we must venture into uncommon territory and see the hidden connections among them.

NOTE

1. G. Davidson and C. McLaughlin, *Spiritual Politics* (New York: Ballantine, 1994): 77.

A SENIOR-LEVEL DIALOGUE ON CLIMATE CHANGE

13

DIALOGUE

Economic Implications of Climate Change Policy

DONALD JACOBS, DEAN, J. L. KELLOGG GRADUATE SCHOOL OF MAN-
AGEMENT: It is a great pleasure to welcome you here today. The students have been very excited that the school is hosting this dialogue
among so distinguished a group of people. And I must tell you that, as
an observer of the scene, Kellogg is proud to assume the role of facilitating this discussion. We have long been developing a specialization in
alternative dispute resolution issues, and I believe that this specialization, coupled with our strong interest in the environment, makes this
an ideal place to conduct such discourse. Finding efficient solutions to
complex problems like climate change necessitates bringing together
people from various sides of each of the issues. So we are looking forward with a great deal of anticipation to today, and we hope that this is
only one of a number of such dialogues that we can host at the Allen
Center and at Kellogg. Thank you for joining us.

ANDREW HOFFMAN, PROFESSOR, J. L. KELLOGG GRADUATE SCHOOL
OF MANAGEMENT: The topic for today is climate change. Few environmental issues have raised such passionate response from industry, environmentalists, and government. And from what we've seen so far there
has been a wild contest between differing views on the science, supported by differing scientists and backed by differing interest groups,
such as environmental and industry associations. Generally these interest groups have adopted intractable and polarized positions on the issue, which leads to a mounting stalemate on meaningful exchange. To

counter this hardening of positions, we at the Kellogg Environment Research Center saw a need for a forum for rational dialogue in order to inject industry into the debate in a more productive fashion. Furthermore, we saw an opportunity to provide the neutral forum for that dialogue to take place. By your presence here today I'll take that as an endorsement that we were correct in our assumption. The dialogue today is to focus on economics. We want to steer clear of a debate over the science. We don't want to talk about what this scientist said versus what that scientist said. We want to focus instead on the economics of a potential climate change treaty and the implications of that treaty for your company, your industry, and the economy. We want to try to focus on the positives. We want to talk about what people in this room can do to foster better climate change policy, rather than discussing how people in this room are going to react to what that policy may do to them. As an outcome of this dialogue we hope that we can develop insights relative to potential policy options, consider what some of the obstacles may be to making those policies, and explore ways that we can work unilaterally and collaboratively to develop better climate change policy. We will start with some opening comments from Mr. Wirth.[1] He has agreed to discuss the U.S. position going into Kyoto, his thoughts on strategy, where there is flexibility, and how those in this room may help to better inform his negotiating position.

The Scientific Debate Is Over:
Now the International Community Must Respond

The Honorable Timothy E. Wirth,
Undersecretary of State for Global Affairs

Thank you very much. I'm delighted to be here and to meet with such a distinguished group of people.

I want to spend my fifteen minutes talking about two groups of three. First, there are the three scientific lessons that are fundamental to how we approach the issue of climate change. And second, there are the three rings of the negotiation process that is leading up to the international conference in Kyoto this December. I'll run through these two triads very quickly, since we have a short period of time. There's a huge amount of material, and I'm assuming a lot of knowledge; but I hope that my comments will help you to think through what is obviously a very complex issue.

The first of the three scientific lessons is that the debate about the existence of climate change is over; there is now a broad scientific consensus that we humans are having a major impact on our planet's climate. The second lesson is that the causes and effects of climate change are global—and that any solution must be international as well. And the third is that the only way to halt the process of climate change is to stabilize the concentrations of greenhouse gases in the atmosphere—so that stabilizing concentrations has to be our long-term goal.

Our negotiation is also being played out in three rings—like a circus. One ring of the negotiations is targets and timetables—the specific limitations over a relatively short-term period of time. The second ring is the instruments that we have to negotiate to implement those targets and timetables; and the third is the commitments that we are asking from the developing world.

I want to start with the science—because scientists were the ones who drew our attention to climate change in the first place, and because we continue to base our policies on the best evidence and the most rigorous scientific analysis available. The International Panel on Climate Change report, to which Andy referred, told us that the scientific debate is essentially over as to whether or not it's going to get warmer—with "getting warmer" being a shorthand for major changes in the climate. There is still a lot of uncertainty about where, how much, and how fast these changes will occur; there's a lot of research now being done on those specifics. But just about every legitimate climate scientist in the world has said that the climate is changing and we have to do something about it. The overwhelming—our overwhelming—sense of the evidence is that we have to move.

Think about this in Cold War terms. We did not know exactly where, with what kind of weaponry, or when the Soviets might attack Western Europe. We did not know exactly where, how much, how fast. But we did think that the threat was significant enough that we began to take out an insurance policy and build our defenses. This is not a bad metaphor for thinking about climate change. We believe that the threat is significant enough that it's time to take out an insurance policy. We don't know exactly where, how much, how fast—but it is time to move.

That leads to the second scientific lesson I mentioned, which is that the threat of climate change is global, involving just about every sector of every economy on earth. It's all one atmosphere, whether it's polluted by American utilities, German steel plants, or Korean traffic jams. That means the negotiations to slow climate change are of extraordinary complexity—domestically as well as internationally. For those negotiations to be successful, we have to put together a package that can go through the following hoops.

Within the administration there are different agencies with different equities; there are different individuals with different histories; there are different political agendas. The administration does not always speak with one voice—usually, but not always. And that's the first negotiation we have to do.

The second is a negotiation on Capitol Hill. I would not say that most members of Congress are disposed to thinking constructively about climate change—either for ideological reasons or because of other agendas. There are a few heroes up there. There are probably 130 votes in the House. There are probably 30 votes in the Senate at this point for what we might end up with. The rest of it is going to be an uphill battle.

The third part of this negotiation is across the country, with all of the veto powers that exist as well as with the constituencies that are coming to understand how severe and major this issue is. Everyone is weighing in from their own perspective, and they each have their own view as to what ought to be done. You can think about this process over the last six months and the next six months as being the longest continuing congressional hearing that you can possibly imagine.

These first three parts of the negotiation are domestic; and there's the fourth, which is international. We're dealing with about 185 countries—including the largest economies in the world. If we were to look at our best buddies in this, they are probably the Japanese. There are differences between them and us, but they will host the multinational conference in December. With Japan in the chair we're going to work out a negotiation that will bring in the key elements in the developed world—the European Union, the Canadians, and the Australians, as well as ourselves and Japan. We also need to include the countries in transition, particularly Russia, who have a very different history. Then there are the developing countries, who are all over the block, with different kinds of perspectives. So the complexity of this negotiation is extraordinary.

By way of comparison, consider the case of the SALT and START negotiations, which were themselves notorious for their complexity. In those arms control talks there were only two countries negotiating. Each side knew what the other had, and they knew what the implications of that might be; it was a relatively certain universe. And they were negotiating in secret. They used press releases to let the world know what the high priests of arms control were saying behind those closed doors. But with climate change you have a negotiation not of 2 countries but of 185. It is being done in public. The players change all the time, because governments change, and these are political actors that are doing this. And we're surrounded by an enormous amount of veto power. Many people have a significant stake in not doing anything. So we shouldn't underestimate the complexity and difficulty of these negotiations.

As we proceed through these negotiations, we need to stay focused on the ultimate goal, which is stabilizing the concentration of carbon in the atmosphere. In contrast, all of the discussions since Rio were merely aimed at setting targets and timetables for emissions. The Rio guideline was to have a target to stabilize our emissions at 1990 levels by the year 2000. And the debate now—where all the newsletters are and all of the environmentalists are pushing and so on—is what we are going to do by 2005 or what we are going to do by 2010? Are we going to stabilize emissions, or have plus 2 percent or minus 5 percent or whatever? These discussions are important in that they signal forward momentum, but if we were to take even the best of what the most aggressive environmental group wants to do, we would not solve the problem. To solve it we need to focus on concentrations.

The way to think about this is to imagine the atmosphere as a swimming pool. We are pouring more and more water into that swimming pool; we're pouring more and more carbon into the atmosphere. The swimming pool can only hold so much water. You can debate about what level that is, but we know that there is an ultimate ceiling to the amount before it starts to overflow. The pipeline that's putting water into that swimming pool is getting bigger and bigger and bigger. We're increasing, the EU is increasing, the Japanese are increasing, and the developing world is increasing. Even if we stabilize emissions, which is the first goal, we're still putting an enormous amount of water into that swimming pool. We're probably going to go past the doubling of concentrations of carbon in the atmosphere at very high speed. Most of the scientific impact work that's been done predicts enormous problems will occur as a result of that doubling. And without aggressive action, we're going to get to tripling and some believe we could even get to quadrupling. We have to understand that the solution to this problem isn't the stabilization of emissions, it's changing the way we fuel the world's economy, in order to stabilize the concentration of carbon in the atmosphere. That is the only way we're going to solve this problem. In thinking about this issue, it's easy to get drawn off at high speeds into targets and timetables right away; but the long-term issue is concentrations.

So the starting points for our negotiating strategy are as follows: first, we believe we have to move, the debate on the science is over; second, we know how complex this negotiation is, but we have to work our way forward in a way that's going to be feasible and reasonable for us in the United States of America; and third, we have to develop momentum that's going to move us toward the focus on concentrations.

There are three major elements in this negotiation. One is the short-term goal—what we are going to do about targets and timetables in the short term to show momentum and to show progress toward dealing with concentrations long-term? Concentrations are an issue that we really will be working on in 2030 or 2040 or something like that, but we have to begin now, and the next steps are targets and timetables, or what we call the emissions budget.

The second ring of the negotiating circus is to develop the instruments that can make these targets and timetables feasible. We have rejected the idea of having uniform international measures that would mean everybody has the same tax or everybody has the same conservation program. We have to maintain the flexibility to implement targets and timetables in our own fashion, in accordance with the needs of our own economy.

We believe the most promising tools for flexible implementation are joint implementation and emissions trading. Joint implementation simply means that we want to have the opportunity to work with other countries, whether they are developed countries or eventually developing countries. If it costs $100 to eliminate a ton of carbon in the United States but you can eliminate a ton of carbon in China for $5, then we want to be able to work with the Chinese. It doesn't make any difference where the ton of carbon comes from. If you burn a ton of coal to stay warm in Shanghai, we all get warm together. So joint implementation is a critical element in what we want out of this negotiation.

We also want to move toward a trading regime. We've learned from the Clean Air Act that it is imperative to have the capacity to trade. We want to move toward the economic flexibility that such an instrument would provide. We know we're not going to get universal trading right away, because it requires an overall global cap on emissions—a step which is not likely to be successfully negotiated anytime soon. So we've focused on a cap for developed countries first, making allocations and allowing trade within that cap. Newly developed countries, such as Mexico and Korea, would be able to trade as soon as they placed themselves under the cap as well.

The third ring of the negotiations is to include the developing world. We grant that the developed world fouled the nest and that we have the first responsibilities as a result. We're the people that have put the carbon up there—the United States is the largest carbon emitter in the world. So it is predominantly our responsibility that the world's temperature is now changing. But if you look out to, say, 2010 or 2020, the Chinese pass us as the number-one emitter. They're growing very, very rapidly. So we have to figure out a way to sequence in the developing countries. We need a maturing instrument that encompasses our responsibilities in the short and medium term while engaging the developing world along the way, so that by the time we get to 2030 or 2035 we're all in this together.

So those are the three imperatives or the three rings in which negotiations are being carried out—the budget issue, the instruments issue, and the imperative of the developing world.

Before my time is up, let me give you a final note about the magnitude of the problem. Over the next twenty-five years, China and India together are projected to build one thousand power plants, each of which will have a five-hundred-megawatt capacity. A five-hundred-megawatt power plant is huge. A thousand of these adds up to 50 percent of the currently installed power generation capacity in North America. So what's going to happen over the next twenty-five years in China and India is extraordinarily important. What kind of power plants are they going to build? Traditional plants that burn dirty brown coal? Or plants that use natural gas, which is much cleaner? Are they going to be moving to the question of nuclear, which ultimately is the kind of devil's bargain that has to be examined honestly?

There are those that say, glibly, that solar is the answer. Solar may indeed be the answer in the long term, but let's think about where we are today. The total installed capacity of solar today is less than one hundred megawatts in the world. That is one-fifth of one of the thousand power plants I just mentioned. That is a tiny amount. Amory [Lovins] knows a lot more about these numbers than I do, but solar costs about four times as much to install, in terms of a central power operation, as a conventional coal-powered plant. How are we going to move down that cost curve rapidly while dramatically increasing our capacity to use solar? We have to think seriously about this issue—because once you understand that the question is concentrations, then you understand that we will eventually have to change the way in which we fuel our economy.

ANDREW HOFFMAN: If there are any questions that could be directed specifically to Mr. Wirth, we'll take them now.

ALLEN KOLEFF, VICE PRESIDENT, STONE CONTAINER CORPORATION: Undersecretary Wirth, when does the administration plan to release its emissions targets and timetables?

TIMOTHY WIRTH: When we're ready. Probably sometime this summer. We have had extensive discussions of the models. We're now trying to make sure that what we come up with is feasible and that we understand the economic impacts. I suspect that the analysis will be released sometime this summer.

DIRK FORRISTER, CHAIRMAN, WHITE HOUSE CLIMATE CHANGE TASK FORCE: Many people focus, as you do in your question, on targets and timetables, or at least on hearing something directional right now. But what really matters is that our negotiators led by Senator Wirth get us the right number in the end. We've got to think tactically about this. Is it to our advantage to actually put one out that we think we can hold all the way until December? You who do business deals don't necessarily start with your bottom line this early in a negotiation. So we have to think through what is in our strategic advantage in the negotiation so that we can end up with the numbers that we would like. But it's true that this summer we should be coming out with analytical information that spans the range under consideration.

TIMOTHY WIRTH: That's a long way of saying when he's ready. [laughter] We live in a democratic society, and you want to be as open and transparent as you possibly can; but you don't want to say this is our bottom line right now and this is where we're going to go. It's not a neat negotiation.

ALLEN KOLEFF: I would like to add that as we move toward December the issue of openness and the opportunity for common review is a rather serious one that the administration needs to consider strongly.

TIMOTHY WIRTH: Over the last year we've had a whole series of seminars. We've met with every industry group that has requested to do so. We discussed where we were with the models before we went to Geneva in July 1996. We've had meetings all winter on the models. I've been in government a long enough period of time to know that people will try to trip you up on procedural grounds and make procedure the issue, to replace a discussion of the substance. We're very aware of that, and we're doing everything we can to avoid that kind of procedural political jujitsu.

RICHARD ABDOO, PRESIDENT, WISCONSIN ENERGY COMPANY: A lot of us agree with what you're doing, but I feel for you because you've got a real credibility problem. The U.S. is the biggest CO_2 emitter, and we say we ought to do something about it. Yet the largest landlord in the world doesn't practice much energy conservation in its buildings. The largest fleet owner in the world doesn't practice much energy conservation with its fleets. The Defense Department is one of the largest violators of EPA regulations. And you say you've got budget problems. Well, I think every industry in this room could say we've got to balance our budget too. And if the government was willing to take a position that said we're willing to practice what we preach, I bet you'd have a heck of a lot better time, not just with people in the international community that you've got to negotiate with but with industry and commerce back here in the U.S. It seems we talk about crisis proportions in this issue, and yet nuclear is not an option because there have been some problems with it. But in the end I think there is a lot of credibility in the U.S.'s position, and I for one would like to demonstrate Wisconsin Electric's support for keeping joint implementation in the U.S. proposal. Can you address that?

TIMOTHY WIRTH: Sure. You're right. It's not smooth sailing. As you know, there are a number of things that we wanted to do when this administration came in with retrofitting—with some very significant incentive programs to move us in the right direction. But these programs require implementing legislation and funding from Congress, which has not been forthcoming.

So, given that, we're trying to move in a different direction. Secretary Perry started to change what DOD is doing and made some progress. DOD is an enormous institution, but it is changing. In many cases I would rather sit and deal with a group of mid-level and upper-level DOD managers than almost anyone else they've got. "Yes sir!": they get their marching orders, and they head off in the right direction.

At State, it's very hard. We have eleven thousand buildings around the world. There's only one that has been retrofitted, and that's the main State building—and even that was a hassle. We've just gotten State to agree to the performance contracting that was in the 1992 energy bill. We're now going to have performance contracts and be able to work on this. We're trying to reach out and make those kinds of changes so that not only can we demonstrate our goodwill, but maybe these hubs around the world could be platforms for U.S. industry. Our automobile purchases at State are now changing. We have not by any means been the perfect manager. These bureaucracies are slow. We haven't had the funds, or there hasn't been as much commitment as there should; but you know we're pushing it.

AMORY LOVINS, DIRECTOR OF RESEARCH, ROCKY MOUNTAIN INSTI-TUTE: In fact, on that point, having just helped the Navy overhaul how it designs its buildings—and it does $6 or $7 billion worth of construction a year—I have to agree with Tim. It was a real lesson for me in the difference between leadership and management. Those folks are terrific.

ANDREW HOFFMAN: I think it is time to bring the rest of those in the room into the center of this discussion. In this first of two sessions, we will focus on the economic implications of climate change policy and how that policy might be developed with the most environmental benefit and at the least economic cost. We will start with presentations in the order in the agenda: Mr. Percy, Mr. Stone, and Mr. Lovins. Then we will open up to a general dialogue, which I am sure will continue to engage Mr. Wirth and Mr. Forrister.

A Call for Action

Steven W. Percy, Chairman, CEO, and CFO, BP America, Inc.

I am going to talk about the implications of global climate change policy, and I want to focus mainly on its strategic and economic implications for the oil industry in general and British Petroleum in particular. To start I'd like to tell you what we at BP believe in order to set the context for my remarks. We acknowledge two facts: first, CO_2 concentrations are rising; second, world temperatures are rising. We feel that the body of scientific opinion now weighs in favor of a connection between the two. While there's still a lot of uncertainty around the timing and consequences of that connection, we can no longer discount the possibility of that connection or of serious consequences. So we, as a company, believe that it is time for action and action on our part.

Having said that, let's just think about a couple of broad strategic issues before we get into some specifics. We feel that this is a long-term and a very complex issue. It is going to take decades to find and implement solutions. It is global. It affects developed countries and developing countries alike. Policymaking is going to take place within a framework

of great uncertainty. And there is tremendous possibility for both un-
derreaction and overreaction. So we have to be very careful about how
we move forward. And in this regard, economic implications are important. We believe that economic growth is a key to the sustainability
of not only the climate but also the planet.

So in order to shape some issues about economic implications, I have
a simple illustration [see Figure 13.1]. This is based on some modeling
work performed by Battelle Northwest Labs. It is just an illustration showing the relative global costs of stabilizing CO_2 concentrations under four
different scenarios. The first scenario assumes no flexibility in either
the timing or the location of emission reductions. The second assumes
flexibility in where emissions reductions take place. The third assumes flexibility in when emissions reductions take place. And the last assumes flexibility in both where and when these reductions take place. As I said, it's
only an illustration, but I think it clearly supports the case that flexible approaches within fixed outcomes will yield the least expensive solutions to
CO_2 emissions. So that's one set of economic implications that should be
addressed as we move forward on climate policy.

Now I'd like to talk about the impact and role of the oil industry. Of
the world's CO_2 emissions, only a small fraction actually come from

Figure 13.1. Global Costs Under Four Alternative Cases.

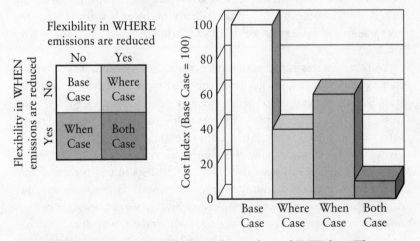

Source: R. Richels, J. A. Edmonds, H. Gruenspecht, and T. Wigley, "The
Berlin Mandate: The Design of Cost-Effective Mitigation Strategies," in
N. Nakicenovic, W. D. Nordhaus, R. Richels, and F. L. Toth (eds.), *Climate
Change: Integrating Science, Economics and Policy.* CP-96-1. (Laxenburg,
Austria: International Institute for Applied Systems Analysis, 1996): 29–48.

human activity. However, this fraction is very important, for two reasons. One, it is the fraction that could tip the equilibrium. Two, it is the fraction we can control. So we are starting with the baseline assumption that human-created CO_2 emissions are a small bit of the overall amount, but the one that we need to act upon. Of the emissions created by humans, roughly 43 percent come from petroleum. And of that 43 percent, one-half come from the use of oil in transportation. So oil in its use must be part of the solution. But it cannot be the only part of the solution. I have these two charts to support this argument, once again produced by some modeling work at Battelle [see Figure 13.2].

This chart depicts several CO_2 scenarios, with emissions on one side and concentrations on the other. The case that's shown by the little dots on the line is a case that extends 1990 technology and its use into the future. You can see emissions and concentrations growing rapidly in that particular case. The second case, the line in the middle, demonstrates the extrapolation of current trends in technology and use. Since we know that our technology actually does improve, this shows that technological development moderates the rate of growth in both emissions and concentrations, but they continue to grow. Finally, the last case shows a shift that takes place in both technological development and its pattern of use necessary to stabilize CO_2 concentrations. This points back to the point that Mr. Wirth made about concentrations being the key issue. I'm not supporting or attacking any of these cases; they are here for illustration. But if you look at the next chart [see Figure 13.3], I am going to talk a bit about how we might contribute towards shifting from the gray line to the darker black line, of stabilizing those concentrations over a period of time.

You can see this is just some speculation about different types of activity which can help us get from the growing concentration levels to stabilized concentrations. There's a couple of conclusions we draw from this work. First, there's a lot of effort that's going to be required to get into that stabilized concentration mode and maintain the economic growth which is underlying these particular scenarios. Second, fossil fuels will continue to play a very important role in our future, a vital role if we're going to maintain economic growth. Other solutions may deflect that role—the black area shows how trees can soak up carbon out of the atmosphere—but the gray shaded area underneath that darker line is fossil fuel–based emissions that are gong to continue for some period of time. We don't know which scenario we will eventually end up with, but there's one picture you might want to look at. So in regards to the oil industry, I am making the point that climate solutions

Figure 13.2. Global CO$_2$ Emissions and Concentrations.

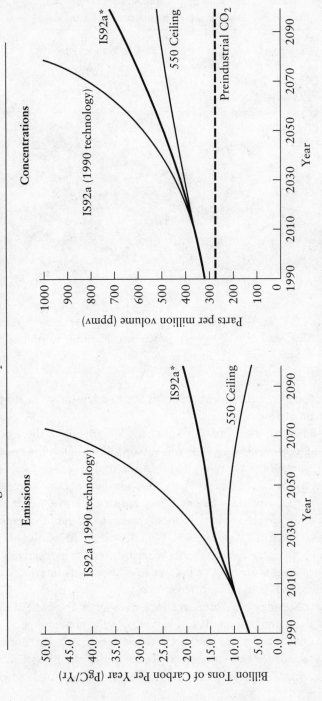

*IS92a is an IPCC scenario documented in Climate Change 1992. It is the middle of six scenarios.
Source: J. A. Edmonds, "Toward a Technology Strategy," unpublished manuscript, Battelle, Pacific Northwest Laboratories, Washington, DC, 1997.

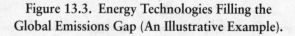

Figure 13.3. Energy Technologies Filling the Global Emissions Gap (An Illustrative Example).

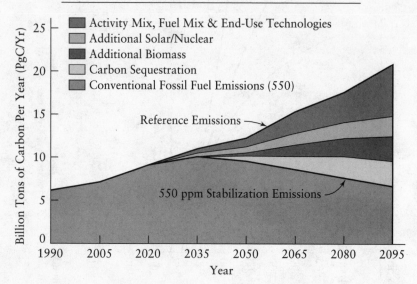

Source: J. A. Edmonds and R. Richels, *A Global Energy Technology Strategy to Address Climate Change* (Washington, DC: Battelle, Pacific Northwest Laboratories, August 1997).

are not necessarily in substitution of oil but in *addition* to the oil that we're consuming today.

Now I'd like to talk a little bit about BP. We are one of the world's largest producers of oil and gas. If you add up all the CO_2 emissions that we make through our operations and then add to that the emissions that are created by the use of our products, we contribute about 1 percent of the CO_2 being produced by humans. So you can say we're too small to solve this issue ourselves, but that doesn't mean we shouldn't be taking some positive actions on our own. We know that the public is concerned, and we share that concern. We want to be constructively involved in what we are calling "a journey to a sustainable future." We've committed ourselves to this journey.

This past Monday our chief executive gave an address at Stanford University that laid out a number of steps that we're taking to begin our contribution to that future. The first is work on conservation, not only for ourselves but for our customers. We're joining the EPA's Climate Wise program. We're going to measure, target, and control our own emissions, and we're going to encourage our customers to conserve energy. Second, we are going to concentrate our effort and resources on new energy technologies. We are soon to be the largest producer of photovoltaics as a company. We're going to emphasize our solar business and try to grow its revenues from $100 million a year to $1 billion a year over the next decade. We're also joining with Battelle, EPRI [Electric Power Research Institute], and the Department of Energy to study future technology strategies. Third, we're becoming actively involved in a joint implementation project with the Nature Conservancy and AEP in Bolivia to protect and reforest four million acres of forest. Our idea really is to learn from this experience and to translate that learning into other places where we're doing business, such as Columbia and Venezuela. Finally, we want to become actively involved in the dialogue leading to the international processes which will carry us forward. We're working with the Environmental Defense Fund and the World Resources Institute on projects regarding the trading of emissions credits, permitting, and so forth. So there's a lot we're doing in the near term. We'll be announcing more over the course of the next year.

A Call for Restraint

Roger W. Stone, Chairman and CEO,
Stone Container Corporation

I am delighted to be on this panel today, representing not only our forty thousand employees but the seven hundred thousand employees that work in the U.S. forest products industry. Frankly, I can think of no other industry that is more qualified to speak on this issue or certainly one that has more at stake. Everything we do—from the trees we grow to the way we make our products—directly affects our nation's environment. Andy asked me to focus my remarks this afternoon on the strategic and economic implications of climate change policy and their effect on the paper industry. But to use my time wisely, we need to consider how we implement this policy. I think we need to focus on a more fundamental question, and that is, why? With all respect to Undersecretary Wirth, I for one do not believe that the science debate is over. I'm curious to know why we as a nation or a world are pursuing a policy that would radically change the way we manufacture our products, potentially burden us with unnecessary technology costs, and ultimately deprive the U.S. paper industry of its global competitive advantage—and to do all that without any compelling evidence that such a policy change is needed or any benefit is derived. I believe there is considerable scientific uncertainty that increases in CO_2 emissions have resulted in an increase in global temperatures. And I am concerned that we are blindly accepting a policy that would result in permanent and destructive changes to our economy.

Further, it appears that this policy is not necessarily being driven by science at all but by a social agenda that is ignoring the large body of facts on global warming. What is the truth on global temperature change? Is the world warming, or is it cooling? Is climate change a natural phenomenon? Or is mankind responsible for changes in temperature? As far as I can tell, the answer to all of these questions seems to be yes. Proponents of climate change policy point to alarming studies predicting that greenhouse gases will raise global temperatures from four to nine degrees Fahrenheit over the next century. I question whether those forecasts are valid. More recent temperature studies by NASA, for example, indicate that the earth has actually cooled, not warmed, over that past eighteen years. Others models clearly indicate that global temperatures are rising at less than a tenth of a degree Celsius per decade, or less than one degree every one hundred years. Much more disturbing than conflicting views and honest views is the appearance that substantial scientific evidence has been ignored or manipulated in order to support the theory of global warming. The final global warming report referred to by Undersecretary Wirth prepared by the UN's Intergovernmental Panel on Climate Change intentionally deleted any statements by scientists that disagreed with the notion of global warming. One statement that was stricken from the report said that no evidence existed to link global warming to man-made causes. This kind of selective editing done in order to advance a social or environmental agenda is hardly in the best interest of this planet or its people. The truth of the matter is that there is no hard evidence to support the notion of global warming.

It would be dangerous, and, candidly, it would be foolish to impose a massive, multinational mandate on a theory that has no scientific basis in fact or one that is being advanced not on its merits but on its perceived social and political attributes. And make no mistake, the potential results of this policy would profoundly affect not just the paper industry but the world's economy.

As we all know, the first UN Framework Convention on Climate Change issued a call on the developed nations to voluntarily reduce greenhouse gases to 1990 levels by the year 2000. As I understand it, the current U.S. position now calls for mandated emissions reduction targets and timetables; we heard that today. This would be accomplished primarily, I think, by setting a cap on energy consumption and may also lead to new taxes on both energy and carbon emissions as well as impose excessive energy efficiency standards and perhaps severely restrict the way we manage our nation's working forests. Massive changes such as these could permanently cripple our pulp and paper industry. A carbon tax could increase our direct costs by as much as 150 percent over the next eighteen years and raise manufacturing costs by up to 14 percent. And if credit is not given to the use of biomass fuels, manufacturing costs could rise as much as 30 percent. Indirect costs would probably be higher than that 30 percent number. I don't think it takes a scientist or a Kellogg School graduate to understand the impact of a 30 percent hike in manufacturing costs. Paper mills could permanently close, thousands of jobs would probably be lost, and our position as the world's leading paper producer would surely deteriorate, if not vanish.

As an industry, paper's payroll is about $26 billion a year, and we export goods worth more than $11.5 billion. In fact, our exports represent more than 2 percent of all U.S. exports. From our perspective it would be just plain silly to jeopardize all of this based on a theory founded on poor or inexact science or someone's complex social or environmental agenda, using the false issue of climate change. What's worse is that the jobs lost in the United States—and I think this is referred to as something that has to be negotiated—will move to the developing nations that are aggressively expanding their pulp and paper capacity, nations such as Malaysia, Thailand, Indonesia, and Brazil. These countries are not a part of the climate change equation as I understand it. And this means that, at the moment, they are not required to reduce their CO_2 emissions, nor do they subscribe to the practice of sustainable forestry. They are free to cut their virgin tropical or rain forests at unsustainable levels. So what would the net effect of all this be? Well, the way we see it is that it will lead to an increase in CO_2 emissions on a worldwide basis and a loss of forests rich in biodiversity. Clearly this is not a level playing field, and we see no environmental benefit in this scenario. In my opinion the loss of thousands of jobs to overseas countries that follow no environmental standard, frankly, is absurd.

It is clear that much more needs to be done before we blindly embrace global climate change policy. Stone Container and the American Forest and Paper Association's position on that issue is that we'd like to see the December timetable to complete changes in policy in Kyoto postponed until more facts about these issues become available. We also suggest that this country never relinquish its sovereignty to a multinational panel. We would also resist any attempts to impose immediate energy taxes or energy use restrictions. And finally, we ask that the government recognize our industry for its positive impact on carbon emissions.

Nowhere in the climate change policy does it mention the unique environmental benefits that the forest products industry provides the world. It is estimated that private timberlands in the United States alone store roughly seventy-five million metric tons of CO_2 annually. Roughly thirty-five million tons are stored in wood products. That's a permanent carbon sink that no other industry can claim. Also, it is a known fact that young growing trees store more carbon dioxide than older trees. As they age, trees stop absorbing CO_2, and then some of them begin releasing it back into the air. If the government mandates that certain portions of private timberlands be set aside for carbon storage, we will see a gradual buildup of older, dying trees that will be a potential tinderbox. And massive forest fires are a major source of air pollutants—CO_2 and dioxins—and perhaps even global warming.

Lastly, I would ask the government to recognize the superb efforts that my industry has already made to limit CO_2 emissions. Our industry's emissions of carbon dioxide from the consumption of fossil fuels and electricity rose just 2 percent between 1972 and 1995. And during that same time period, the industry's production rose 67 percent. We, like most other industries, are working with the EPA to develop comprehensive air quality emissions standards, and our industry is spending more than a billion dollars every year on new environmental measures. We're also developing technology that will further reduce CO_2 emissions in the coming year. But implementing those changes takes time; you can not make them appear by a certain date by waving a magic wand. The pulp and paper industry is one of the most capital-intensive industries in the world. It's simply not possible or even desirable to scrap our current technologies and expect to replace them with new systems overnight. I am encouraged by Undersecretary Wirth's measured approach, but these things can have a momentum all of their own. In closing, I guess we would ask Undersecretary Wirth to reconsider our policy, and, in fact, we'd go just a little further than that—we'd ask you, Undersecretary, to just say "no" when you get to Kyoto.

Stabilizing the Climate Is Not Costly, but Profitable

*Amory B. Lovins, Vice President and Director of Research,
Rocky Mountain Institute*

I find myself both in sympathy and in disagreement with all three of the previous speakers. If I heard correctly, they all like to do things that make money and make sense; they all like flexibility; and they all assume that protecting the climate will cost more than what we're doing now. I'd like to suggest that actually protecting the climate will be highly profitable rather than costly if we do the cheapest things first, and that pursuing that profit motive will put industry in its rightful place as the largest part of the solution.

Let me give a trivial example. This is what a "nega-ton" of carbon dioxide looks like [holding up a compact fluorescent light bulb]. This lamp over its life will keep a ton of CO_2 out of the air, but it also makes you tens of dollars richer than if you used an incandescent bulb to produce the same light. That's one of a zillion examples—actually one of the costlier examples—of the simple idea that *it's typically cheaper to save fuel than to burn fuel.* Therefore the emissions avoided by not burning fuel can be avoided not at a cost but at a profit. And since they are profitable, they can be beneficial to the marketplace.

I would therefore suggest that the cost of a climatic "insurance policy" is actually negative—the insurance company pays *you* for the insurance—and that the uncertainties in the climate science don't matter at all because we ought to do the same things about this issue just to make money, whether we think the problem is real or not. That is, the no-regrets measures are enough. If we look in fact at all the things you can do about stabilizing climate, we find that over half of the problem, if there is a problem, can be avoided by using energy in a way that saves money. That's a negative cost, because it costs less to save the fuel than to burn it. Another quarter or so can be avoided by sustainable farming and forestry practices, which are at least as profitable as carbon mining or soil mining—let's call that one roughly a break-even. And you can get rid of the rest of the problem, if there is one, by getting rid of CFCs, but we have to do that anyway to protect the ozone layer, so it doesn't matter what it costs—although that one turns out to be about zero anyway. So if the cost of protecting climate ranges from strongly negative to roughly zero, what are we arguing about? We ought simply to be taking economics seriously. And therefore I believe that industry pursuing its economic self-interest is a key part of the solution, if industry understands and grasps its opportunities.

We've already gone quite a ways in this direction. Twenty-one years ago I was heavily criticized for suggesting in *Foreign Affairs* that rather than following the official forecast, which heads up towards the Northeast corner[2] [see Figure 13.4], U.S. primary energy use over the next half-century might stabilize and decline as we gradually wrung out the losses in converting, distributing, and using the energy. The heavy line here is what actually happened. The energy used per dollar of real GDP has actually gone down one-third more than I said it might; and yet we now know that we've barely scratched the surface of how much efficiency is available and worthwhile, thanks to the leadership of many companies represented here.

One of the things we've found lately is that the standard mental model—that the more you save, the more and more it costs; marginal cost rises steeply until you hit the limit of cost-effectiveness at the end of diminishing returns and you stop—is not the whole story [see Figure 13.5]. This is indeed often true, up to a point. But by good engineering, not by

Figure 13.4. An Illustrative U.S. Soft Energy Path
Versus Actual Consumption (1975–1995).

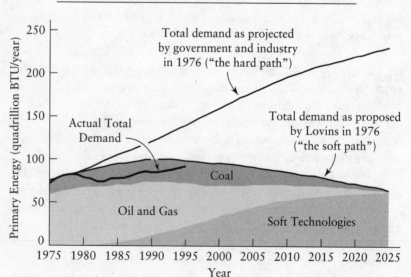

Source: Soft path data is from A. Lovins, "Energy Strategy: The Road Not Taken?" *Foreign Affairs*, 1976, *55*(1): 65–96.

economic theory, we discover another interesting thing. If you keep going and save even more, very often you find yourself "tunneling through the cost barrier," and the cost comes down again, so you get *bigger* savings at *lower* costs.

Let me give you a few examples. I was recently working with a Dutch engineer designing a pumping system for a carpet factory in Shanghai. He adopted a practice I imported from Singapore of using big pipes and small pumps instead of small pipes and big pumps and of laying out the pipes first and then the equipment. This is not rocket science, but it saved 92 percent of the pumping energy, cost a lot less to build, and worked better in all other respects. We recently applied similar principles in re-designing a major chemical plant. We got about half to three-quarters electrical savings, and the plant costs less and works better. Here's a couple of Alaskas worth of oil and gas savings in a super window [holding up a piece of superinsulated glass]. These have now been used to make new houses which require no heating or cooling in temperatures ranging from minus 47 degrees Fahrenheit to plus 115 degrees Fahrenheit, but they're more comfortable, and they cost less to build. You can use the same techniques to save three-quarters of the energy used by new or existing office buildings, with about a 6 to 16 percent gain in labor productivity, which adds an order of magnitude more to the bottom line than eliminating your entire energy bill. This is simply because people

Figure 13.5. Systems Approach and Leapfrog.

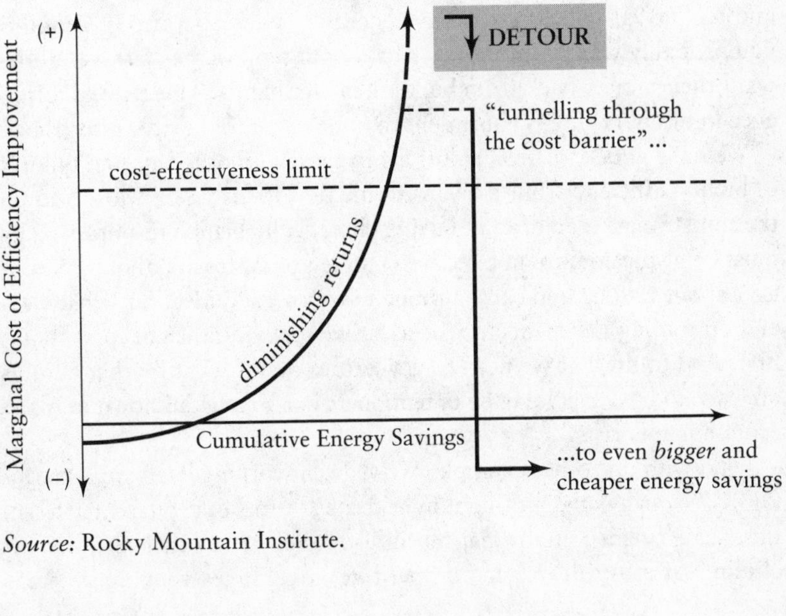

Source: Rocky Mountain Institute.

who can see what they're doing because of better lighting design and natural light, people who can hear themselves think and feel more comfortable because the building is designed better, can also do more and better work. This is great for competitiveness. We recently saved, cost-effectively, about 97 percent of the air-conditioning energy of an existing office building and made it more comfortable. You can save about half of existing motor systems energy—motors use about three-fifths of all electricity—by doing thirty-five things that pay back in an average of about sixteen months of a nickel rate.

You'll find fifty such examples in a new book coming out next week called *Factor Four: Doubling Wealth, Halving Resource Use.*[3] It's a sort of an ecocapitalist manifesto. The important thing about it is not that it gives these case studies of how do you do more and better with much less, but rather that it also asks, why doesn't everybody do it already? What are the market failures that are making this not happen? Let me mention a few of them. Obsolete rules of thumb used throughout engineering practice are typically wrong by half to one order of magnitude compared with whole-system life cycle optimization, because they're optimizing a little piece of the system and therefore pessimizing the whole system. Most of our building design is "infectious repetitis," not real engineering or architecture at all—partly because architects and engineers are rewarded for what they spend, not for what they save. Similarly, our utilities, in almost every jurisdiction, are rewarded for selling more energy and penalized for cutting your bill. We have split incentives between builders and buyers of equipment or buildings, and between landlords and tenants. If you invest to save energy in your operations or home, you probably want your money back about ten times as fast as utilities want their money back from building power plants. This tenfold difference in discount rate is equivalent to about a tenfold price distortion.

We have good practical solutions to these and other market failures in buying efficiency. But it seems to me that focusing on those and on the similar market failures in buying climatically benign resources really must be at the core of an effective climate policy. It isn't about taxes. It isn't about trading and caps, although that's a good idea. But what we'll end up trading is benefits, not costs, if we really do the cheapest things first. And to do that we need to get serious about what market failures are encountered every day by practitioners but largely unknown to many economic theorists.

I end with one other example. We've been working lately on a "nega-OPEC," which is the ultralight hybrid car. It turns out to be three to six times as efficient as a normal car and superior in all other respects, including offering dramatic competitive advantages that make early adopters win. It's a better car: people will buy it as they buy compact disks instead of vinyl records. Therefore we had the rather sneaky idea that rather than patenting and auctioning the hypercar idea, we would just put it in the public domain where nobody could patent it, and get everyone fighting over it. That was in mid-1993. We now have about $2.5 billion, doubling every year, committed to this line of development by a couple of dozen existing and intending automakers. You should see early ones on the market around the end of this decade. In fact, some of the companies represented here already have important work in this area.

I think this suggests that if we take market economics not literally but seriously, it can be the best friend of climate protection. It can solve the problem, if there is a problem. You'll all make money on the deal. The technologies to do this already exist, although they're not very widely known. And therefore if we recognize that protecting climate is at root not costly but potentially very profitable, I think we will find that the negotiations get an awful lot simpler. But this is a different focus for discussion than arguments about how much do we need to tax carbon. I would give you the analogy that the oil and car industries have been in gridlock for years. The car industry wants higher gasoline taxes to make cars efficient. The oil industry wants tighter standards to make cars efficient. And they've fought each other to a draw. It turns out, in a way, they're both right, they're both wrong, and it's all irrelevant. If you engineer the car better as a clean-sheet design, you get a superior product with decisive competitive advantages for the manufacturer. You can therefore implement it in the market without changing prices or public policy. That's what's actually starting to happen. I think we can do the same thing on a much broader front in climate protection.

ANDREW HOFFMAN: As hoped for, we've heard a wide range of ideas on the economics of climate change policy. Now I'd like to open the floor to general discussion. Please introduce yourself and feel free to engage both the people on the panel as well as the people around the room. Let's begin.

MAX BAZERMAN, PROFESSOR, J. L. KELLOGG GRADUATE SCHOOL OF MANAGEMENT: Amory, could I ask you why these corporate folks aren't picking up these hundred dollar bills on the floor?

AMORY LOVINS: Some of them are. Some of them are our clients. Some of them work with other designers, achieving exactly these kinds of savings.

MAX BAZERMAN: Why aren't the masses of corporations doing what you say?

AMORY LOVINS: Well, let me go back to that 92 percent savings on pumping energy, because it's a nice example. This was done by a Dutch engineer using Singapore practice, and when he got through he said, "You know, this is so obvious! Why doesn't everybody do it this way?" Well, it turns out that the rule of thumb that mechanical engineers use to optimize pipe size is based only on pumping energy. It's not based on the life cycle cost, both capital and operating, of the whole system. Now, he was given an initial design that the designer swore was optimized. The designer was supposedly the best in the business, but by making the pipe bigger—which makes friction go down as almost the fifth power of diameter—he had this 92 percent energy saving with a sixteen-day payback before he started making the equipment smaller. And then the pump, motor, inverter, and electricals got smaller, so the whole thing cost a lot less to build. I see some nodding heads. I think there must be some engineers in the house.

Why doesn't everyone do it that way? Well, we have some real problems with engineering education. It's slice-and-dice, it's not whole-system thinking. I already gave you a long list of market failures. But very little attention is paid to them. And I'm afraid the climate debate has been hijacked by the sorts of economic theorists who doubtless lie awake at night wondering whether what works in practice can possibly work in theory. Those of you who are practical industrialists will, I think, recognize that you've heard some of the engineering innovations before, and I daresay we could go into any of your factories and find very similar opportunities. That's not what the argument is about. Tim, you're stuck in a very different kind of negotiation about allocating costs, not benefits. I don't know quite how to break out of that, but I hope this meeting will be a start.

JAMES OLSON, SENIOR VICE PRESIDENT, TOYOTA MOTOR SALES, USA, INC.: I can add to what Amory said. We will be introducing a hybrid car in Japan late this fall. And it's exactly as he said. We optimize the motor and optimize the engine. When you optimize the engine you get an engine that you can make lighter, has less friction. It's 80 percent more efficient. You can keep it below four thousand rpm, so it doesn't need to be as strong. That keeps the lightness as well. And if you have electronics that activates this, you end up with a motor and engine together. You can use each one in the driving cycle where it

from at least some developing countries that "we don't like the idea of joint implementation because this is a way for you guys to come along and pick off all the low-hanging fruit so that n-years from now"— where n is fifteen, twenty, or thirty—"when we become part of this we're going to have to climb to the top of the tree after you guys have picked off the easy opportunities"? Do you see that as a big obstacle to joint implementation and trading?

TIMOTHY WIRTH: Well, that's one obstacle, and another one is their fear that we're going to try to load everything on joint implementation and do nothing ourselves. They're going to say, "you're just ducking your responsibility." That's part of the political response we hear. We hear that political response as much as we hear the response on the other side that says we're unilaterally disarming.

I've been negotiating parts of this for the past four years, and I have seen a dramatically changed perception in China. A number of things are happening in China. One, they're looking out at their enormous projected energy needs, and they understand that they would like to have as much modern technology as possible. Second, there is increasing political power in the hands of people at the regional and local level. If you talk to the mayor of a large city in China, almost invariably he will speak of the health problems that are caused by a polluted atmosphere; those mayors want to make changes to deal with this. They are more and more responsive. Of course, as you get further toward Beijing, outside of the science agencies, there is more resistance, because there are a lot more constituencies—coal constituencies and rail constituencies, or whatever.

AMORY LOVINS: Well, I think the important thing to undergird what Tim's saying is that the economics and logistics are very much against the traditional development patterns. Countries like China are starting to realize very rapidly that they could afford either to build lots of coal-fired power plants or to develop, but not both. They have to make resource efficiency the cornerstone of the development process if they're going to avoid enough supply-side investment to have enough money left to buy the things that are supposed to use all that energy.

ANDREW HOFFMAN: We've got two lines of argument going: one is the-developing-versus-the-developed countries, and the other is the technological development that Amory is talking about. Steven Percy brought up the idea that more flexibility on where we're going to reduce emissions and when we're going to do it is the key to solving climate change in the most cost-efficient way, while Jim and Amory are suggesting that the technology is already there for automobiles. But is it there for utilities? Is it there for oil? And what kinds of time frames and what kinds of targets are going to be able to spur that kind of technological development for the industries represented in this room, both here and abroad?

JAMES OLSON: I mean to say that we can get there if we can meet enough customers' needs without intruding on what they really want, which is just what they've had in the past. Make it look like just what they've always had, and make sure they can afford it.

ANDREW HOFFMAN: Are we ignoring the idea that behaviors have to change? Are we going to continue to give them technologies that allow them to do what they want to do?

AMORY LOVINS: Yes, and then it means that instead of running out of oil, air, or climate you keep building cars and driving them until you run out of roads, land, and patience. Some Chinese officials really want to try that experiment. But I'd rather have them do it with cars that don't endanger everyone's climate.

RICHARD KLIMISCH: Certainly one example of the answer is the PNGV program [Partnership for New Generation Vehicles], which is in fact working very well. Many of the things in that program are things that Amory's been talking about. Nobody's happy with how fast it's going, but at the end of the day technology is the answer not just for us but for India and China as well. The most noteworthy goal of PNGV is the eighty-mile-per-gallon vehicle. But it's forcing us to look at hybrids, lightweight materials, manufacturability, and the like. Ultimately at the end of the day it's that first-cost problem: the first cost of those light bulbs, the first cost of these cars. Our behavior is first-cost-oriented. That's the way people behave. It's hard to get over that.

AMORY LOVINS: We actually think these efficient cars will cost the same or less because they're a lot simpler; they take a tenth as much capital to make, and so on. And that's the "tunneling through the cost barrier" idea. The CAFE standards cut our fuel intensity in half [see Figure 13.6]. Then it stagnated for a decade. PNGV wants to get to here, hypercars are down here, and it turns out that those are cheaper and easier to do. So they're happening very quickly. The market and

Figure 13.6. "Trend Is Not Destiny, But What Is?"

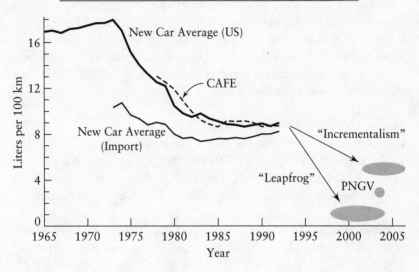

Source: Rocky Mountain Institute.

PNGV itself may go slowly, but I think it will be overtaken by what the "black" programs of the automakers and new automakers are doing behind the curtains. And that's starting to peek out, as in Toyota's hybrid program. That's very exciting. I think it shows what industry is really good at.

JAMES OLSON: You know our car will be close to PNGV and will get about sixty miles per gallon.

AMORY LOVINS: And in 1997, not in 2003.

JAMES OLSON: And it'll perform the same as the Corolla I drove here.

TIMOTHY WIRTH: The puzzle to me is knowing whether it is a different conservation technology, different automobile technology, or different utility pattern. This thing is going to get solved only if we make these kinds of very significant shifts. We know we have to do this. This is a long-term issue. It's not going to get solved in Kyoto in December. Kyoto is just opening the doors.

The frustration I have is that it's extremely difficult to have any kind of conversation with much of the automobile industry, who are largely saying, "don't do anything; get out of our lives." Or with the pulp and paper industry, which, with exceptions, reflects a view that has recently been echoed to many of you. Now, there's frustration on the industry side, and I feel it on our side. How do you get to a point where we can more rationally figure out how we're going to solve the problem? We're trying to say that this is an open instrument. We're trying to give as much flexibility as possible. It isn't going to get done unless there are a series of innovative partnerships. Some are emerging. I'd like to see them develop more rapidly.

JAMES OLSON: Well, I think that's what you did with PNGV. We looked at it and said, "whoops, we better get going." And we're going to get there, with a car, that is. We've hit three-quarters of PNGV a little earlier. And that's competition. That's what all the companies do. We see a market developing, and we go after it. Its driven by self-interest.

ROBERT MASSIE, EXECUTIVE DIRECTOR, COALITION FOR ENVIRON-MENTALLY RESPONSIBLE ECONOMIES: My question comes from my experience yesterday at the UN conference in New York on the relationship between financial investment and environmental performance. There was a lot of interest among the various securities analysts, commercial bankers, investment bankers, and insurance companies about how to get a handle on the environmental performance of companies so that the markets can function more efficiently, investing in companies that are showing long-term performance and improvement—the kinds of things that Amory is talking about. There's a real sense that the market is misallocating capital right now, and a desire to find the opportunities. They want to identify those who are performing poorly and whose cost of capital ultimately will go up. There is a very interesting report that was just released yesterday by the World Business Council for Sustainable Development on environmental performance and shareholder value that suggests that if you take a progressive stance towards environmental technology, you're going to show some kind of improvement in your long-term rate of return. So my question is about government policy and its direct impact on business. What can be done to correct the market failures in capital markets so that they are able to allocate resources more efficiently and promote the kind of changes we're talking about, changes that are obviously necessary if we're going to make real improvements? We haven't talked about the capital markets, and it seems to me that on a global scale they're very important. Amory, I'd like to know your observations about that.

AMORY LOVINS: I'll give a couple of quick examples of some neat folks in DOE [Department of Energy] who actually came out of our shop.

They've worked with the financial community to develop the North American Measurement and Verification Protocol. This is like FHA rules for mortgages: it lets you package energy-efficiency financing in a standard way so that you can originate loans to do the work as fast as you can sell them on the secondary market. It lets you securitize, bundle, and aggregate streams of energy savings. You therefore don't need your own capital to do it anymore, so if you're capital-constrained, you can still get all the cost-effective savings. I think one of the most important things we could do—which about eight states have already done and the rest have not—is to decouple utilities' profits from their sales volumes and let them keep part of what they save as extra profit. Now, I'm saying this in traditional, regulated terms, because a lot of states will probably stick with that for quite a while: the supposed wave of restructuring is actually quite uneven. But the basic idea is to align shareholder and customer incentives by rewarding utilities for cutting your bill, not for selling you more energy. Dick Abdoo has had experience with this in Wisconsin, and it really changes behavior. Why didn't the rest of our states do this? It would be a very fundamental way of reallocating capital to the best buys first.

ALLEN KOLEFF: In responding to Undersecretary Wirth in what he might do to cooperate, and coming from the basis that something will be done in Kyoto regardless of whether something should be done, I suggest that paying close attention to one of the slides that Mr. Percy put up is of primary importance to our industry. The flexibility in when and where we spend capital becomes extremely important when you happen to be operating in the most capital-intensive industry in the world in terms of cost of installation per unit of output. As Roger Stone pointed out, our industry has increased its CO_2 emissions only 2 percent in the last twenty-three years from fossil fuel and purchased energy consumption. This was in spite of a 67 percent increase in output, which has occurred because we have had the flexibility to apply new technology, when it was available, in a cost-effective manner. We've not been forced to abandon the very serious investments that we've had to make before their time. And if we have that flexibility to move forward, then progress is possible. But if we are faced with mandated time frames and mandated solutions, this industry's going overseas, pure and simple.

TIMOTHY WIRTH: It would be very interesting to know what kind of a differentiated set of responsibilities for domestic industries you would recommend and you think would work. As I understand what you're saying, those industries that have become very efficient over a certain period of time get X and X, and industries that are less efficient get Y and X. If there is a framework like that, one which you think is feasible and we ought to consider, it would be interesting to look at.

ALLEN KOLEFF: I don't think I'm preparing to advocate civil war here.

TIMOTHY WIRTH: As I understand the proposal, that's what you're suggesting. Isn't that right? Aren't you suggesting that you were efficient and so you ought to be rewarded for being efficient compared to other industries who wouldn't be rewarded because they weren't efficient?

ALLEN KOLEFF: No, I'm sorry; that was not the intent. The intent was just to point out what we have been able to do with the flexibility we've been afforded. I'm not suggesting that different standards are at all appropriate.

ROGER STONE: It was all motivated by self-interest.

ALLEN KOLEFF: Sure.

AMORY LOVINS: But would the sort of cap and trading system that Tim says is the administration approach meet your needs for flexibility? When and where and how?

ALLEN KOLEFF: I'm not sure it would. To be perfectly honest, I haven't analyzed that question. But the kind of statistics I'm quoting are industrywide averages. There are six hundred, more or less, paper mills in the United States, and every bloody one of them is different. For example, you run into competing environmental goals. Increased recycling is loved by the whole world. It's one of the most popular issues from a public perception standpoint with respect to how they feel about our industry. And yet paper mills that use 100 percent recycled waste paper as their raw material have higher fossil fuel consumption.

AMORY LOVINS: I can't resist one comment, because I've worked in your sector for quite a while. This industry is very good at using fuel efficiently, it saves a lot of steam, it saves fiber and water better and better all the time. It still has not done very well on saving electricity. I was working with the chief engineer of a firm that designs most of the North American mills a few years ago and told him how I would approach motor systems. He said, "Well that's really interesting; we've never looked at it as a whole system like that. And if we did, we'd save more than the 50 percent you're talking about." There's a long way to go.

ALLEN KOLEFF: The consumption of purchased electricity in our industry as a percentage of our total BTU consumption per ton of product has increased from about 4 percent or so in 1972 to about 6.5 to 7 percent today. And a very large part of that increase is from the installations required for environmental management. So we're giving ourselves the luxury today of talking about this issue in isolation, without taking into account the kinds of capital allocation decisions that managers face on a day-to-day basis to meet their customers' quality concerns, productivity, improvement concerns, and so forth.

AMORY LOVINS: And this gets back to my earlier question, because most of the mill managers I know are held to a two-year payback horizon on saving energy.

ALLEN KOLEFF: Yes, but if there isn't enough capital to go around and the payback on the quality improvement or productivity improvement is six months, then the energy is not going to get a very favorable conclusion.

AMORY LOVINS: Oh, but if that's the case then you're describing a massive misallocation of capital, societally, and we all need to fix it.

HOWARD (BUD) RIS, EXECUTIVE DIRECTOR, UNION OF CONCERNED SCIENTISTS: I'm desperately trying to avoid engaging in debate on the science of climate change, and I'll stick to the rule here and do that. But nobody has mentioned restructuring of the electric utility industry, and there are a lot of utility people here, and I wonder where or how you see that issue intersecting with climate change. I think the basic question is, as utility restructuring proceeds in its many different forms and many different states, is that going to enhance CO_2 reduction in the future or make it more difficult? And I'll add one piece of background to the discussions: we have had maximum flexibility with a 1992 treaty on climate change which essentially was voluntary. It has not worked. We will miss our goals by 5 or 6 percent in the next several years. But the basic question is where does this fit with utility restructuring?

JAMES O'CONNOR, CHAIRMAN AND CEO, COMMONWEALTH EDISON CO.: Maybe I can answer that. There are now forty-nine of the fifty states that either have considered or are in the process of considering utility restructuring. And it's fair to say that this question of climate change is not foremost on the agenda. That's a reality. The states which have gone through with it—California, Massachusetts, Rhode Island, and Pennsylvania—are the ones that are behind us. It's very active in another dozen states, and it's on the agenda in still a great number more. It's like a forest fire. Honestly, Amory, you suggested that it's going rather slow. It is, in fact, going like a forest fire.

AMORY LOVINS: I said it was uneven, happening all over the map.

JAMES O'CONNOR: But it is happening, and it's happening quite rapidly. And environmental issues are not at the top of the agenda. And climate change is clearly not even in the subset in most of the discussion thus far. What does that portend for the future? I think it's very hard to tell at this point in time. But, if used, it is something that is going to have to be factored into what's going to happen if you had all the major New England companies and the California companies getting rid of their generators. Who's going to assume the responsibility for climate change and for environmental matters going forward?

AMORY LOVINS: Basically, it's good for gas, it's good for some coal, it's bad for nuclear, and, surprisingly, I think it can be very good for distributed renewables, because financial people who understand risk-adjusted discounting rather than making decisions on weighted-average-cost-of-capital terms are going to start making the decisions. Then the fifty or so distributed benefits that can increase the value of a lot of renewables by half to one order of magnitude can start to express themselves in the market. That'll be completely new.

STEPHEN PECK, VICE PRESIDENT, ELECTRIC POWER RESEARCH INSTITUTE: I have a question on the concentration target. Senator Wirth made a very interesting comment about pursuing a concentration target. People who've looked at how to do that have found that in the short term there should be relatively low incentives to reduce emissions and that the incentives should increase over time as the concentration target is actually approached. This is not consistent in the short term, with stabilizing U.S. emissions. In fact, U.S. emissions and world emissions under an approach to achieve stabilized concentration targets should rise for the next two to three decades. Some of us were recently privileged to hear the early results of some analyses which were being done by the federal government about options to stabilize emissions.

We heard that those analyses implied a carbon tax of $100 a ton. A hundred dollars a ton would lead to a 25 percent increase in the price of most delivered energy. This $100 a ton is not consistent with analyses that look at stabilizing concentrations over the next hundred years. So I would ask the government to look much more seriously at concentration stabilization approaches rather than emission stabilization approaches, because such approaches imply smaller differences between current activities and what we ought to do in the short term to stabilize concentrations. Therefore they would be more likely to be acceptable within the United States and the developed world, while we work to bring in many of the other players—China, India, and Brazil. So the approach of focusing on concentration targets is more likely to be achievable.

AMORY LOVINS: Could I ask you for an analogy from your utility experience? Doesn't this hundred-dollar-a-ton number sound an awful lot like the huge estimates for where the market would clear in the SOx and NOx markets, and it just didn't turn out that way? People got smart when they started competing in that market, and the price was driven right down to the best buys.

STEPHEN PECK: That $100 a ton doesn't just come out of the air. The Energy Modeling Forum at Stanford University used something like fifteen or twenty energy models over the last two to three years in a study of this issue.

AMORY LOVINS: But they're economic models. They're not engineering models. That was my point.

STEPHEN PECK: No, they're a variety of models, some of which have considerable engineering detail. And $100 a ton is a consensus number.

DIRK FORRISTER: I'll respond to this because I think there's been a lot of misinformation out there. The administration has come out with nothing recently in the $100 a ton ballpark. A year ago—returning to the chart from Battelle on the "where" and "when" flexibility that Steven Percy put up—we put out a range that said, without flexibility, we're looking at what we believe domestically to be something between $100 and $200 a ton. We did not think that was acceptable. This is one of the reasons the United States is so bullish on both "where" and "when" flexibility. In fact, it ties directly to the point that you raised about concentrations, because our eye is definitely on the ball of concentrations as the ultimate thing that makes sense to look to. And in fact this kind of flexibility allows the capital to do the most good by actually protecting the broadest range of possibilities on concentrations that we would consider wanting to achieve. Without that flexibility, we don't have a prayer of meaningfully addressing concentrations. As Tim sometimes says, "business as usual" will see doubling in the rearview mirror. We will charge past it so fast. And we're headed toward a tripling of concentrations. But with flexibility, you begin to convert some of those options, because with "where" and "when" flexibility you're talking about cutting that $100 or $200 by 85 percent. The U.S. policy has already been influenced by this "where" and "when" flexibility analysis.

STEPHEN PECK: Paul [Portney] and I were at a meeting a month ago in which we heard $100 a ton as being a focal point of current government analyses.

DIRK FORRISTER: Without flexibility?

STEPHEN PECK: No, with flexibility.

DIRK FORRISTER: No, that is incorrect based on what I've seen.

STEPHEN PECK: A hundred dollars a ton for stabilizing emissions. This addresses this point of openness that Senator Wirth talks about. It's very difficult for all of the people around this room to engage in this debate when you're not sharing these analyses with many of the people—people who are a very important audience for what you want to try to achieve.

TIMOTHY WIRTH: Let me say again that we're being very open with what we have. Other stuff just isn't done yet. It just is not done yet. We had a very difficult time attempting to reconcile the various models that were being used for projecting what the economics of various paths were going to be. There were the family of models that EPA had and the family of models that the Department of Energy had and the family of models on the outside, and we had to get them into some kind of reasonable combination. That was done in the Department of Commerce. We've been extremely open about that—about what the models are, what we're dealing with, what they say, how they work, and all that sort of thing.

To respond to the first request, that the models be peer-reviewed—we were trying to peer-review those models till the cows came home. I understand your frustration that they weren't peer-reviewed at high speed and then we didn't have a lot of other things in there, but that peer review has taken longer than we thought it would.

Having said that, as a response to the procedural attack on this front, let me remind us all of the context in which this negotiation is taking place. We are not the only player in this business, and the assumption somehow that we, the United States, are going to determine where and when things are going to happen is simply not the reality. The problem is a significant one, and we have to move on it; and the earlier we start to move on it, the easier it's going to be to get to that point where the curve starts to bend down and we focus on concentrations. That means that we have to maintain the current climate treaty, which was very difficult to negotiate. All of you have been in negotiations of one kind or another. We have a treaty that's been negotiated and been agreed to. We're afraid that if we don't do anything, then we will have an enormous credibility problem in the developed world; if we don't act, then probably a number of other countries in the developed world won't act either. Then the whole climate treaty falls apart. Now, there are a few people who would like to see that happen. But it is our judgment that that would be an irresponsible thing for the United States to do. We've got to maintain the climate treaty; and maintaining the climate treaty means requiring reasonable action by those who are currently putting the most carbon up into the atmosphere. We're trying to figure out what that reasonable action is.

In addition, there is no way that we are going to obtain what we would like to have in terms of flexibility and in terms of developing-country commitments—the other two rings of the circus—unless we are able to demonstrate that we are willing to take some kind of action. That's the only way we can get the other countries on board. So let me ask those of you who are reflecting a kind of skepticism—and there's a lot of skepticism—to remember the context. This is not Uncle Sam alone. We may be producing 22 percent of the carbon going up into the atmosphere from man-made sources, but we are but one of a whole series of players in this process. I hope that you keep that in mind.

HOWARD RIS: To follow up on the concentration goal and maybe for Tim or for Dirk: if we ultimately accept and choose a concentration goal, and putting aside whether it's 450, 550, or 800 parts per million, what's the next step, and how is that implemented? If we go that route—and let's say we don't have an emissions reduction goal—how do we put it into place? Is it possible?

TIMOTHY WIRTH: We don't know how to do that yet, so therefore we're not saying that we can frame this around a concentration goal. I don't think the world is even close to doing that. We're still negotiating targets and timetables, based upon some kind of stabilization of emissions sometime in the first couple of decades of the twenty-first century. That's the kind of world we're looking at now. We've begun to think about stabilizing concentrations, but there is no way that this negotiation is going to get from here to there.

ROBERT BANKS, VICE PRESIDENT, SUN COMPANY: A couple of comments for the senator: I would agree with Steven Percy's comments about energy conservation, as Sun is both a consumer of fossil fuels and a producer of fossil fuel products. Energy conservation is our top priority for reducing greenhouse gases at our facilities, and this is backed by economic justification. One of the frustrations we encountered in developing reformulated gasoline was the impact of unintended consequences. When we began to roll out our reformulated gasoline to the public, the consumers rebelled against the anticipated higher prices, and a number of voluntary state opt-in areas were withdrawn. We took a tremendous financial bath because we were not permitted to sell the reformulated gasoline or to recover our costs. My concern about climate change is that this issue is much longer-term and there is far more uncertainty involved than the ozone issue. Unless great care is taken, there could be many unintended losers resulting from climate change policy. As a company, and as an industry, we are concerned that we could become a major loser, so we need to be represented at the table as climate change policy is developed.

TIMOTHY WIRTH: I'm very familiar with that particular issue. We had it in Denver with the whole problem of low-level pollution. We attempted the same kind of solution, and we had some similar backlash but not nearly as much as you had there. We're mindful of what you say. What we're trying to do is develop a set of instruments that have as much flexibility as possible, and a budget—targets and timetables—which is going to be doable.

We're not going to do something that is going to damage the economy. I can assure you, Mr. Stone, that there's nobody out there with some kind of ideological motive to try to destroy the economy. That is,

I would say, a preposterous notion, and I might add personally some-what insulting.

We are mindful of the kinds of problems Mr. Banks is suggesting. I was talking with Norm Augustine the other day, the CEO of Lockheed Martin. Lockheed Martin, then the Martin company, invested an enor-mous amount in solar in the late seventies and early eighties. They thought there were certain requirements, and they made great invest-ments at that point and took a big bath on it. We talked about it and Norm said we were burned once, but we realize there is this problem, and we want to come back again. So let's figure out how we are going to take this on based on our earlier experiences. As Norm said, this is a problem we've got to take on.

ANDREW HOFFMAN: As much as I hate to interrupt this discussion, I think it's time to take our first break. In this first session we've heard a lot of ideas and concerns, but it has been slightly unfocused and has not included input from several people in the room. But I hope that some common interests have been stirred and we can explore those in the second session.

NOTES

1. Timothy Wirth is a public servant whose words are part of the public domain. They are excluded from any copyright claim on the rest of this book and may be freely copied by anyone.
2. A. Lovins, "Energy Strategy: The Road Not Taken?" *Foreign Affairs,* 1976, 55(1): 65–96.
3. E. Von Weizsäcker, A. Lovins, and L. H. Lovins, *Factor Four: Doubling Wealth, Halving Resource Use* (London: Earthscan Publications, 1997).

14

DIALOGUE

Seeking Common Ground

ANDREW HOFFMAN: Welcome to Session 2 of the climate change dialogue. In this session we hope to draw off the ideas presented in the first session and use them to search for areas of common ground where collaborative efforts can lead those in this room to help develop and implement better climate change policy. We will open with remarks from Jim O'Connor and Paul Portney.

The Role of Voluntary Programs
in Collaborative Climate Change Mitigation

James J. O'Connor, Chairman and CEO,
Commonwealth Edison Company

Before beginning, let me remark very briefly on our earlier discussion on utility restructuring. I do think this has thrown a little bit of a curve into utility's thinking about where we go on environmental issues. In fact, I have to leave this meeting to go downtown to talk about the restructuring legislation in Illinois. And it's fair to tell you that in the top ten items in the restructuring debate, you do not see the word *environment*. I see Dick Abdoo nodding his head, and I think the same is true in Wisconsin as it is in most other states. That's an important point, and it's an issue that I plan to raise when we go to our industry meeting in a couple of weeks, to see just exactly what the consensus is on how we, as an industry, should approach a lot of the environmental issues that are of great concern.

I fortunately worked with Andy in developing part of the approach that we have tried to take today. I suggest that the question that we're addressing is not whether action should be taken. Roger [Stone], I guess I'm a little bit more toward the middle in believing, not necessarily that all the debate on the science is over, but clearly much of the science is in. And we as an industry are prepared to do what we believe to be our part to address the issue. In response to Undersecretary Wirth's question as to whether or not we would subscribe to mandated objectives, we would have a very hard time doing so. We would be reluctant as an industry to support mandated programs. And part of the reason for this is that we've had pretty good success in our own voluntary efforts on climate change, which were initiated five years ago in 1992. We worked with others, and I guess Dirk [Forrister] cut his teeth on our particular program over at DOE. We developed a climate challenge program where we went out and got about a hundred of our largest companies to develop commitments to reduce carbon emissions by over 160 million tons between then and the year 2000. That's not insignificant, and what it suggests is that if we put our minds to it as an industry and are willing to subscribe to certain goals—not mandated targets but goals—that we can accomplish much. Now, we have to factor in what the restructuring of the industry might mean with respect to our ability to reach those voluntary goals in the future. And that is a tough question. But a lot of things have been done along the lines of what Amory [Lovins] has suggested by some of the more progressive companies in our industry. Things that we've done in the area of building structures, power plant efficiency, and availability improvements have been significant in the last several years. I mentioned to Amory during the break that we're viewed as one of the most recent builders of power plants in the country. The last plant that we completed was ordered in 1973, twenty-four years ago. You're simply not finding a great deal of power plant construction of the size that we were accustomed to building in the sixties and seventies— not the huge five hundred or a thousand megawatt units that became very standard in the seventies. And in fact it has been suggested that in the future, between now and the year 2010, the majority of new energy supplies from the electric utility industry will come from distributed generation. It's estimated that 40 percent of new generation between now and the year 2010 will be in small increments at seventy-five or a hundred kilo-watts. We have to assess whether or not that's a positive or a negative with respect to the global warming issue. I think lot of people would conclude that it's a positive.

We also believe that immediate and significant reductions by the developed countries is not necessarily where the majority of emphasis should be placed. And this goes back to the question, is it better to spend $5 abroad or $100 here in getting to the same result? And that's a very serious question on the minds of people in our industry.

While cost impact is relevant to our discussion, so too is the fact that world energy consumption, driven largely by growth in the developing countries, is forecast to increase 34 to 46 percent over 1993 levels in a decade and a half. That continues a worldwide increase of roughly 2.5 percent that we've experienced since the year 1991. Taken in isolation these facts portend some pretty ominous global impacts. It's interesting to note, however, that during the same period CO_2 emissions have increased at the rate of 2.1 percent. I think the reason for this divergence is relevant to our discussion because of the large nuclear complement of plants that was put on-line over the past twenty-five years. That clearly has made a contribution to not having a proportional increase in CO_2 emissions. Now, I know that a lot of folks in this room have varying opinions on nuclear power, so I won't get into that subject. But the fact is that it has averted roughly two billion metric tons of CO_2 during the past quarter of a century—not an insignificant contribution.

There are a lot of things that are involved in our ability as an industry to work with other industries and to work with our customers that we think can lead to a better environment and in the process lead to a reduction in CO_2 emissions. Amory talked about the light bulb: we're the last electric company in the United States that has a light bulb program. We have 1.1 million of our customers who pay 68 cents a month for the opportunity to get four light bulbs, and we have constantly tried to get more efficient light bulbs. Amory, I don't know if we have the kind that you pointed to in stock, but we have some pretty interesting things, and it's an attempt to be responsive to what we think a number of our customers—not all, but a number—feel is important with respect to the environment, energy efficiency, and in lowering their cost in using energy.

We do think that the electrical utility industry will support a flexible, voluntary, and cost-effective policy to address global climate change, and I underscore the word *flexibility*, which we heard a number of times in the earlier session. For this reason we urge that any agreement adopted in Kyoto in December of this year reflect the following fundamental principles. Commitments for action beyond the year 2000 must include both developed and developing countries, and in this vein it's important to permit the transfer of emission credits between participants in joint implementation projects. We talked about the success of the SO_2 trading system developed some years ago [in the 1990 Clean Air Act amendments]. Second, national policies and measures for emission reductions should be voluntary. Legally binding targets imposed only on the developed countries will impede the development of cost-effective global solutions. And finally, some credit should be given to utilities for the successes that they have enjoyed and the kinds of things that they have embarked on, as an incentive for future industry commitments.

Dick Abdoo's company and mine are involved in a major project in Czechoslovakia which will significantly reduce the emissions from a rather large fossil-fired facility in a town so polluted that none of us would ever want to live there. It's been quite successful. We're also both involved in some tree-planting activities which are of modest scale but are not insignificant. In our own company we are constantly looking for other ways. This coming week we will be completing the conversion of a five-hundred-megawatt oil-burning machine, so it will be capable of using gas. That is the fifth of these large machines that we will have been able to convert. We will continue to try to find ways in our self-interest that at the same time will contribute to environmental betterment.

Let me mention one other thing that is exciting and has clearly caught the attention of a lot of people. We now have the largest chilled water-making facility in the world here in downtown Chicago. The first of our facilities came on-line three years ago, and it offers a major benefit to the large commercial buildings in Chicago. For those of you who are familiar with the building stock in our downtown area—the Merchandise Mart, the Board of Trade, the First National Bank—these are some of the facilities who have adopted this technology, which replaces their old air conditioning system and avoids the expensive need to retrofit to meet the new CFC standards. We are now taking that technology— it's nothing terribly exotic—and partnering with people in Boston, Houston, Nevada, and Windsor, Ontario, in developing similar kinds of schemes which over the long haul will make a major difference in reducing the CO_2 emissions in those downtown areas. We are quite excited about what this will contribute and think it demonstrates what successes the utility industry has to show in controlling climate change.

The Role of Research and Development in Setting Collaborative Climate Change Goals

Paul R. Portney, President, Resources for the Future

I will limit myself to four observations. Some will deal directly with what we talked about already; some will introduce new wrinkles. I want to say a brief word about the seriousness of the problem that we are discussing here today. I want to say a few words about the administration's proposals that Senator Wirth so admirably laid out earlier. I want to talk a little bit about the cost of the implied commitment that we would be making by pursuing the administration's proposals. And finally, I want to raise a point that we haven't talked much about to this point—the need for expenditures on research and development into less carbon-intensive technologies. I will plunge right in.

In regards to the seriousness of the problem, I would only state that I talk to no one privately who does not express concerns about global climate change and the increasing concentration of CO_2 in the atmosphere and who doesn't acknowledge that we need to begin to do something about this problem. I mention this because this includes many people who in public still say that the science is not conclusive on the need to do something about this right now: businessmen and women, people in government, fellow economists. At any rate, regardless of people's public pronouncements, virtually everybody that I talk to says that this is a serious problem and that we need to begin to think about the size of the insurance policy that we're going to buy. This is a big change from the situation even as recently as three or four years ago.

Having to do with the administration's policies, I want to say that I think the administration deserves a great deal of credit for the overall structure that they have laid out here, and in particular I congratulate Tim Wirth and other people in the administration for emphasizing the long-term nature of this problem. It's taken us a long time to get into this, and it will take us a long time to get out. It's silly to think about doing things impetuously without thinking carefully about them. The administration has established a fairly long-term framework to address this problem, despite the fact that they are constantly beaten about the head and shoulders by people in the environmental community who want much more precipitous action. Second, I congratulate them for talking about a policy in which flexibility with respect to where and when emissions reductions are made is a key linchpin. This includes the notions of joint implementation and trading in lieu of mandatory, specific energy conservation requirements, technology-based standards, etc. If they continue to adhere to that, they will deserve high praise. Their insistence on joint action, including the developing countries, and their commitment to a modeling approach are also sound. But this framework, I think, reflects an awful lot of learning by people who previously would have been wedded to command-and-control. I think the lessons learned from the acid rain trading program, where marketable permits have shaved off nearly 50 percent of the annual costs in comparison to forced scrubbing, have not been lost on the administration, and they deserve credit for that.

Having said that, I would certainly prefer at least a little bit more specificity about the targets and timetables that the administration would like to get in the agreement in Kyoto. This, in part, is because it's very hard to do the economic modeling on the administration's commitments unless we have more specific information about targets and timetables. I would also like to see more from the administration on the research and development that would be done in the interim, because I think everybody realizes that more R&D is essential if we're going to develop less carbon-intensive technologies. I'm going to come back to this point as I conclude.

Let me say a word or two about the cost of doing something. We're in Illinois, and when I was a graduate student here, the late Senator Everett Dirksen was one of the senators from Illinois. In talking about one government program he said, "a billion here, a billion there, pretty soon you're talking about real money." We're talking about real money when we talk about stabilizing CO_2 emissions anywhere near the levels that we have talked about so far. Two days ago I had a conversation with someone in the administration who's playing a prominent role in this modeling exercise. I asked what was the general consensus of the models with respect to the cost of stabilizing emissions in the year 2010 at about 1990 levels. The response I got was, about a $100-per-ton carbon tax. Admittedly this does not take into account the point that Amory made earlier. We have about a $7 trillion GDP right now. A $100-a-ton carbon tax, according to the models that the administration is looking at, would shave—for some period of time, not in perpetuity—about one percentage point off the annual rate of growth of GDP. That's about $70 billion per year. This is not enough to bring the U.S. economy to a halt, but on the other hand, we currently spend about $140 to $150 billion per year on all of the regulatory programs that have been put in place in the United States since 1970. So the climate stabilization measures that we're talking about now, using the best information that we have at our disposal, would be equal to about half of what we've spent to this point annually on all environmental measures. That's a lot of money. So we need to think seriously about this.

This leads me to my fourth and final point, which is the importance of research and development in all of this. I would imagine, although I haven't heard this from Senator Wirth, that when businessmen and women talk to him about waiting to act on this until more research and development is done, they are conspicuously absent in testifying before Congress for larger research and development budgets for the Department of Energy, the Environmental Protection Agency, NASA, etc. So I think that, to make business's position in the climate policy debate even more credible, you ought to be up there shoulder to shoulder with people from the administration and the environmental community, lobbying for more expenditures on research and development. I would add, in the spirit of what Steven Percy said earlier about BP's commitment, that you should begin to commit your own resources, perhaps in industry consortia, into research and development efforts designed to look at ways that we can reduce the carbon-intensity of economic growth in the United States. We clearly need to know more, to be smarter, and to find ways to get these costs down. It is going to be difficult to sell a $70-billion-a-year program to the United States people when some of them feel that climate mitigation will benefit Bengalis two hundred years from now but not themselves or their children in the here and now. This is a very tough political sell.

RICHARD KLIMISCH: Why in the world would you ever give research money on this subject to EPA or DOE?

PAUL PORTNEY: First of all, you wouldn't necessarily have to. Some parts of industry now contribute a lot of money to MIT for their climate modeling program. I think that's a good program. In addition, as the focus of the debate moves to economics and away from the science, there are a lot of other places, including RFF [Resources for the Future], that can do this kind of research. But I'm not going to stand up here and say that I don't think any of the research that's been funded by DOE or EPA has been any good. I think there have been good research programs there. But the money doesn't have to be run through there alone. The important thing is that the research gets done.

RICHARD KLIMISCH: I forgot about the National Labs. And of course, Research for the Future came to my mind right away. [laughter]

JOHN DELL, SENIOR VICE PRESIDENT, DUFF & PHELPS CREDIT RATING CO.: We may be on the course of an endless debate unless we reverse the order of things. I don't think that the attainment levels and the tax levels are likely to be decisive within any time frame that makes sense unless we decide how to apportion what the burden is around the world. And I'd have to say that I find it hard to accept the government's notion that the underdeveloped world shouldn't kick in pretty early in the game, if not immediately. I don't know whether it's at the same level or some other level, but the notion that the underdeveloped world, which is growing a heck of a lot faster in terms of energy use than the developed world, gets off the hook because the developed world fouled the nest is a premise that I don't think has any economic basis. Maybe it sounds fair, but it leaves most of industry in the U.S., Western Europe, and the rest of the developed world at a distinct economic disadvantage. And I don't think that any CEO in this room or any CEO in the rest of the developed world will settle on anything that gives them an economic disadvantage. The battle will never end. I think we better decide on a better way to apportion the cost and then decide on the cost in the opinion polls.

ROGER STONE: Even if you get the less developed world and emerging economies to agree, the act of agreeing and actually doing are two different things. How many in this country can say with any kind of assurance that once you did agree to this grand master plan—which could be very difficult to come to grips with anyway—what kind of enforcement scheme can make sure that it will happen? In my experience it has a higher probability of happening in the Western world once it's agreed upon. And in the less developed world it has very low probability of happening once it's agreed upon.

DAN MARTIN, DIRECTOR, WORLD ENVIRONMENT AND RESOURCES PROGRAM, THE MACARTHUR FOUNDATION: It strikes me that in very capital-intensive industries, such as paper, a large degree of capital is sunk in the United States, where you have a democratic procedure, a more educated market, and not many state enterprises. American manufacturers who are in a competitive situation with manufacturers in developing countries have a major interest in an agreement that will level the playing field. The American manufacturer is always going to be subjected, because of the nature of the consumers and democratic politics, to pressures that state enterprises don't experience. Given that, I don't understand why international climate change agreements are not seen as something very much in the interest of firms in the United States or Western Europe. This would suggest that, far from the United States' giving up something, we need negotiated agreements more than the competing enterprises in Malaysia or Indonesia, who would have advantages in the absence international agreements.

JAMES OLSON: I'd like to underscore what's been said. I, speaking for Toyota, and the auto industry are so afraid that we're going to end up with an agreement, supported primarily by the U.S. and Japan, where we have 70 percent of our global sales based on a command-and-control system to enforce it, and we will never get the developing Third World to enforce it unless the economics minister is sitting next to the environmental minister at the table. It just isn't going to happen.

AMORY LOVINS: But that split is exactly what puzzles me about this discussion, and it puzzled me in John Dell's remark, which is about costs and burdens and the need for (as you put it) possible command-and-control interventions to make people do things that are more expensive. I thought I heard Allen [Koleff] say that in his industry people are passing up six-month paybacks on energy efficiency because they're capital-constrained.

ALLEN KOLEFF: Let me correct that impression, Amory. I was trying to point out that in an industry as capital-intensive as ours there is a hierarchy of priorities for spending money. The projects at the bottom of the list don't get funded, and wherever the cutoff occurs is immaterial. The point is that if energy efficiency happens to be below the cutoff point, it's not going to happen.

AMORY LOVINS: Of course, but the point I'm making is that whatever that number is, something that pays back is not a cost, it's a profit. Let me go back to first principles. A certain distinguished economist said a few years ago that it would cost the U.S. about $200 billion a year to meet the Toronto target. That number got stuck in John Sununu's head and paralyzed policy for about eight years. Now, where did that number come from? It came from economic theories which said that if energy efficiency were cost-effective at present prices, people would have done it already, because we have an essentially perfect market. So it must not be cost-effective at present prices, and we need some kind of tax or trading system to raise the energy price and make it cost-effective. Then, as Paul [Portney] described, you just turn the crank on the model and say how much does this cost, how much does it depress GDP—especially if you don't reinvest it but rebate it—and then that's viewed as the "cost" to the economy. Well, that $200 billion was about right except for the sign. It actually *saves* about $200 billion a year, if you use the empirical data from industry and utilities that save energy every day and you simply ask them, "What does it cost to save energy?" So I asked this economist, "Why didn't you use the empirical data on what it actually costs to save energy?" And he said, "Oh, I just used an assumption from economic theory. That's an interesting hypothesis you have, Mr. Lovins, that maybe there's all this unbought efficiency out there because of some kind of hypothetical market failures. Of course, if you made that assumption, you'd reach a very different conclusion." Well, what the hell is a fact, if it isn't a measured number? I think we keep slipping back into theoretical assumptions rather than the everyday experiences that many of your companies have about the cost-effectiveness of efficiency opportunities that haven't all been captured yet—in fact, we've barely begun.

JAMES OLSON: We have already recognized the inevitable, with 70 percent of our sales exposed. We upped our R&D budget by nearly $1 billion last year, and that's going entirely into alternative power plants.

JOHN DELL: If Amory's right it would make it pretty easy to spread the burden on an even basis.

ROGER STONE: It would be self-funding.

AMORY LOVINS: *It isn't a burden* if in fact there's no cost.

JOHN DELL: If you could sell that to the rest of the world, Amory, then you would see a drop in the resistance level from the undeveloped world to get on board. And that's the point. It isn't spreading the burden, it's spreading out the attainment requirements.

AMORY LOVINS: And especially in a world where a quarter of all the development capital is going into more supply of electricity, and that investment is taken away from other vital development needs. A lot of economics ministers are struggling with macroeconomics competition for capital. If they can see a way not to build those plants because they find they can build a super-window factory or a compact fluorescent lamp factory for three orders of magnitude less capital than expanding the supply of electricity to provide the same services, that's just irresistible.

PAUL PORTNEY: I'm willing to make a concession to Amory: it is that markets are not as perfect as at least some people in the economics profession sometimes suggest that they are. If I could just get you to concede that businessmen and women are not as stupid as you persistently suggest that they are. The notion that we have to put a gun to businessmen and women's heads to get them to take advantage of all this free money is silly.

AMORY LOVINS: The people aren't stupid at all; it's actually an organizational failure. There are very well known issues in economic theory, principal-agent problems and so on, that explain exactly why companies full of smart people often don't do what makes great economic sense.

PAUL PORTNEY: And in some cases they don't, and in some cases they are able to take advantage of efficiencies that Milton Friedman would say they would have taken advantage of twenty-five years ago. But to say that on the one hand some people think that this will cost $200 billion a year to address, and to hear you say that we're going to get rich laughing to the bank while we're reducing our CO_2 emissions, is a big source of frustration to me. I've spent twenty years looking at alternative estimates of the cost of complying with various environmental regulatory programs. Business estimates are traditionally on the high side, not always out of mendacity but because they often say, "If we had to do this today, here's what this would cost us." If they're given the time and the flexibility, those cost estimates come down. On the other hand, I've seen estimates in the past that this will cost as little as that, and often it costs more than the lower-bound estimate. Somehow research is so important here because I've never seen a public policy issue where the range of cost estimates is so large between making a ton and going bankrupt. This lends itself to research, and I hope everybody would agree that one of the components of a climate policy program is investing more in research to begin to narrow this range of uncertainty.

AMORY LOVINS: And I hope we'd agree that it should be an empirical question.

MAX BAZERMAN: This goes back to my earlier question. We may not be home free, even if Amory is right. There are political, social, organizational, and cognitive barriers toward implementing it. So there's a fundamental point in the decision tree. If Amory's right, then we should be looking at the market imperfections and how to solve those, in order to get the technology solved. If not, then we have this trade-off issue. So one is an educational issue and getting through all these barriers, and the other one is a trade-off issue between this environmental problem and the economy. But there are two fundamentally different problems to address.

HOWARD (BUD) RIS: One of the clear lessons of this meeting is that we need some developing-country people representatives in the room. Let me try to make their case, just to throw it out on the table. Having heard all this, I think they would say the following: First of all, you all fouled the nest, which Tim said earlier. Number two, I'm from China, I recognize that my country is now probably the number-two emitter of carbon dioxide in the world, and our emissions are growing on a total country basis. But number three, our emissions per capita are probably one-fifth to one-tenth of yours in the United States, and so if we want to talk about burden sharing, we need to keep track of that. And number four, something you don't hear very much about, greenhouse gases have a very long residence time in the atmosphere—fifty to a hundred years or more. And if I asked you, being from China, to go back and look at the emissions of carbon dioxide that you have put in the atmosphere to date, even though I am now number two and might even surpass you in the next several years, it will be a very long time before the quantity of emissions I put in the atmosphere anywhere near approaches what you have put there for the last fifty years. So what some of us in the environmental and scientific community fear is that this is a big red herring. I'm not suggesting that any of you are doing this, but if industry puts forth this party line, I think most of the developing countries are going to take a hike very quickly for their own political reasons. And it's likely that we won't have a treaty. So it seems to me that if we believe this is a problem, that we have to adopt some kind of sequencing approach. I'm not sure it's exactly the one that Tim, Dirk, or the administration puts forward, but we have to somehow demonstrate that the developed countries will lead and demonstrate some level of commitment. But then there has to be a trigger mechanism that says, as soon as you have done that, the developing countries have to come in. I would just predict that we will not have a treaty if we simply just keep on saying that it's not fair, because the developing countries have a much stronger argument to say it would be unfair to saddle them with the biggest burden right off the bat.

RICHARD KLIMISCH: It's a little bit more complicated than that. I've seen a gentlemen from the India Energy Institute put up a chart of CO_2 cumulative emissions since 1870. It shows that they've got a long way to go before they're up to Europe. The one thing that keeps coming up is the issue of marketing, and trading in sulfur in particular. It was my impression that most of that cost reduction was due to deregulation of the railroads so that they could bring low-sulfur coal from the Powder River basin. How much of that was trading? I mean, I'm a big fan of trading, but I thought a lot of it was deregulation of the railroad.

PAUL PORTNEY: Well, briefly, the deregulation of the Railroads Act was 1979 or 1980, so a lot of the estimates that were made during the 1980s were made predicated on a deregulated rail industry. I think there still was a big surprise element there, and I think the idea of giving flexibility was important—giving utilities the opportunity to dual-fuel boilers with either coal or natural gas. The truth is that the cost of scrubbers fell dramatically once scrubbing was no longer the only way you could reduce SO_2 from flue gases, and so I think that shows the beauty of competition and the wonderful thing about a market approach. We learned after the fact what the costs are. If you do this by fiat, we never know ex post facto how expensive it was to do this, and to me that's why a marketing approach to a carbon emissions policy, whether it's a tax approach or a marketable permits approach, is so useful.

JAMES O'CONNOR: But the answer to your question is that railroad deregulation and the entry of new railroads was a major contributor to dropping prices. It took a while to build just the trackage. This made all the difference in the world. Competition worked. It worked by about 40 percent.

DAN MARTIN: Getting back to Bud's comment about the developing world, even without the consideration for prior cumulative emissions, we still have the differential per capita. If we ignore the number of people involved and only look at the percentage of emissions, the United States is now producing 25 percent of the total emissions, while China and India are growing. In that light, you might have a relatively neutral way of resolving this controversy. The cumulative argument is persuasive to the people who are making it, but in a political process it would be hard to implement, because it's hard to track. We can't escape the fact that the United States, which accounts for 4 percent of the world's population, is still producing 25 percent of the world's emissions. And then you get the competitive question about the trade-off between energy use and efficiency practices in the United States, Japan, and Europe. We operate at a considerable competitive disadvantage with the other industrial centers of the world because of our inefficiencies. But if we only looked at the contribution to the total emission, I think you could have something more of a serious negotiation with India and China.

JOHN BOBEK, VICE PRESIDENT, JOHNSON CONTROLS, INC.: I don't mean to sound Pollyannaish, but I am optimistic about the developing world. I work for Johnson Controls and travel the world frequently. The statistics that I've seen suggest that the new construction of work space, office space, and industrial space in particular in Shanghai alone is four times more than the construction activity going on in the U.S. Shanghai seems to have the construction crane as its national bird. It's the same thing in Kuala Lumpur, Jakarta, and at least half a dozen other cities. I've visited them and counted cranes. And yet, my experience in dealing with those who are putting up those buildings indicates that they do have an emphasis on total life cycle cost, and in fact energy efficiency is sometimes easier to sell in developing countries than it is in developed countries, particularly the U.S. So in some ways the developing countries are already getting ahead of the curve, which may portend for competitive issues downstream, since they are building energy efficiency into their industrial plants and commercial buildings up front.

ANDREW HOFFMAN: Is that because they have higher energy costs?

HOWARD RIS: They don't have much energy. They have to save it.

JOHN BOBEK: It varies from country to country. There seems to be a renewed emphasis on total capital and operating costs in the long term, including energy costs. Many developing countries do have higher energy costs per unit as output. But most of this cost problem is due to energy inefficiencies, not high fuel cost. Energy efficiency is also the quickest, least expensive way to lower carbon emissions.

RICHARD ABDOO: And the numbers we're talking about here may also have the unintended result of making nuclear the cleanest, most inexpensive source of electric energy.

ANDREW HOFFMAN: Well, it looks like the common ground we've agreed upon here is that it's us versus them, the developing world versus the developed world. Am I reading this wrong?

ROGER STONE: Is it reasonable to assume that we can even come to an agreement? Because of these diverse issues and diverse plans, is it reasonable to expect that agreement is possible?

RICHARD KLIMISCH: It isn't a question of us versus them. It isn't a question of fairness. I think the issue is, even if the Annex 1 countries do all the things imaginable, it's not going to make any difference. China, India, and Brazil are going to blow us away. So the question is, what's the point? Unless we find a proper incentive for them to join this, it's not going to work. It's naive to think that if we go ahead and do all this then they'll somehow say, "Oh, what a great idea, we'll do it too."

BRET MAXWELL, MANAGING DIRECTOR, FIRST ANALYSIS CORP., AND BOARD MEMBER, ENRON RENEWABLE ENERGY CORP.: I am surprised no one raised the issue of education, particularly for the average citizen in the United States. As I visit other parts of the world, the average person on the street seems to be much more aware of these issues than the average American citizen. Given that we are by far the largest generators of CO_2 per capita, it's important that we set an example to the rest of the world. But the average American citizen is unaware of these issues or doesn't seem to care. We are simply energy pigs, for a lack of a better way to describe it. Does the administration have a plan for educating people on this issue?

The other point I wanted to raise was Mr. O'Connor's point on deregulation. While utility deregulation is sweeping the country, the actual deregulation process is somewhat erratic. Consider California, where the initial deregulation strategy set by the Public Utility Commission was going to give a four-year window to generators who use renewable energy sources. That is, they would have allowed those generators to begin soliciting customers at the beginning of 1998 while those using fossil fuel sources would have had to wait another four years before they could begin soliciting customers. This would have been a tremendous benefit to the renewable energy industry. But in the next iteration of regulation, this renewable benefit was taken away, without any explanation, effectively deincentivizing the further deployment of renewable energy sources.

JAMES O'CONNOR: I wasn't aware of that.

JOHN BOBEK: But even without such government incentives, our fastest-growing business at Johnson Controls is performance contracting, which is the fine art and science of squeezing energy out of buildings without compromising the indoor environment. Our biggest market for that is K through 12 schools, and in many of our school district contracts there is a specific requirement for us to make the energy conservation experience not only economically sound for the school district but also an educational experience for the students. So folks in the United States are trying to build energy awareness into the educational programs at a very early age.

JAMES O'CONNOR: After deregulation, as we enter the competitive arena and those gates open up, you're not going to see a lot of electric utilities in this country raising rates. It's just not going to happen. In fact, you're going to see them going in the other direction. That's caused a lot of companies to get into performance contracting, and we hope that Johnson Controls stays in Kuala Lumpur and Shanghai and not in northern Illinois. [laughter]

We estimate that in northern Illinois alone there's about $1.2 billion dollars in performance contracting as a market. So our utility, as well as a whole host of others, are looking at this area, because our revenue increases are not going to come from increasing rates, and they're not going to come, in many instances. from increasing usage. We don't see that. We see things like the electrification of factories, the electric car, and a few others, but we do not see usage increasing at the rate that it's been increasing on an average annual basis over the last twenty years. So you'll find utilities looking for other avenues. One of the foremost will be performance contracting.

DENNIS PARKER, VICE PRESIDENT, CONOCO, INC.: Conoco's position is generally in line with the BP position described in Steven Percy's presentation. I feel there are two main focus areas: clarifying the technical aspects of greenhouse concentrations in the environment, and the impacts of proposed controls on the world economy. Currently some are alleging greenhouse gas environmental impacts that have not been scientifically determined. We need to understand the scientific impacts before jumping to draconian solutions.

But the most important area for our focus is the world economy. The community and industrial infrastructure of the developed world is tied to fossil fuels. The developing countries are trying to grow rapidly to get the basics of life for their citizens. Accompanying this growth is an increase in their use of fossil fuels. I believe that this growth needs to continue for the well-being and quality of life of all world citizens. Having said that, it is imperative that the administration take a firm stand in requiring both developed and developing countries to share in any commitment, rather than to move unilaterally. When actions are taken, I believe they should involve more incentives and less punitive measures. For example, U.S. tax structures are one of the reasons Amory's optimal engineering solutions are not implemented. Capital investments are written off slowly over many years, versus expenses like energy use being written off in a single year.

DAVID KEE, DIVISION DIRECTOR, U.S. EPA REGION V: But in the end we need to start setting an example for the rest of the world. Our pattern of urban development in this country is one of sprawl, and we're going to have to start talking about that issue. In the Chicago area we have a village called Naperville which will probably soon annex Peoria, and it just seems to me that we haven't talked much about transportation issues in terms of emissions, but that has to be on the table.

PAUL PORTNEY: There is an existing pricing mechanism that sends an awfully strong signal that influences sprawl, energy use, and investments in research and development on energy conservation. Maybe we need a little bit more backbone and more willingness to use the pricing mechanism as a way to direct development in these areas. Pricing mechanisms convey a heck of a lot of information, there's no question about it.

JOHN BOBEK: Is there an official opinion among our executives from the electric utility industry as to whether the pricing mechanisms of utility deregulation will have a positive or negative effect on emissions? The signals are that the price of electricity may come down, which actually may encourage more usage. If deregulation, as Amory said earlier, does not favor nuclear, then as the nuclear plant base gets retired prematurely, it seems the only substitute is a carbon-based fuel.

AMORY LOVINS: That is simply not true. What you would buy now is either a combined-cycle gas plant at about 2.5 to 3 cents a kilowatt hour, or renewables—whose cost is all over the map, depending on what they are, but they're worth a lot more than they look like because of distributed benefits—or efficiency that's typically a cent or less per kilowatt hour. You'd never buy another nuclear plant, and if you did, it would make global warming worse. Why is that? Because as long as there are cheaper options available, every dollar you spend on a more expensive instead of a cheaper option means that you're releasing more carbon into the air than if you bought the cheapest thing first, because that would displace the most coal burning per dollar. It's a simple opportunity-cost argument.

RICHARD ABDOO: That is not a universally held view in the electric utility industry.

AMORY LOVINS: From straightforward economics, I think Paul would agree with me about that. If there's a cheaper option, you can displace more coal per dollar by buying it.

RICHARD ABDOO: And even if you decided all of these wonderful things tomorrow, they are not available. My view is that the "green smokestack" that some people in the Northeast and other high-cost areas have hidden behind is somewhat bogus. Markets will, in fact, work over a period of time. There may indeed be more requirements on NOx, for example, where there are controls and things you can do. But you're going to have to compensate for them. To assume that the existing environmental infrastructure will be adequate in a restructured, deregulated industry is unrealistic. But the "antis" are using that as a reason for a green smokescreen to simply say, "We can't do it, because there may be modifications required and new environmental regulations." We would argue that at the appropriate level you could actually benefit the environment with less pollution and the customers with lower prices.

ANDREW BERMINGHAM, MANAGING DIRECTOR, MONTREUX ENERGY CORP.: I'd like to get back to the developing-world issue. India provides essentially free power to a great percentage of its population. But India, China, and many other places around the world have got a 20 percent or more savings rate. Is there not some way that we can tap into that momentum? Is there not a way that we can understand that perhaps in this country, if we had a little bit higher savings rate, we wouldn't have the problems we have with caring for our growing elderly population and a number of other things? Is there not a way we can position ourselves to be a little bit more open to learn what the developing countries have to teach us? And in doing so, can we gain their trust and openness and get away from the idea that we've got to teach them and that we know it all? I'd love to hear Paul's [Portney] thoughts on the savings rate.

PAUL PORTNEY: That's a problem that a lot smarter guys than I have puzzled about for a long time. The savings rate in the United States is deplorably low. We need to raise it. I think it comes back to investments in education as being the key not only to the savings rate issue but also to understanding the seriousness of climate change. We need to bring public understanding to the point where we can have a debate in the United States about people's willingness to commit resources to this problem as opposed to any number of other pressing needs that we have to deal with.

RICHARD ABDOO: But in terms of education, the government has to take the lead. People in this country and developing countries alike respond to the signals they get. Where do they get most of them from? The U.S. government. And when the Clean Air Act says you can move five hundred feet over the county line and build a stack free of certain regulations, people do that. You get this over and over again. We've got the world's cheapest energy crisis. There are disincentives to conservation, as Amory pointed out. That's the point I was getting to with Tim. I wanted to badger him a little bit. If this is really important, then the U.S. government needs to take the lead. The U.S. government must establish policies that when people study them, they will decide that there is an advantage to doing this, not a disadvantage. If it's important to do it, they will respond.

CLEMENT ERBMANN, MANAGING DIRECTOR, FIRST ANALYSIS CORP.: I was born and grew up in Zimbabwe and feel I have a good understanding of the mentality of politicians in underdeveloped countries. I do not believe that there will be a big problem convincing these governments to comply with the regulations. There is an understanding that an infusion of foreign investment capital is necessary for economic development and that this infusion does not come without concessions. This linkage is politically acceptable and is beneficial to the country in the short term through capital infusion and in the long term through a decrease in health costs. I think acceptance of the solution will be a lot easier than we anticipate.

ANDREW HOFFMAN: We are running out of time and must bring some closure to these discussions. Dirk Forrister has been listening to this dialogue and has agreed to offer concluding remarks on what he's heard and how it can be integrated into the U.S. position going into Kyoto.[1]

Integrating Industry Concerns into
the U.S. Negotiating Framework

Dirk Forrister, Chairman,
White House Climate Change Task Force

Before I begin I want to tell Dick Abdoo that there's good news. This headline ran in the *New York Times* yesterday: "U.S. to Renovate Federal Buildings to Cut Energy Bills by 25 Percent." My hat goes off to Federico Pena for launching a program that's going to save energy, on the order of $1 billion a year, at federal facilities across the country. We are going to beef up our efforts to try to lead by example. But Amory's right, some of his former colleagues who are now in the energy-efficiency area at the Department of Energy would probably say that it's only a start, that there's much more that could be done.

A well-known senator said of Tim Wirth's negotiation over the Berlin mandate, "If this were a game of strip poker, the U.S. had negotiated itself down to its skivvies." I think this view grew from his perception that the cards that we were holding would cost $100 to $200 billion per year. This is the point raised by some in this room that a $100 billion cost could cause, according to one model, a 1 percent drag on GDP for a short period of time, after which the economy will start to rebound on the investment. I can't really talk a lot about the administration's draft analysis while it undergoes peer review. Yet I'm going to stand by what I said earlier to my friend from EPRI, Mr. Peck, that the $100 billion cost does not relate to the position that we are advancing in the international forum.

The cards we are actually playing in the international forum are not based on $100 billion and an inflexible, command-and-control policy. In fact, we favor global flexibility that drives the cost down significantly. EPRI worked with Battelle on some of the cost-saving analyses that I was referring to earlier. The $100-billion-per-year cost estimate flows from an assumption of no flexibility. You do it all at home; you don't get any international trading. But actually, three of the partners in one of the greatest joint implementation pilot ventures in the world are here today: NIPSCO, Commonwealth Edison, and WEPCO. They are proving on a pilot scale that flexibility works. Our critics also presume that the cards we are playing are based on no developing-country actions. I agree that if these were the cards that we're holding, we're not going to get anywhere very fast. The point raised earlier about simply transferring problems to other places becomes more valid under such dismal assumptions. That's probably the scenario that some in this room have been looking at. Well, this is not the set of cards that we in the United States government believe that we are playing in the international forum. We think that we're playing with something that is more akin to the "where and when" flexibility that was referred to earlier by Steve Percy.

Now, we aren't talking about setting a global budget for the whole century, which that study looked at. And a lot of people in this room would not want us to set emissions budgets without developing countries' having the same kind of binding obligation. So if we get the "where and when" flexibility that these models show us, even with the flawed systems that Amory pointed out, we can get up to 85 percent cost reduction by rationalizing where and when we do it. Maybe we won't get the whole 85 percent, but that's what the cards tell us right now. We're looking for full flexibility, and we are looking for several things from the developing countries.

Let me describe the three things that we're doing to bridge this into our position, things that we're trying to get from developing countries to enhance performance under their existing commitments in the Rio Convention. First, they should begin taking no-regrets action early. Second, we're trying to launch a voluntary category for some of the more developed of the developing countries to step in and voluntarily take binding emissions budgets at some level or time frame. Third, we're looking for a certain date, such as 2005, when all nations would have negotiated binding commitments. Remember that the framework Tim laid out earlier required that developed countries take binding commitments in the medium term. We've basically ruled out 2005. So we're looking at a medium-term clump of years that probably spans 2010 to 2015 or 2020, when we would start to take our binding obligation. Our view is that everybody will have binding obligations set. We've got this in brackets and it's negotiable, but we've started out saying, maybe 2005.

So we have the view that we're taking an important step forward and everybody else is starting to move along with us. And when you think about where Tim Wirth stands in these negotiations, this is where we begin [see Figure 14.1]. Per capita emissions is how the developing world wants to look at this. And you'll notice that we lead the pack. Notice where China comes in. This is the top twenty CO_2 emitters [pointing at

Figure 14.1. Per Capita CO$_2$ Emissions, 1992
(Fossil Fuel and Cement Sources Only).

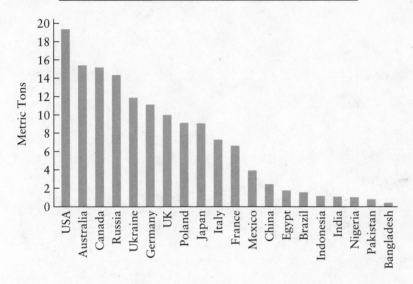

Source: World Resources Institute, *World Resources 1996–1997* (New York: Oxford University Press, 1996): 326.

chart], and they come around twelve or fifteen. But let me show you another chart. This is total emissions [see Figure 14.2]. This is the way we tend to look at it more often, because this shows that in 1992 China was number two. So it's true they're growing into a more and more important player. But any way you cut it in these negotiations, the United States is the number-one emitter. This shows our standing over time from 1970 to 1994 [see Figure 14.3].

. So what we're talking about in this set of negotiations is the next step for all of the higher emitters. Then we want to see a graduated system where the others come in steadily over the following few years. I'm going to show you one more version of the cumulative picture that makes Bud's [Ris] point even more graphically. The way many developed nations look at the negotiations, the developed world has been fouling the nest [see Figure 14.4]. We in the developed world have pumped 74 percent of what's up there. So it's right that the developed world should take the first step and show some leadership.

And just for posterity, I want to underscore that this is not something that we invented in Berlin. This goes right back to the Framework Convention on Climate Change negotiated by the last administration in 1992

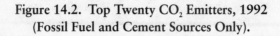

**Figure 14.2. Top Twenty CO_2 Emitters, 1992
(Fossil Fuel and Cement Sources Only).**

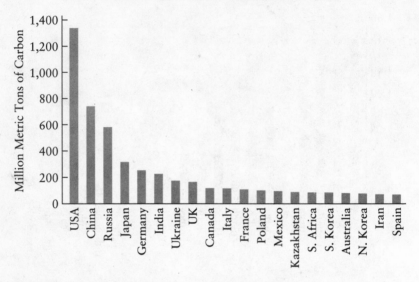

Source: Oak Ridge National Laboratory, *1992 Estimates of CO_2 Emissions from Fossil Fuel Burning and Cement Manufacturing Based on the UN Energy Statistics and the US Bureau of Mines Cement Manufacturing Data.* File CDIAC-25, NDP-030, 9/95. (Oak Ridge, TN: Oak Ridge National Laboratory, 1995).

in Rio. The concepts of developed countries' taking the lead and going first with "common but differentiated responsibilities" and developing countries' having more time to develop before they take on responsibilities are all in the 1992 convention. This convention was already ratified by the United States Senate. It is there. It is U.S. policy. So that's one of the cards that we started with, common but differentiated responsibilities. Most of all, it's right that we should be stepping forward in taking responsibility to lead on this next step. Not in perpetuity, but as the beginning of an effort to manage this problem for the long term.

I actually found John's [Dell] comments some of the most interesting in terms of—let's get real about this—developing countries are growing to be more and more part of the problem and must be included in the solution. I once saw a chart that compared growth between now and 2015 from all of the OECD in one bar and China in another bar, and guess which one was bigger? It was the China bar. They're going to add more capacity and more emissions than all the OECD combined. If we

Figure 14.3. Energy-Related
CO_2 Emissions by Region, 1970–1994.

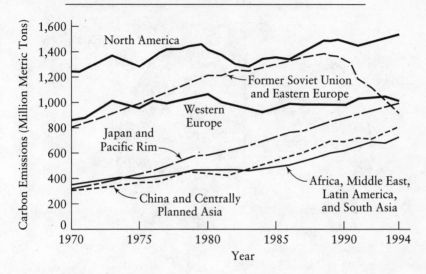

Source: Energy Information Administration, *Emissions of Greenhouse Gases in the US, 1995* (Washington, DC: Energy Information Administration, 1995): 9.

suck up all the capital that we have available to address this problem by directing it only within the OECD, that's not really a smart solution. And that is not what the United States has been pushing. We are not pushing to begin with budgets that go with per capita emissions, for example. We're talking about using real 1990 emissions as a baseline—what your historic emissions were in 1990 and trying to measure improvements off of that. Now it's true that we haven't said whether we're looking to stabilize or whether we're looking to reduce emissions, but we're seeking a rational approach. It is not in our self-interest to use a per capita basis or a differentiated scheme but rather a formula based on 1990 emissions levels with all the developed world taking a uniform percentage of that. Maybe it's 100 percent times however many years are in our budget. Maybe it's some amount plus or minus. But we're analyzing that, and you'll see what our analytics show very soon. But directionally, what this combined with a joint implementation strategy allows us to do is get that capital to the places where it can do the most good. It allows "where and when" flexibility in world compliance.

This is the another version of the chart that Steven Percy showed us based on the analysis that EPRI and Battelle did [see Figure 14.5]. We can save ourselves 85 percent—I put 80 to be conservative. This is the

Figure 14.4. Cumulative Global Emissions of CO_2, 1950–1992 (Fossil Fuel and Cement Sources Only).

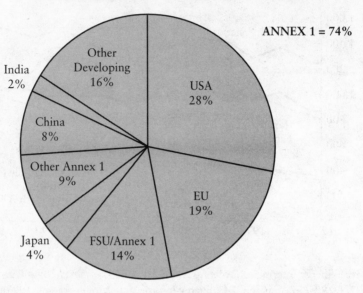

Source: G. Marland, R. Andres, and T. Boden, "Global, Regional and National CO_2 Emission," in T. Boden, D. Kaiser, R. Sepanski, and F. Stoss (eds.), *Trends '93: A Compendium of Data on Global Change.* File CDIAC-65. (Oak Ridge, TN: Oak Ridge National Laboratory, 1994).

real world that Jim O'Connor and Dick Abdoo know well, showing what's going on in international power markets. I think it's a good surrogate for making my point. We have some existing plants that may have opportunities for retrofit to reduce emissions costs effectively. But most of our fleet of power plants are relatively modern and efficient by world standards. New plants being constructed tend to be in developing countries right now. Dick, when was your last power plant built?

RICHARD ABDOO: It was ordered in the mid-1970s and went into service in 1980.

DIRK FORRISTER: How about NIPSCO?

PATRICK MULCHAY, EXECUTIVE VICE PRESIDENT, NORTHERN INDIANA PUBLIC SERVICE CO.: The last one went into service in 1986.

Figure 14.5. World Climate Change Compliance Costs.

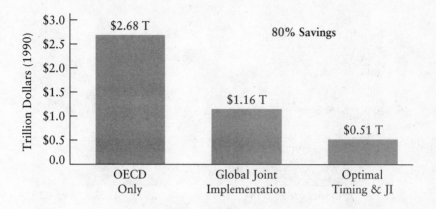

Note: The $2.2 trillion savings between the first and third columns is roughly equivalent in value to one-third of current annual U.S. economic output.
Source: A. Manne and R. Richels, "The Berlin Mandate: The Costs of Meeting Post-2000 Targets and Timetables," *Energy Policy,* 1996, *24*(3): 205–210.

DIRK FORRISTER: So there hasn't been a whole lot being built in the United States lately. This chart shows what power projects have been built in developing countries, projects that actually reached financial closure over the ten-year period from 1985 to 1995 [see Figure 14.6]. What's really interesting about this chart is that the amount of money coming out of international private sources—which is the top—has tripled since 1992. This is the marketplace that so many U.S. electric utilities now have subsidiaries entering. What joint implementation creates is the possibilities for these types of investments to go toward higher-end technologies that reduce emissions and provide an opportunity to swap credits. Overlaying U.S. climate policy on top of this type of a market reality is going to create strong incentives for getting capital to the places that it can do the most good. A lot of our power plants are not at the end of their useful life. A lot of the ones in the former Soviet Union, China, or India are.

I want to talk about what I think are the leading points to take from this discussion today, points that would be valuable for continuing dialogue about the construction of policy in the future. One is that we

Figure 14.6. Power Sector Finance for Developing Countries.

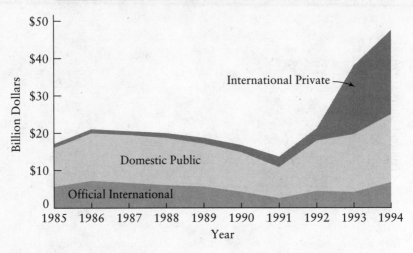

Source: Resource Dynamics Corporation, *Financing Worldwide Electric Power: Can Capital Markets Do the Job?* Contract DE-AC01-92FE62489. (Vienna, VA: U.S. Department of Energy, 1996): ES-3.

should stick to our guns in the negotiations and bring home a protocol that has features of flexibility, features that make business sense and enable us to comply at an affordable cost. What hasn't been said is that a climate protocol must go through Senate ratification. We're talking about sixty-seven votes in the United States Senate before the U.S. is committed to this. We're also talking about a domestic implementation strategy to go with it. Well, we're not going to develop it in a strictly partisan fashion. We've got to be able to show that this is an economically sensible approach. That's why we're going to stick to our guns and try to bring home a protocol that has these marks of economic rationality. Climate policy should look like what bipartisan majorities supported in the past, like the Clean Air Act or the acid rain program.

I also think that our policy is likely to maintain the kind of flexibility for companies that we've seen up until now. Jim O'Connor talked about the Climate Challenge Program that is near and dear to my heart. I spent a lot of time at the Department of Energy working on that program. It has achieved by far the largest reductions of any of the voluntary programs launched so far. For those of you who don't know, it's a program where electric utilities take on voluntary commitments—like BP has just done in the Climate Wise Program—to look across their company for cost-effective reductions that make sense. Our policy is going to try to honor those commitments. In fact, one way or another we must provide the same kind of flexibility to go across sectors, across gases, and into sinks, to bring home the reductions that make the most sense. Now, whether we go voluntary or mandatory, that's something we need to talk more about. The binding nature of this convention may mean that we need to look at more serious types of commitments or legislation. Certainly, as electric utility restructuring continues, this is a conversation that is going to occur.

As a matter of fact, it is interesting that the first foray into connecting climate and electricity restructuring was not made by a Democrat. The first foray on this was by Senator Jim Jeffords, who introduced a bill that would give the EPA administrator the authority to cap CO_2 emissions. So it's already in the debate, and I think it will continue to be part of the debate for that sector. But this type of flexibility approach may also have a place for other industries in this room. I am particularly impressed with what BP did earlier this week. I had the privilege of being in California that day at another forum and got to hear John Browne's remarks. Browne's remarks, combined with some of the other remarks I have heard in this room, make me believe that there's hope of avoiding a confrontational debate over this environmental problem. Instead we are seeking a more cooperative solution. We heard a great deal about that today.

I want to pick up on one other point about our domestic policy. We're going to look to reward those type of players that have stepped forward and tried to work with us. But the other thing I heard here today from Paul Portney was a strong endorsement for research and development. I haven't seen any model or talked to anyone who's serious about work on the climate change issue where research and development doesn't come up as a high priority. It's in the BP commitment; it's in a number of other places; it's coming up as a regular theme among opinion leaders. I think there's a model out there that some of you in the room are familiar with that others ought to take a look at. It takes the Partnership for a New Generation of Vehicles program and applies a similar approach to other sectors. It's the Industries of the Future Program at the Department of Energy. The paper industry has participated in this partnership, coming together to determine where it wants to be in the year 2020 in terms of its energy, environmental, and economic performance. They agreed upon a vision of where they wanted to go and delivered a technology road map on how to get there. This is giving government as well as industry a very valuable tool to use in designing a more rational research and development strategy. I think this approach is likely to be part of the answer.

The other thing that I've heard here today that I think is important is education. We recognize that in this country the thinking on this issue is more advanced than it is in some countries. But it is not as advanced as it is in others. The European Union, for example, sees this as an urgent issue. Ultimately, the ratepayers, shareholders, and purchasers of automobiles have to have some better understanding of this. That's part of why my task force exists to try to improve our outreach and dialogue with the public on this issue. I hope we'll see more public education going on. But there's another point that I think is really valuable, and I will close with this, the opportunity in the international arena for sharing experiences that have worked in this country. Maybe it's the Climate Challenge program or the Industry Visions of the Future program, or maybe it's just knowledge transfers. I was privileged to conduct energy bilaterals in India last fall when I was still at the Energy Department. They have electric power shortfalls on the order of 14 percent a year, and it was very interesting to learn that they've got installed capacity to meet that need. They just haven't got the know-how and, in some places, the technology. But they aren't even operating the existing power plants to spec. There's tremendous opportunity for sharing knowledge abroad that could help reduce emissions and could conceivably be credited in a joint implementation venture. I think the education piece is a very important one and one that we all ought to look at again.

NOTE

1. Dirk Forrister is a public servant whose words are part of the public domain. They are excluded from any copyright claim on the rest of this book and may be freely copied by anyone.

15

DIALOGUE

Responding to the Public

ANDREW HOFFMAN: I want to take a minute to set the context of what we are doing here. First of all, we are sitting in a hall in a business school to talk about an environmental issue. I want you to appreciate the significance of that, the importance of environment in business today. We have a list of senior executives, CEOs of oil companies, paper companies, and utilities coming to talk about an environmental issue. More importantly, coming to engage environmental activists and government in this debate. Let there be no mistake about it, environmental management and corporate strategy are inextricably intertwined. Environmental management is a significant part of corporate strategy in the 1990s. That's the general context of what we're doing here.

The specific context is the topic of climate change. Just to get you up to speed, for those who aren't familiar with it, we are talking about greenhouse gas emissions. The burning of fossil fuels produces carbon dioxide and other greenhouse gases, which trap heat in the atmosphere. The scientific consensus is pretty solid that the gases are building up, and now there's some political momentum that we should try to do something about it. So I want you to consider some of the things that have been happening in the past two or three years that are leading up to what is going to happen in December, which is why we're coming together today.

First, in 1995, twenty-five hundred scientists of the Intergovernmental Panel on Climate Change presented a report concluding, and I quote, "The balance of evidence suggests a discernible human influence on the global climate, and that climate is expected to continue to change over the next century." In 1996 the Clinton administration agreed to a negotiated treaty in which *binding* timetables and targets would be set for reducing the emissions of greenhouse gases. Then, earlier this year, two thousand economists, including eight Nobel laureates, endorsed a report saying that carbon dioxide emissions could be reduced with little or no effect on the economy. This all leads up to December of this year, when the United States will send negotiators to Kyoto, Japan, to negotiate a treaty on carbon dioxide emissions and controlling those emissions worldwide.

Now, there are many aspects of that treaty which we're going to talk about today. Aspects that have tremendous implication for industry. Simply put, controlling CO_2 means controlling energy use. In one way or another, when shifting to alternative energy sources or putting taxes on energy, it fundamentally impacts energy. And when you impact energy, you impact every single sector of the economy. Because of that, the response from industry has been strong and passionate. Anyone who has been following the debate knows that the stir over the scientific evidence has been vigorous over the past couple of years, and now we're starting to shift from a focus on science to a focus on economics and the competitive position of the United States relative to other countries. That's what we're trying to focus on today. We're trying to get past the science and focus on what this means for corporations in the United States. We worked on this over the last four and a half hours in private, and now we're going to share some of our thoughts in public.

Energy Efficiency, the "No-Regrets Policy," and Market Failures

Amory B. Lovins, Vice President and Director of Research, Rocky Mountain Institute

There is some very good news about the climate problem: we do not need to worry about how the climate science turns out or whether this is a real problem or not. I happen to think it is; I have been following it in some detail for thirty years. But it doesn't matter who is right about it, because we ought to do the same things about it anyway just to save money. That is, what are called in the trade the "no-regrets options"— the things we ought to do anyway because they are profitable—are, I think, enough to stabilize climate very nicely. The obstacles to achieving this profitable resolution are not technological or economic. Rather, they are cultural and procedural. They are what economists call "market failures"—the silly rules and practices that do not mean anyone is dumb but rather that the normal way we do things does not let us use energy in a way that saves money.

I live in a house at 7,100 feet in the Rockies, where the temperature goes to minus 47 degrees Fahrenheit and it can be cloudy for thirty-nine days at a time in midwinter. The growing season between hard frosts is fifty-two days. You can get frost any day of the year. We are currently harvesting our twenty-fifth passive solar banana crop. We get them all winter too, yet there is no heating system, and the house is cheaper to build that way. We have done the same thing at 115 degrees Fahrenheit: a house that does not need heating or cooling equipment is more comfortable and costs less to build.

There are many more examples of the astonishing results of modern techniques for making big savings of energy cheaper than small savings. We had a 97 percent energy saving by retrofitting an office air conditioning system, and it became more comfortable. We just got a 92 percent energy saving on a pumping system in a Chinese carpet factory just from using big pipes and small pumps instead of small pipes and big pumps and from laying out the pipes first, then the equipment, so the pipes were short and straight, without the friction of extra bends. About twenty-five current and intending automakers are developing ultralight hybrid electric "hypercars" that start at one hundred miles a gallon and go up to two hundred or more, burning whatever fuel you want. They have zero or zero-equivalent emissions; they are superior in all respects like performance, comfort, and safety; and they probably cost about the same to build, or less. Those hypercars should start hitting the market in early models in the next few years, just through market competition— no government policy, no taxes, no mandates.

The whole climate debate ignores this kind of advanced engineering development. In fact, it is not based on technology at all. It is based on a theoretical economic assumption that saving energy, or doing the other things that protect the climate, like sustainable farming and forestry practices, must cost more or we would have done them already. It is the story of the economist who doesn't pick up the $20 bill off the street because such things could not possibly exist; somebody would have picked it up already. Well, I go into factories all the time, of every imaginable variety, and there are figuratively $10,000 bills lying all over the floor. For example, if a single watermelon-sized motor were spec'd properly, it would add about $10,000 of present value to the bottom line, and the whole factory is full of hundreds of such motors. This is not at all unusual. Even companies that are relatively efficient and countries that are relatively efficient have the same potential, although the biggest potential is in the developing and formerly socialist economies. Developing countries are on average about three times less energy-efficient than, say, the United States, which has an overall energy efficiency of a few percent compared to what is theoretically possible: for example, only 1 percent of a car's fuel energy actually moves the driver. America's materials efficiency is only around 1 percent. There is clearly a lot of room for improvement.

So what I think we ought to be focusing on is not the economic theory that says energy efficiency must not be worthwhile or we would have done it already, how much do we have to raise the price to make it worthwhile, and then how much does that depress the economy and cost jobs, etc. Rather, we ought to be focusing on the specific market failures that prevent people from doing what makes economic sense. For example, we reward utilities in almost every state, including this one, for selling you more energy, and we penalize them for cutting your bill. We reward architects and engineers for what they spend, not for what they save, and in general they don't get any of the savings they achieve. We require energy savings to pay back about ten times as fast as energy supplies—that's like a tenfold price distortion. We don't smooth out the split incentives: why should you fix up your house if the landlord owns it, or why should the landlord do it if you pay the utilities?

I think once we get to grips with these practical obstacles to implementing existing technology, obstacles which practitioners of energy efficiency and other climate-protecting measures butt their heads against every day, we will find that the climate problem becomes not a cost but a profit. Solving it will take a lot of work, but not nearly the kind of burden that is commonly discussed. Quite the contrary, we will find it a source of prosperity and competitive advantage.

The Need for "Where" and "When" Flexibility

Stephen C. Peck, Vice President,
Electric Power Research Institute

I want to talk about the advantages that can be bought in "where" and "when" flexibility. Any policy to stabilize carbon dioxide concentrations in the atmosphere will be expensive, but proper application of the principles of "where and when" flexibility has the potential to save a lot of money, trillions of dollars, in fact, between the cost of an arbitrary policy and the cost of the optimal policy. But they are difficult to implement, and so, although the U.S. policy in general supports "where and when" flexibility, there are many details in getting them right so that we can, in fact, save those trillions of dollars. And it is important to manage them well, because if in fact climate policies are too expensive, then there won't be the will in the world to implement them. So let's talk about the principles involved.

This analysis is based on four computer models of the world over the next couple of centuries and what happens to carbon dioxide in the atmosphere [see Figure 13.1]. The base case shows one hundred as the level of cost of an arbitrary climate policy. If in fact you can go to a policy of "where" flexibility, it will enable you to find the cheapest places in the world to reduce those carbon dioxide emissions, whether they are in the developed world or in the developing world. Now, one of the things we heard about the U.S. policy is that initially it is going to include the developed world—that is, the OECD, and possibly the former Soviet Union and Eastern Europe—but it is going to leave the developing world out for a while. Now, if we leave the developing world out for a while, the costs shown here will be closer to the one hundred than they are to the much lower level in the diagram associated with "where" flexibility. To include the developing world, one argument is that we have to make a commitment in the developed world and then later on, if we are lucky, the developing world will join us. But what that does is tilt the playing field. It means that you are paying a lot to reduce carbon emissions in the developed world and not too much in the developing world. When that happens, we are going to get a transition of industry away from the developed world and into the developing world. That is both expensive and disruptive to jobs in the developed world.

The second thing is "when" flexibility. If you add "when" flexibility to "where" flexibility, that actually can reduce the costs to about half again. But there are details in how you implement "when" flexibility. The principles behind "when" flexibility are exactly the same as the principles behind "where" flexibility, except with "when" flexibility you are trying to equalize the present value of the marginal cost of emissions reductions over time. And that means you should take low-cost efforts now and higher-cost efforts in the future. In fact, the intensity of your efforts should get higher and higher until you get to the concentration ceiling you are aiming for.

Now, the U.S. climate plan at the moment has a certain limited amount of flexibility in time, but probably not enough. Again, the problem is that you may lose that extra reduction in costs because the program does not allow for enough flexibility in time. Those modelers and analysts who have looked at this problem have found that for the next twenty to thirty years you can allow emissions to rise, although somewhat below the baseline, depending on the concentration target, and then subsequently you can take advantage of all the new technologies which Amory [Lovins] told us are just around the corner to cut back emissions very significantly. This is the cheapest way to manage the climate problem. The advantage of this approach is that it enables the existing capital stock, built before we were particularly concerned about climate, to live out its useful life and then to be replaced with a new set of technologies. It is very important, as you will probably hear from Paul [Portney], to establish private, government, multinational initiatives to work hard on developing a new set of technologies which can provide the energy we need and produce considerably less carbon dioxide emissions than we do now. The Electric Power Research Institute, along with our partners—BP, the Department of Energy, and others—is very committed to working on such a technology strategy.

Seeking Consensus Among Industry, Environmentalists, and Government

Richard L. Klimisch, Vice President,
American Automobile Manufacturers Association

Discussions like this tend to focus on disagreements, but we have many more agreements than disagreements in this group. For example, we all agree that this is an incredibly complex problem. It is really *the mother of all environmental problems:* the most complicated environmental problem you can imagine, because it involves the whole earth. It is very dangerous; many people believe it could stop economic growth if abatement is done wrong. Obviously we don't want to do that. There is a lot of potential to impact employment and jobs, and some suspect that some countries' positions are based on trying to gain competitive advantage through this. That is very dangerous. We all agree that it must involve less developed countries. This problem cannot be solved with just the Annex 1 countries. If the Annex 1 countries do all that is considered possible, you would not be able to see the difference in the climate. Obviously the solution must be cost-effective—we all agree on that—and it must be flexible. The timing problem is one where we have concerns. This is likely a one-hundred-year problem, and the question is, do we need to do things right away? Premature retirement of capital stock is a very expensive pastime. It doesn't make any sense.

We also all agree that we need to get the incentives right and prices and taxes. We cannot expect people to behave the way we want them to when the incentives are backwards like they are, for example, in energy prices. Probably nothing is more important than research and development. We have managed to cut back on R&D in this country, particularly in the private sector and in the university sector, for a long time. We need to turn that around, particularly for this problem. One of the fundamental issues is to help countries like China and India develop. How do you tell them they cannot use fossil fuels like we did? And yet, if they continue to use fossil fuels as projected, they are going to overwhelm everything we do in the Annex 1 countries.

Finally, I agree with almost everything Amory [Lovins] said. When people buy vehicles, they make more than an economic decision. Vehicles provide lots of things. There is the whole emotional and cultural thing. We need to change that behavior. We have vehicles out there that get fifty miles per gallon, but there are very few of those vehicles sold. That is a very small segment of the market, and it is not growing. It may have something to do with the price of gasoline, but I do not want to get into that, because it might upset some people. Of course, the Constitution says gasoline can never rise above $1.10 a gallon in 1980 constant dollars, I think—just kidding.

Anyway, I feel a lot better about this, particularly after listening to Dirk Forrister. We want to work cooperatively on this. We, in fact, have a program in the auto industry called the "Partnership for New Generation Vehicles" which is working on many of the things that Amory talked about. It is aimed at getting vehicles to eighty miles per gallon and is working on many of the things that are contained in the hypercar that Amory talked about. It does not quite go that far, but we are trying to catch up to him. It's pretty hard.

ANDREW HOFFMAN: So far, we have controlled the agenda, and now I turn it over to you. We have two microphones. If anyone wants to ask a question of anyone on the panel or any of the other attendees seated in the first three rows, you may do so at this point.

QUESTION 1: I hear a lot of generalities, but I don't hear any specifics. As I look at real estate around the Chicago area, it seems they are building urban sprawl. Urban sprawl means you have to use a car to get places. They are not really dealing with some of the things we have to deal with. I am wondering if people can comment about specific things that can be done. There are a couple of things that come to my mind. One would be shifting from use of oil to natural gas in cars and then, maybe, a shift to hydrogen.

DIRK FORRISTER: The experience thus far in the Clinton administration is that it is a lot of little things and probably some major things. Certainly we are going to take a look at some of the questions you raised as part of the reauthorization of the Intermodal Surface Transportation Efficiency Act in this next Congress to make it as CO_2-efficient as possible. One of the more interesting programs that we have had under way is with some of the electric utilities that are present here today. It is called the Climate Challenge program. Companies have made a commitment to try to mitigate greenhouse gases, taking advantage of the flexibility to look across their operations and do it however they could. Most of them have adopted a portfolio approach, where they have made improvements, sometimes switching from oil to gas in power plants, sometimes taking a power plant that is burning coal and cofiring with biomass or natural gas. Sometimes they have improved efficiency of an existing power plant. They have also done a lot of things with renewables and a lot of things on the demand side, going out and working with customers, whether they be homeowners or commercial entities or industries, to try to improve emissions through adoption of some of the technologies that Amory was talking about earlier. This problem is not like other kinds of environmental problems where one can slap technology on the end of the pipe to deal with it. It requires efficiency across a lot of activities, and there will be a lot of little answers.

RICHARD KLIMISCH: Over the past five years there has been a movement to try to use more alternative fuels and natural gases. The three companies I represent—GM, Ford, and Chrysler—have all had natural gas vehicles. They are slightly more expensive because of high-pressure tanks, but you save money on fuel costs. Unfortunately the sales have been very poor. Very few vehicles have been sold. There is some cost in convenience. You lose a little trunk space. That is what the experience has been, and some of the companies have withdrawn the products. You can get a car converted to natural gas. That can be done, but not very many people are doing it.

RICHARD ABDOO: People respond to the incentives or mandates of the government. The Clean Air Act is probably the biggest single reason we have urban sprawl, because of the way they set things up. And I am not criticizing. But the way they set it up, they decided on specific geographic areas. You can be five hundred feet into an attainment county and build your plant without any of the difficulties [you would have] if you moved into a nonattainment area. If you look where the nonattainment areas are, they are all where the people are. People respond to these things, and I think we really have to do a much better job with things like brownfield development in getting the right signal from government. We need leadership and focus if we are going to take these things seriously so that all of us can respond with better research and better education.

QUESTION 2: Several of you talked about the imperative of being able to maximize the efficiency with which you make CO_2 reductions. What that really involves is a transfer of payments from the developed world to the developing world and the nations that can least afford it. I wonder if you could comment on the political feasibility of those sorts of transfers?

PAUL PORTNEY: Maybe we were a bit unclear in talking about this "where" flexibility. The idea is that if there is a cheaper opportunity to reduce carbon dioxide in some other country, it is not that the burden is shifted from a U.S. company to the foreign country; rather, the U.S. firm has the opportunity to go to that country and invest and spend its money to improve the efficiency of a coal-fired power plant in China or agricultural practices someplace else. The idea would not be to pass the financial buck but just to enable the firm that has a responsibility in the United States to look all around the world to see where it could most inexpensively reduce its financial commitment. One of the things we talked briefly about earlier today was the fact that some developing countries do not like this idea, insisting that the U.S., which will have its obligations to be met first, will go to other countries and pick all the low-hanging fruit so that when it comes time for the developing countries to make their CO_2 emissions reductions, they will be left with the fruit that is on the top of the tree and it will be relatively more expensive for them to pursue it. The idea is not that the obligation shifts but rather that we be able to spend that money someplace else.

DIRK FORRISTER: We in the administration are completing an economic analysis that, among other things, looks at the question that you raised. There would be payments, as Paul described, and we are trying to look at their magnitude and location. My supposition is that if transfers achieve a less expensive route out of the problem, they may not bother the American people. Right now, even though we are importing over half of the oil used in this country, the economic efficiency seems acceptable to the general public. Oil is a very strategic asset, and yet we accept the transfers that go to places like the Middle East right now. The amounts of money we are talking about on this problem are, I think, going to turn out to be just a small fraction of what we already see in the marketplace and in other sectors of world trade.

QUESTION 3: It seems to me that reasonable people possessed with the same facts will often disagree about causes, especially with complex problems. In terms of global warming, scientific opinion has not been unified. Does everybody on the panel and everyone who came here today believe that, in fact, climate change is occurring for certain? And would somebody who took the opposite side misrepresent the facts?

STEPHEN PECK: The Intergovernmental Panel on Climate Change, a body of about one thousand or more scientists, presented their last report, which was three volumes. There is one sentence in it that most people quote: "The balance of evidence seems to suggest that there is some perceptible human influence on the climate." I think that there was also a lot of other material about [such questions as] how much is temperature likely to rise over the next one hundred years? What sort of damage is that likely to do over the next one hundred years? There is an enormous range of uncertainty about those things. And there will continue to be an enormous range of uncertainty about those things for twenty, thirty, forty or more years. The important thing about climate policy is that it needs to remain flexible. And we need to take a policy which appropriately balances the risks and the costs. We need to keep an eye on the development of science, both as to how inexpensive it is to reduce emissions, as Amory talked about, but also science about what is going on in the world climate system. We need to be prepared to adjust our course as time goes on.

HOWARD RIS: I will just comment briefly that I think in simplest terms there is a consensus within the scientific community and certainty within the community of climatologists that this is a serious problem. I think there are a few skeptics out there, but they are fewer and fewer than even a few years ago.

QUESTION 4: First, Mr. Lovins presented new technology as saving us in a certain way. I think that solution has been being presented to us for a long time. But it still has not come. It is always around the corner but never happens. Second, let's say you are able to reduce your emissions by 50 percent through a new technology. That is great for everyone. We have less pollution, but if that also saves you money, then you are going to turn around and expand production. If you double your production and now have twice as much pollution, you are back to where you started. I think this points to an underlying point, which is that increasing the use of technology as a Band-Aid is not the ultimate and best solution. I am wondering who here is willing to commit to not always keeping economic growth and capital expansion as an underlying goal. I don't think anyone is, but I would say that from my perspective as someone on the other end of corporate pollution, I am wondering if that approach is really the best thing to go after?

PAUL PORTNEY: You raised a very difficult question, and I don't think anyone here would disagree with it. There is some evidence to suggest that at least part of your premise is not right: as we improve technology, we are overtaken by growth and output. If you look at emissions of sulfur dioxide, particulates, nitrogen oxides, and other major criteria pollutants (as the EPA calls them in the United States), both on a unit-of-GDP basis and also in absolute terms, emissions are considerably lower in the United States than they were ten years ago and dramatically lower than they were in 1970. So it is not necessarily the case that as we invent new, lower-pollution technology that we're overtaken by economic growth. Can we continue into the indefinite future to use technology to bail us out? I would be remiss if I said I am absolutely confident that we can. We can only look at past experience, and in the United States, over what geologically is a short period of time, technology has enabled us to enjoy a higher standard of living. At the same time, we have begun to take much better care of the environment. The real question for all of us is figuring out a way to get people in the developing world to begin to enjoy higher standards of living—which, incidentally, will help them care more about the environment—while at the same time skipping some of the highly polluting stages that people in the U.S., Germany, Japan, and the UK went through. That is really the critical question that faces mankind. I tend to be technologically optimistic, but there is no guarantee that we will pull this off.

QUESTION 5: I realize that the world is not yet ready for really strong action, but I feel that through my lifetime that point will be reached. My question is regarding the feasibility of growth and flexibility. Today, a U.S. consumer consumes seventeen times more than a consumer in Latin America. They consume one hundred times more than a rural consumer in Asia. If the corporate world continues on this strategy of growth with globalization, this will necessarily involve growth in the developing countries. This growth will need the consumer market to expand and with it infrastructure and resources to fuel that consumption. Regarding flexibility in "where": nowadays, multinationals are only a small fraction of the developing-world economies. Most polluting industries are in transportation and energy producing, and those are mostly locally owned. So even if the First World forces their own industry to be more efficient in the Third World, this will not bring fast solutions. How is the corporate world going to slow growth in a global economy, and how is the First World going to work together with the Third World in low pollution development?

RICHARD KLIMISCH: I think it is not the corporate world that is driving growth; it is the consumer who is driving growth. If some company decides they are not going to sell something, someone else will. That is the way capitalism works, and that is why we have a better standard of living here than we had before and it is continuing to improve. You always come up with trade-offs. The trade-offs are jobs and standard of living versus the environment, and we decide many trade-offs in the political system. But I think the consensus is that people want to see continued growth.

STEPHEN PECK: And I think insofar as the problem is continually increasing CO_2 emissions, you heard a number of us say that we think that a major research effort to find ways to produce energy without producing so much CO_2 is a very worthy long-term research effort.

STEVEN PERCY: I think that multinationals have a key role to play in this idea of transferring technology from the developed world to the lesser-developed world. Speaking for BP, it is our intention and has been our practice that we maintain the same standards no matter where we operate. So the standards to which we march here in the United States, which has strong regulations, are the same standards that we apply in other places. I think that through this kind of activity we can help transfer the technology and the best practice to where it is most needed.

ANDREW BERMINGHAM: It was recently said that electricity is more addicting than cocaine, cigarettes, or alcohol. The point is that there is a tremendous demand. More than two billion people on this earth are off the grid. They have no access to commercial electricity. One-third of the world's people, in spite of living close to a phone, have yet to make their first phone call. So they want so much, and as Dick responded, if companies don't sell, someone else will. There is a real opportunity for education, and there has been a lot discussed about partnerships between government and industry, but how about getting the consumers of this world to take a real ownership in their future? If I buy a box of corn-flakes, I see my recommended daily allowance in terms of carbohydrates and fat on that box. Well, how about labeling the carbon content? We have an odometer on our car; wouldn't it be nice if somehow we had a way of automatically knowing how much carbon we just emitted? Then we would think about it. But we do not think about what we are consuming. So as consumers, we have to take more responsibility.

QUESTION 6: It seems to be a basic tenet of human philosophy that when there is a crisis, there is concerted action. Then the flip side is that when there is no crisis, there is lethargy. Are we getting toward the crisis point? Is that why we are here? If so, how do we measure our progress from here on out? If we are just now coming to agreement that there is a problem and establish a response, how do we measure ourselves, and how do we know that we are doing a good job?

RICHARD KLIMISCH: We rarely get a clear-cut crisis. The only environmental one that I recall recently is the hole in the ozone layer, and I am proud that our industry and every other industry responded. We have taken CFCs out of the system. In global climate change there is one possibility, that the ocean currents could turn around. That would really get everybody's attention and would wreak havoc in Europe. While we don't understand what drives the ocean currents, it might take something like that to get people's attention, because then it would really be a threat. Climate change is a big deal, but there really isn't a crisis. The statement that "the balance of the evidence suggests a discernible effect on climate" really is not going to get people excited to say, "I am not going to drive anymore. I am going to walk to work."

DIRK FORRISTER: As we approach the international negotiations, all negotiators come from different political situations back home. My sense is that in Europe, "Joe Six Pack" believes this is a real problem, and that he is feeling the effects of it right now. The United Kingdom just went through one of the longest droughts they have had in recent memory, and Joe Six Pack in England now associates weather problems with climate change. In this country, based on the polls I have seen recently, climate change has not quite reached the kind of fever pitch you are talking about. I think people are getting more aware. But it is not quite at the crisis point. I think that is why you hear a lot of us talking about taking out responsible insurance that allows us to learn over time. It hasn't quite sunk in here in this country. We have experienced a warming over the last one hundred years—an increase in some places, some regions, and decreases in others, but on balance the United States has gotten warmer over the last one hundred years. It has also gotten wetter, which is part of what happens with warming temperatures: more evaporation, more water in storms, more flooding, that kind of thing. So we are starting to see that fingerprint more. I think what is going to happen over the next couple of decades is that we are going to start seeing that imprint more and more, and people are going to start making the connection.

STEPHEN PECK: It is true that the Intergovernmental Panel on Climate Change also said that as far as available evidence, the evidence is not very extensive, there is no relationship between the concentration of CO_2 in the atmosphere and the extremes of weather.

HOWARD RIS: You asked how we can measure progress, and I think one of the grand ironies of this issue is, as complicated as it is and as global as it is, it is quite measurable. Globally we have a very good handle on what the concentration of carbon emissions in the atmosphere is, and we measure it regularly. Nationally, at least in the developed countries, there is probably more data on the energy and transportation industry than any other sector in America in terms of how much energy is used and produced each year and the components of it and the emissions that result from it. Individually or locally, all you have to do is look at the kilowatt hours on your electric bill every month or the miles you drive your car. It is a very measurable area, in which we can measure progress in the future.

QUESTION 7: In talking about "when" flexibility, one of the goals is to sustain or increase production in order to use that money to go back and use it for environmentally safe technology. But historically, because of the pressure from investors, capital has been going into industrial expansion instead of environmental technology. How do you plan to convince investors to invest their money in something that is potentially going to decrease their returns?

DIRK FORRISTER: The kind of approach we are looking to implement as protocol in the United States will send a powerful signal that you have to be in compliance, or else. We have not decided whether that is going to be with a cap that is legislated on certain sectors, or R&D strategies with certain sectors, or just what we are going to use. But the model we are looking at, the closest is one that we used on acid rain, where we set a cap for the industry as a whole and then allowed them to have the flexibility to trade permits among themselves to achieve reductions jointly across the industry. What makes that work is the cap. It is that requirement. In that case, it is legislated and set in stone. Investors would then try to pick who are going to be the environmental winners, the ones that know how to manage the environment at the cheapest cost. They are going to note that Dick Abdoo came to Kellogg way back here and that Steve Percy has been looking at it for so long, and weigh that in their investment decisions.

STEVEN PERCY: Since CO_2 emissions are bound up with the consumption of energy, there is money to be made in reducing the consumption of energy. So there is an investment. There are other new ideas that may be, in fact, more efficient forms of energy, like solar power. Investors are going to buy into that eventually too. So there are some positives as well.

RICHARD KLIMISCH: One of the problems with our environmental laws is that they tend to focus on new plants, and that is a disincentive for building new, more efficient plants. So people keep old plants open longer than they would otherwise. The same thing is true with vehicles. If the price of vehicles goes up, people tend to keep their older car longer, and we would like to see turnover occur more rapidly. Please tell everybody to buy a new car. [laughter]

RICHARD ABDOO: That's an excellent question, because as it has been said, you can get two kinds of regulations. You can get the old command-and-control, where nobody makes money and everybody loses. Investments in environmental stewardship are non-revenue-producing.

But in the Clean Air amendments of 1990 we've got performance-based regulations. Those companies that had been progressive early with new technology and reducing sulfur emissions actually developed a competitive advantage in the market in terms of being able to sell power. We could provide an emissions reduction for the power, which made it more attractive, plus we inherited a lot of sulfur credits that we could use if we had to buy or swap power in the market. So again, I come back to the government. It really has the leadership role. If they are willing to provide incentives, whether tax-based or performance-based, investors and corporations respond to the signals from an environmental standpoint and make a dollar in the process.

PART THREE

CLOSING THOUGHTS

16

THE ART OF CLIMATE WAR

Industry's New Battle Plan

Andrew W. Bermingham

TODAY'S CLIMATE CHANGE DEBATE has provided people with yet another reason to dislike foes they already distrust. Climate change has become one more battle in the continuing war over environmental protection. The protagonists from both camps have moved to obscure the climate issue, like some kind of deep-sea squids, by spreading murky black ink over the ongoing rhetorical, political, and scientific debate. There are those from industry who deny the reality of anthropogenic climate change and sabotage any chance for progress in assigning responsibility and accepting solutions. They seem to suggest that the economy can progress without any regard for the scientific concerns that it is damaging the environment. And there are those from the environmental camp who take a "sky is falling" approach, hoping to turn back the clock on the formidable historical contributions made by industry in delivering heightened standards of living for all. They seem to suggest that the world economy could get along just fine powered by photovoltaic cells and backyard compost piles.

Andrew W. Bermingham is managing director of Montreux Energy Corporation.

On this newest and perhaps greatest of environmental and political battlefields, climate change has mobilized armies not only from industry and the ranks of the environmental movement but also from governments, the developing world, producer states, and the media. On all sides great sums of money are being spent mounting campaigns and training forces. Chieftains have dispatched their infantrymen, soldiers, and scouts. It is a battlefield that is beginning to produce regretful behavior in even the best of us.

In setting a battle strategy, we in industry must begin by acknowledging that global warming poses grave dangers and could prove to be the ultimate of all human trials. Some would claim it is Armageddon, on the scale of a nuclear holocaust. Not only is the planet challenged physically, but equally frightening, new political instabilities could arise if climate change wreaks havoc in some regions and not others, causing some to win while others lose. As history has shown, this kind of inequity leads to instability and ultimately to conflict. Climate change, it should be argued, is a potentially dangerous and lethal game—environmentally, economically, and politically.

The potential threats of climate change to industry are indeed serious: loss of profits, early capital stock retirement, new operating rules, and new competition. The debate that surrounds these threats appears to expose the soft, unprotected underbelly of the private sector—a perception that it is driven only by profit, focused on shortsighted horizons, and founded on an aversion to change. But the private sector also has strengths and armaments that can be mobilized in this war: technological expertise, international operating experience, financial acumen, risk analysis, information technology, research and development, intelligence gathering, the ability to take initiative, the ability to operate in competitive markets, and access to funding for projects of any size. To channel this vast array of proficiencies onto the battlefield of the climate war, the issue and the terms of the debate must be reframed, not as an absolute threat but as a chance for opportunity. Climate change can offer potential profits through new markets, new customers, and new technologies. For example, economic growth in the developing world is expected to be rapid in the coming decade, and climate change will be just one factor in the overall shifts this growth creates toward a global marketplace. The energy industry can provide cleaner sources of energy to fuel this economic growth. The infrastructure industry can combat shortages of food and water and add to the momentum of standard-of-living improvements.

So—what is the war, and who is the enemy? Is it the climate change issue and the environmental movement? Is it the economic threat of climate change policies and international political regimes? The war is no different than that fought over any other economic transition. It will yield winners and losers, as is so often played out in our rapidly changing business environment. In this battle industry must aspire to be on the winning side. And to be on the winning side we must stop playing the role of the naysayer and positioning ourselves as an obstruction, not only to action but even to analyses of what action might be needed. Rather than asking, "How can we win the climate war?" we might ask, "How might we lose?" We could lose by continuing to adhere to a win-at-all-costs mentality in the rhetorical sparring match. To continue on this path is to announce that we cannot be counted on as part of the solution but rather are an obstacle to it that must be brushed aside.

In *The Prince*,[1] Machiavelli asserts that human beings are naturally wicked and require a strong government to keep them from reducing society to ruin. I do not believe this to be true. The private sector must work to find economically and technologically feasible solutions to climate change, lest governments find them for us. But at the moment we lack a global patriotism to take responsibility for this and other environmental challenges. Society has to change, to become more efficient and better informed, and industry must be a constructive part of that process. The great ability of the private sector to design goods and services for which consumers will pay is a tremendous asset that must be utilized to guide consumers toward less energy- and carbon-intensive products. Businesses can realize the economic opportunity in this social need and act to seize it, or they can wait for government to mandate ways for them to meet that need.

In all likelihood the governments of the world will soon pass a binding climate treaty—if not in Kyoto in 1997 then soon in the next century. Those with a stake in the climate change debate, regardless of their position, must adopt a collective boardroom—or war room—attitude. How can we choose generals and lieutenants who have the courage to lead? And how can we educate those who will follow them? How can we devise a battle strategy for the long haul of this long-term political challenge? And how can we engage all the combatants in this war on terms of our own choosing, built on trust and cooperation?

In the end climate change is an issue with serious consequences for all. Industry cannot win by denying the scientific community. Environmentalists cannot win by turning back the clock, hoping to simply turn off the technology and progress we have made to date. And society cannot win if all sides do not come together as one to seek solutions that satisfy our need for economic and environmental stability. We cannot think about sustainability without growth, and we cannot think about growth without potential environmental hazards. Solutions to the problems we face must come from all who understand the complexities of what today seems a dichotomy.

Instead of new lobbying efforts to block progress, industry must move to turn a weakness into a strength, a disadvantage into an opportunity. This will entail a new battle plan, one that includes the engagement of those who think they have no stake or say in the matter. Globalization holds the promise of new markets and competition. But it also means that more responsibility must be accepted by all stakeholders. Oil, gas, and electricity companies must take environmentalists seriously, even if the disagreements between them are wide. Shell Oil learned this lesson with their Brent Spar debacle. While they rested on their scientific analysis that the oil rig would make a suitable reef, and the government supported that decision, Greenpeace took the battle to the field of public opinion and won. Shell got the terms of the battle wrong. Industry cannot make this mistake in the battle over climate change. We must adopt a strategy that will win from the beginning and win in the end. We must engage all who have an interest in this issue and present our case. British Petroleum has begun this process with a dialogue with Greenpeace, committing top management time and resources. The result has been a new level of understanding on all sides.

An ancient Chinese proverb states, "The best time to plant a tree is twenty years ago. The second best time to plant a tree is today." We may have missed our opportunity to plant the tree twenty years ago and become embedded in a system of distrust and denial, but business leaders can correct this missed opportunity. They must spend time thinking about what they will want twenty years from now. They must then endeavor to begin making it happen today. For their part, environmental leaders must consider the future they imagine and recognize that for all involved that future must include the cooperation and contributions of the industrial community. In this kind of a battlefield we can all win. As Sun Tzu wrote in *The Art of War,* "If you know the enemy and know yourself, you need not fear the result of a hundred battles."[2]

NOTES

1. N. Machiavelli, *The Prince,* ed. and trans. R. Adams (New York: Norton, 1992).

2. Sun Tzu, *The Art of War,* ed. J. Clavell (New York: Delacorte Press, 1993): 2.

17

THE LONG ROAD TO INSTITUTIONAL CHANGE

Andrew J. Hoffman

CLIMATE CHANGE IS NEITHER an environmental nor an economic issue: it is both. Climate change mitigation policy is designed to protect the global environmental systems on which we depend for our survival. But such policy must also protect the world's economic systems, on which we equally depend. In today's world the two are interconnected. Business executives cannot conduct their affairs without an integrated awareness of both. And now, as the five-year policy debate over climate change is about to culminate in the December 1997 negotiations in Kyoto, business leaders find that they must defend both their environmental and their economic interests. The task of fashioning an appropriate national and international climate change mitigation program cannot be left to governments alone. All must participate in the policy development process.

Acknowledging this need for participation, the Kellogg Environmental Research Center organized the dialogue recounted in this book. In terms of facilitating exchange on the economics of this environmental

Andrew J. Hoffman is assistant professor in the Organizational Behavior Department of the Boston University School of Management.

issue, the forum was a success. Rather than reaching consensus, however, we exposed many of the issues surrounding climate change that are of concern to business leaders: the level of scientific consensus, the costs (and opportunities) of control, "where" and "when" flexibility, the inclusion of the developing world in a negotiated treaty, the need for more research and development, and the importance of education and behavioral change in bringing about sustainable environmental controls.

One common underlying theme uncovered in the dialogue is that we *all* must change—industry, environmentalists, government, and the public. In short, the institutions through which our societies operate must be adjusted to mitigate the effects of climate change and to create a stable environment and economy. But we must patiently accept the fact that broad societal change is slow and incremental. Government cannot simply mandate it; it has neither the knowledge nor the capability. Change must occur at the level of the fundamental beliefs by which we guide our lives and our business activities. Today's corporations must increasingly consider the social and political implications of their technological and strategic decisions. To accomplish this transformation, exchange with diverse (and increasingly powerful) stakeholders is critical.

The most direct way to bring about such exchange is face-to-face dialogue, such as that described here. The Senior-Level Dialogue at Kellogg was not a unique meeting, but it was a vital step in the continuum of institutional change and in the process of restructuring our social institutions. As I first considered the attendee list I was struck by the concentration of institutional power in the room. The individuals that were there control the actions, strategies, and cultures of the large institutional organizations that drive our society. As managers of hundreds of thousands of people whose activities have a direct impact on the climate change problem, they have disproportionate influence on any attempt to control it. Bringing them into contact with respected individuals who hold differing ideas and beliefs about the state of the environment and the role of the corporation in managing it represents an important step in the process of institutional change.

As an illustration of the extent to which institutional change has occurred thus far, consider the fact that this kind of dialogue was not always possible. Just eighteen years ago the chairman of the Getty Oil Company, Harold Berg, publicly proclaimed the Environmental Protection Agency to be "the worst enemy the oil industry has."[1] At the same time, the slogan of the Environmental Defense Fund was "sue the bastards."[2] Today it would not be surprising to find these two organizations engaged in a joint alliance. This is a reflection of the institutional change process that has been under way. Originally perceived as enemies, these allies now acknowledge each other as legitimate partners in the dialogue on finding solutions to complex environmental problems. And as environmental issues—like climate change—become more and more global, the need for this type of dialogue will become even more urgent.

Ultimately the contribution of this dialogue will be measured by the extent to which minds are changed and new ideas influence the U.S. negotiating position at Kyoto. But it will not stop there. If a treaty is signed in December, the institutional change process will only progress to the next phase. New issues for dialogue and action will center on questions such as these: How do we measure and disseminate national and global carbon emissions levels? How do we verify those measurements? How do we enforce national goals and timetables? How do we apportion national goals among individual industries? How do we establish an international trading system that efficiently minimizes transaction costs? The answers to each of these questions are extremely complex and will require input and contributions from every sector of the economy and society.

The need for more meetings like the one described here will only grow. Some organizations, like the Keystone Center, the Aspen Institute, and Montreux Energy, are providing forums for such meetings to take place, bringing people together to exchange ideas and learn from one another. But it is also time for business schools to step up to the plate and become a more central part of this process. Their unique mix of specialized business skills and political neutrality give them the ability (and the responsibility) to facilitate these types of forums and to help search for universally acceptable solutions.

In the end the success of such forums rests on the exchanges of ideas, the public articulation of interests, the development of networks, and, ultimately, the contributions to the process of institutional change that they produce. The interactions documented here suggest such an outcome for the Kellogg dialogue. For all the participants there emerged a new awareness of the diversity of interests and perspectives on this complex issue. Furthermore, the connections that crystallized at the Kellogg Center will form the foundation for continued dialogue in the future. And as we face issues that pose ever-mounting concern for the global community, it is through these connections and dialogue that the solutions will be found. If we are to find solutions to problems like climate change and strive for sustainable environmental and economic systems, we must keep talking with, listening to, and learning from one another.

NOTES

1. "Getty's Berg Calls EPA US Oil's Worst Enemy," *Oil and Gas Journal,* October 15, 1979: 89.
2. R. Gottleib, *Forcing the Spring* (Washington, DC: Island Press, 1993): 138.

APPENDIX

U.S. DRAFT PROTOCOL FRAMEWORK
As of June 1, 1997
(submitted without prejudice to ultimate form of agreement)

The Parties to this Protocol, have agreed as follows:

Article 1
Definitions

For purposes of this Protocol:

1. "The Convention" means the United Nations Framework Convention on Climate Change done at New York on 9 May 1992.
2. "Party" means Party to this Protocol.
3. "Greenhouse gas" means any greenhouse gas covered in Annex C of this Protocol.
4. "Tonne of carbon equivalent" means one metric ton of carbon, or a quantity of one or more other greenhouse gases equivalent to one metric ton based on the global warming potentials decided by the Parties in accordance with Annex C of this Protocol.
5. "Net anthropogenic emissions" of greenhouse gases is the calculated difference between emissions by sources and removals by sinks.
6. [other definitions to be developed or cross-referenced to the Convention as necessary]

Article 2
Emissions Budgets

1. Each Annex A and Annex B Party shall ensure that its net anthropogenic emissions of greenhouse gases do not exceed its emissions budget for any applicable budget period, as specified in this Article.

---

2. For each Annex A and Annex B Party, its emissions budget shall be denominated in tonnes of carbon equivalent emissions allowed and shall equal:

    (a)   the tonnes of carbon equivalent emissions it is allowed under paragraph 3 or 4 below, plus

    (b)   any tonnes of carbon equivalent emissions allowed that are carried over from a prior budget period under paragraph 5 below, plus

    (c)   up to [__ percent] of the tonnes of carbon equivalent emissions allowed under paragraph 3 or 4 below, such as may be borrowed from the subsequent budget period under paragraph 6 below, plus

    (d)   any tonnes of carbon equivalent emissions allowed that are acquired from another Party under Article 6 (International Emissions Trading) or Article 7 (Joint Implementation), minus

    (e)   any tonnes of carbon equivalent emissions allowed that are transferred to another Party under Article 6 (International Emissions Trading).

3. (a)   For the first budget period, [20__ through 20__], each Annex A Party shall have a number of tonnes of carbon equivalent allowed equal to [a percentage of] its net anthropogenic emissions of tonnes of carbon equivalent in 1990, multiplied by [the number of years in this budget period].

   (b)   For the second budget period [20__ through 20__], each Annex A Party shall have a number of tonnes of carbon equivalent emissions allowed equal to [a percentage equal to or less than the percentage in subparagraph 3(a)] of its net anthropogenic emissions of tonnes of carbon equivalent in 1990, multiplied by [the number of years in this budget period].

   (c)   [possible subsequent budget period(s)]

4. For the budget period [20__ through 20__], each Annex B Party (see Annex B for States included) shall have a number of tonnes of carbon equivalent emissions allowed equal to [options for Annex B Parties include: budget periods, base years, and percentages different from those applicable to Annex A Parties].

5. At the end of a budget period applicable to a Party, any amount by which the Party's emissions of tonnes of carbon equivalent is under its emissions budget for that period may be carried over and added to its emissions budget for the next budget period.

6. At the end of a budget period applicable to a Party, any amount of tonnes of carbon equivalent emissions allowed that is borrowed from

the subsequent budget period shall be subtracted at a rate of [1.2:1] from the subsequent budget period.

6.bis. At the end of a budget period applicable to a Party, any amount of tonnes of carbon equivalent emissions over its emissions budget shall be subtracted at a rate of [rate greater than that in paragraph 6] from the subsequent budget period.

7.   Any State not listed in Annex A may, in its instrument of ratification, acceptance, approval or accession, or at any time thereafter, notify the Depositary that it intends to be bound by obligations of Annex A Parties. It will then be an Annex A Party. The Depositary shall inform the other signatories and Parties of any such notification.

8.   Any State not listed in Annex A may, in its instrument of ratification, acceptance, approval, or accession, or at any time thereafter, notify the Depositary that it intends to be bound by obligations of Annex B Parties. It will then be an Annex B Party. The Depositary shall inform the other signatories and Parties of any such notification.

Article 3
Measurement and Reporting

1. Each Annex A and Annex B Party shall have in place by [the first year of its first budget period] a national system for the accurate measurement of anthropogenic emissions by sources, and removals by sinks, of greenhouse gases.

2. For the purposes of implementing paragraph 1 and promoting comparability, consistency, and transparency, the Parties shall, not later than their first Meeting, decide on agreed best available methods for the measurement by Parties of anthropogenic emissions by sources, and removals by sinks, of greenhouse gases, taking into account the best available methods determined by the IPCC and other expert bodies. They shall also decide on appropriate adjustments to measurements of emissions and removals where agreed best available methods have not been used. The Parties shall periodically update agreed best available methods and adjustments based on evolving scientific knowledge, including advice from the Subsidiary Body for Scientific and Technological Advice referred to in Article 12.

3. Each Annex A and Annex B Party shall put in place, if it has not already done so, national compliance and enforcement programs relevant to its implementation of the obligations under this Protocol.

4. Each Annex A and Annex B Party shall submit to the Secretariat, as part of its communication under Article 12 of the Convention, information on its implementation of this Protocol, including policies and measures it is taking to meet its obligations in Article 2. Such submission shall be in accordance with guidelines which the Parties adopt at their first Meeting, taking into account any relevant guidelines adopted by the Parties to the Convention. Such submission shall also contain the following information:

   (a) once the obligation in paragraph 1 above becomes effective, a description of the national measurement system that it has in place;

   (b) once the obligation in paragraph 1 above becomes effective, the results of its national measurement system;

   (c) a quantitative projection of its net anthropogenic emissions of greenhouse gases through the budget periods; and

   (d) a description of relevant national compliance and enforcement programs it has in place pursuant to paragraph 3 above, as well as a description of their effectiveness, including actions taken in cases of non-compliance with national law.

5. In addition to the information required to be submitted under paragraph 4, each Annex A and Annex B Party shall submit to the Secretariat, on an annual basis and in accordance with the guidelines referred to in paragraph 4, its current calculation corresponding to each of the subparagraphs in Article 2.2 and its remaining emissions budget for that budget period. With respect to any tonnes of carbon equivalent emissions allowed that are acquired or transferred under Articles 6 or 7, the Party shall specify the quantity, Party of origin or destination, and the relevant budget period.

6. The first of the submissions referred to in paragraph 5 shall be part of a Party's first communication that is due after the Protocol has been in force for that Party for two years. The frequency of subsequent submissions shall be determined by the Parties.

7. Information communicated by Parties under this Article shall be transmitted by the secretariat as soon as possible to the Parties and to any subsidiary bodies concerned.

8. Without prejudice to the ability of any Party to make public its communication at any time, the secretariat shall make information communicated by Parties under this Article publicly available at the time it is submitted to the Parties.

Article 4
Review and Compliance Process

1. In addition to the review of communications conducted under Article 10.2(b) of the Convention, the Meeting of the Parties shall consider the information submitted by Annex A and Annex B Parties under Article 3 in order to assess those Parties' implementation of their obligations.

2. Reviews will be conducted by expert review teams, which will be coordinated by the secretariat and composed of experts selected from those nominated by Parties and, as appropriate, by intergovernmental organizations.

3. Reviews will be in connection with the review of communications conducted under Article 10.2(b) of the Convention and will be in accordance with guidelines to be adopted by the Parties at a meeting. These guidelines shall, *inter alia,* provide for how information will be made available to the public and define mechanisms by which observers and the public may provide comments, supplemental data or other information to facilitate and improve reviews. The guidelines shall be periodically reviewed by the Parties for appropriate revision.

4. Review teams will review all aspects of a Party's implementation of this Protocol, including the likelihood that a Party will achieve its emissions budgets obligations. They will be authorized, *inter alia,* to review pertinent information and consult with the Party in question and others as necessary. They will prepare a report assessing a Party's implementation of its obligations, identifying any areas of apparent non-compliance, as well as potential problems in achieving obligations.

5. Such reports will be circulated by the Secretariat to all Parties. In addition, the Secretariat will identify for further consideration any report indicating a question of implementation.

Article 5
Advancement of the Implementation of
Article 4.1 of the Convention

Recognizing the progress that has been made to date in implementing commitments under Article 4.1 of the Convention:

1. The Parties reaffirm their commitments under Article 4.1 of the Convention and the need to continue to advance the implementation of such commitments.

2. Each Party shall strengthen its legal and institutional framework to advance the implementation of its commitments under Article 4.1 of the Convention.

3. Each Party shall take measures to facilitate investment in climate-friendly technologies.

4. Each Party shall report, as part of its communication under the Convention, on how it is promoting public education and participation in the development of climate change policy.

5. Each Party that is neither in Annex A nor Annex B shall identify and implement "no-regrets" measures for mitigating net anthropogenic emissions of greenhouse gases, including any identified through the review process under paragraph 7 below. In this regard, each such Party shall also:

   (a) quantify the effects of the measures it implements;

   (b) evaluate barriers to the adoption of potential measures; and

   (c) report to the Secretariat, as part of its communication under the Convention, on the measures it has implemented, plans to implement, and barriers to the adoption of potential measures.

6. Each Party that is neither in Annex A nor Annex B shall submit to the Secretariat, on an annual basis, its inventory of greenhouse gas emissions. Such inventory shall be consistent with any guidelines adopted by the Parties.

7. The Parties shall establish a process for reviewing communications received under the Convention from the Parties identified in paragraphs 5 and 6. The process shall be designed to:

   (a) enable the review of the effects of individual measures described in paragraph 5;

   (b) assist such Parties in identifying and implementing "no-regrets" measures for mitigating net anthropogenic emissions of greenhouse gases;

   (c) seek to identify key sectors and technological options within them;

   (d) consider possibilities for promoting voluntary arrangements with industry aimed at identifying and encouraging implementation of "no-regrets" measures; and

   (e) explore various means through which such Parties could obtain both the know-how and the technology needed to implement options identified.

Article 6
International Emissions Trading

1. Except as otherwise provided below, any Annex A or Annex B Party may transfer to, or acquire from, any Annex A or Annex B Party, any of its tonnes of carbon equivalent emissions allowed for a budget period, for the purpose of meeting its obligations under Article 2.
2. An Annex A or Annex B Party may not transfer or acquire any of its tonnes of carbon equivalent emissions allowed if it is not in compliance with its obligations under Article 3 (Measurement and Reporting) or if it does not have in place a national mechanism for certification and verification of trades.
3. An Annex A or Annex B Party may not transfer in a given budget period any of its tonnes of carbon equivalent emissions allowed if it has exceeded its emissions budget for that period.
4. If a question of a Party's implementation of the requirements referred to in paragraph 2 or 3 above is identified by either the review process under Article 4.5 or by the Secretariat under Article 11.2(b):
   — transfers and acquisitions of tonnes allowed (in the case of paragraph 2) and transfers of tonnes allowed (in the case of paragraph 3) may continue to be made after the question has been identified, provided that any such tonnes may not be used by any Party to meet its obligations under Article 2 until any issue of compliance is resolved. Issues of compliance shall be resolved as expeditiously as possible.
5. A Party may authorize any domestic entity (e.g., government agencies, private firms, non-governmental organizations, individuals) to participate in actions leading to transfer and acquisition under paragraph 1 of tonnes of carbon equivalent emissions allowed.
6. The Parties, at a meeting, may further elaborate guidelines to facilitate the reporting of emissions trading information.

Article 7
Joint Implementation

1. Any Party that is neither in Annex A nor B may generate tonnes of carbon equivalent emissions allowed through projects that meet the criteria set forth in paragraph 2.
2. In addition to any criteria adopted by the Parties to this Protocol, the following criteria shall apply to projects:

(a) Projects must be compatible with and supportive of national environment and development priorities and strategies, as well as contribute to cost-effectiveness in achieving global benefits;

(b) Projects must provide a reduction in emissions that is additional to any that would otherwise occur.

3. [Additional provisions to be added on calculation, measurement, monitoring, verification, review, and reporting]

4. Any Party that generates tonnes of carbon equivalent emissions allowed consistent with this Article may:

(a) hold such tonnes of carbon equivalent emissions allowed; or

(b) transfer any portion thereof to any Party.

5. Any Annex A or Annex B Party may acquire tonnes of carbon equivalent emissions allowed under this Article for the purpose of meeting its obligations under Article 2, provided it is in compliance with its obligations under Article 3 (Measurement and Reporting).

6. Any Party that is neither in Annex A nor Annex B that generates or acquires tonnes of carbon equivalent emissions allowed under this Article shall notify the Secretariat annually of the quantity, origin, and destination of such tonnes.

Article 8
Science

The Parties shall periodically review this Protocol, and guidelines established thereunder, in light of evolving scientific knowledge related to climate change.

Article 9
Progress Toward Long-Term Goal

The Parties shall cooperate in the establishment of a long-term goal with respect to atmospheric concentrations of greenhouse gases.

Article 10
Meetings of the Parties

1. The Parties shall hold meetings at regular intervals. The secretariat shall convene the first meeting of the Parties not later than one year after the date of the entry into force of this Protocol and in conjunction with a meeting of the Conference of the Parties to the Convention.

2. Subsequent meetings of the Parties shall be held, unless the Parties decide otherwise, in conjunction with meetings of the Conference of the

Parties to the Convention. Extraordinary meetings of the Parties shall be held at such other times as may be deemed necessary by a meeting of the Parties, or at the written request of a Party, provided that within six months of such a request being communicated to them by the secretariat, it is supported by at least one-third of the Parties.

3. The Parties, at their first meeting, shall:
   (a) adopt, by consensus, rules of procedure for their meetings;
   (b) [other].

4. The Parties:
   (a) shall periodically review the adequacy of this Protocol;
   (b) shall review the implementation of this Protocol, including the information submitted in accordance with Articles 3 and 5, reports received from the review teams referred to in Article 4, and any other reports and recommendations received from processes under this Protocol;
   (c) shall implement an appropriate regime to address cases of non-compliance with obligations under this Protocol, including through the development of an indicative list of consequences, taking into account the type, degree, and frequency of non-compliance;
   (d) may establish an implementation committee consisting of a subset of Parties to assist them, including by making recommendations, in carrying out functions referred to in subparagraphs (b) and (c) above.

5. The United Nations, its specialized agencies and the International Atomic Energy Agency, as well as any State not party to this Protocol, may be represented at meetings of the Parties as observers. Any body or agency, whether national or international, governmental or non-governmental, qualified in fields relating to climate change which has informed the secretariat of its wish to be represented at a meeting of the Parties as an observer may be admitted unless at least one-third of the Parties present object. The admission and participation of observers shall be subject to the rules of procedure adopted by the Parties.

Article 11
Secretariat

1. In accordance with Article 8.2(g) of the Convention, the secretariat of this Protocol shall be the secretariat of the Convention.

2. The functions of the secretariat shall be:
   (a) to maintain and administer records relating to the accounting of the emissions budgets of Annex A and Annex B Parties, including

initial budget allocations, adjustments to budgets consistent with Articles 2, 6, and 7, annual emissions, and remaining budgets in a given budget period;

(b) to facilitate the review of implementation of this Protocol through, *inter alia,* coordinating the review of Annex A and Annex B implementation; coordinating the reviews under Article 5; identifying for the Parties questions of implementation, including whether individual reports are consistent with reporting criteria; and preparing an annual compilation and synthesis report that contains inventory and budget information, and notes any discrepancies in accounting.

(c) [other].

Article 12
Subsidiary Body for Scientific and Technological Advice

1. The Subsidiary Body for Scientific and Technological Advice of the Convention shall serve as the Subsidiary Body for Scientific and Technological Advice of the Protocol.

2. When the Subsidiary Body for Scientific and Technological Advice exercises its functions with regard to matters concerning the Protocol, decisions shall be taken only by those of its members that are, at the same time, Parties to the Protocol.

3. When the Subsidiary Body for Scientific and Technological Advice exercises its functions with regard to matters concerning the Protocol, any member of the bureau of the Subsidiary Body for Scientific and Technological Advice representing a Party to the Convention, but, at the same time, not a Party to the Protocol, shall be substituted by an additional member to be elected by and from the Parties to the Protocol.

Article 13
Subsidiary Body for Implementation

1. The Subsidiary Body for Implementation of the Convention shall serve as the Subsidiary Body for Implementation of the Protocol.

2. When the Subsidiary Body for Implementation exercises its functions with regard to matters concerning the Protocol, decisions shall be taken only by those of its members that are, at the same time, Parties to the Protocol.

3. When the Subsidiary Body for Implementation exercises its functions with regard to matters concerning the Protocol, any member of the

bureau of the Subsidiary Body for Implementation representing a Party to the Convention, but, at the same time, not a Party to the Protocol, shall be substituted by an additional member to be elected by and from the Parties to the Protocol.

Article 14
Multilateral Consultative Process

[The Parties, at their first Meeting or as soon as practicable thereafter, shall consider the establishment of a multilateral consultative process to promote effective implementation of the Convention.]

Article 15
Dispute Settlement

[Silence, with the result that Article 14 of the Convention would apply to this Protocol.]

[In addition, mandatory, binding dispute settlement (with specific consequences flowing from a violation) among Annex A and Annex B Parties, as well as against other Parties as appropriate (for example, host countries under Article 7)]

Note: this process would be without prejudice to the review and compliance process under Article 4.

Article 16
Evolution

The Parties shall adopt, by [2005], binding provisions so that all Parties have quantitative greenhouse gas emissions obligations and so that there is a mechanism for automatic application of progressive greenhouse gas emissions obligations to Parties, based upon agreed criteria.

Views on Certain Final Clauses

Adoption and Amendments of Annexes:

Depending upon what type of material is eventually included in annexes, it may not be appropriate to restrict the content of all annexes to "lists, forms and any other material of a descriptive nature that is of a scientific, technical, procedural or administrative character." For any substantive annex, it may not be appropriate to provide for tacit adoption/ amendment.

Signature:

This provision should state that only Parties to the Convention may be Parties to the Protocol.

Entry into Force:

To ensure effective implementation, as well as to minimize the potential "free rider" problem, this provision may need to stipulate an entry into force trigger that requires ratification by States that account for a particular percentage of global emissions of greenhouse gases.

Annex A

This Annex would include the same States as those listed in Annex I of the Convention, plus those that join subsequently pursuant to Article 2.

Annex B

This Annex would include those States not listed in Annex A that indicate before adoption of the protocol that they want to be included in this Annex, plus those that join subsequently pursuant to Article 2.

Annex C

All greenhouse gases, their sources and sinks, with global warming potentials as decided by the Parties at their first meeting (taking into account the IPCC's global warming potentials for 100-year time horizons) and as subsequently updated by the Parties to reflect evolving scientific knowledge.

INDEX

C